Fallen Eagle

Rochefort and the Charente estuary

Fallen Eagle

How the Royal Navy Captured Napoleon

Norman MacKenzie

Best regards

[signature]

A BELLEROPHON BOOK

ISBN 978-0-9562611-0-6

Printed in Great Britain by the
MPG Books Group, Bodmin and King's Lynn

First published in the UK in 2009 by

BELLEROPHON BOOKS
Lewes Book Centre
38 Cliffe High Street
Lewes
East Sussex
BN7 2AN

For Christopher Justice
Who piped the Billy Ruffians on board

Norman MacKenzie is an emeritus professor at the University of Sussex. One of his previous books was *The Escape from Elba*, which is matched by this new volume on Napoleon's subsequent fall. He has also written a number of biographies and books on social and educational problems.

Preface

The idea of this book was suggested by Christopher Justice, whose ancestor, Thomas Wall Justice, was one of the midshipmen on *HMS Bellerophon* in 1815 who performed two plays to entertain Napoleon on his voyage into exile. Christopher Justice launched the Bellerophon Project for resurrecting and performing these plays, and urged me to write an accompanying history of Napoleon's flight from Waterloo and his apprehension by the Royal Navy. As I wrote I became more aware that Napoleon's detention and imprisonment on St Helena raised an important and overlooked issue that remains current today: the question of extraordinary rendition.

This legal problem has arisen most recently in the case of Moslem jihadists and Guantanamo Bay, but it applies alike to the arrest of Saddam Hussein and any other 'state prisoner' such as Napoleon. It is not the same thing as ill-treating prisoners-of-war, as happened on a tragically large scale in 1939-45. It is an act of doubtful legality committed outside the rules of law, as laid down in such forms as the Geneva Convention, and outside the laws of the state which commits the denial of human rights that it professes. It is an act which denies any legal redress by due process. By its nature it raises serious moral and practical difficulties to a state seeking to escape its toils. This is the situation in which Britain found itself when it seized and detained Napoleon in 1815 and kept him aboard a ship anchored in British waters.

I am grateful to my wife, Gillian, for consistent support, to Christopher Justice, Juliana Saxton and other members of the Bellerophon Project team; to Julia MacKenzie and Geoffrey Moore, Commander John Pritchard and the Naval Club, John and Rosemary Tarry, and Judith Burns, of the Home Office in Brighton, who produced an impeccable manuscript.

Norman MacKenzie
Lewes 2009

Contents

Napoleon Bonaparte

Principal Characters

Captain Charles Baudin	1784 – 1854	Antarctic explorer, later Minister of Navy.
Hortense de Beauharnais	1783 – 1837	Daughter of Josephine, late and divorced wife of Napoleon, some time Queen of Holland.
General Lenard Becker	1770 – 1840	Elected deputy, and commander of the guard at the Chamber of Representatives.
General Charles de la Bedoyère	1784 – 1815	Commanded first troops to defect to Napoleon on his return from Elba. First defector shot by returning royalists.
General Henri Bertrand	1773 – 1830	Manager of Napoleon's court and his household on Elba and St Helena. Noted for both loyalty and administrative skills.
Frances 'Fanny' Bertrand		The temperamental wife of Bertrand, daughter of Dillon, an Irish officer in the French army murdered in the revolutionary wars. Wished to settle back in Britain with her three children.
Field Marshal Blucher		Prussian Commander.
Joseph Bonaparte	1768 – 1844	The senior brother and a man of cultural and domestic inclinations, who disliked being made King of Naples and Spain and happily settled in the United States.

Lucien Bonaparte	1775 – 1840	The only Bonaparte to decline royal status. Hotheaded, he was for drastic action in July 1815. His tranquil detention in England 1809 – 1813 encouraged Napoleon to hope for similar generosity.
Casimir Bonnefoux		Maritime prefect of Rochefort
Viscount Castlereagh	1769 – 1822	Notoriously reactionary Foreign Secretary and bitter opponent of Napoleon. Committed suicide in 1822.
Marquis de Caulaincourt	1772 – 1827	Accomplished negotiator of the first abdication: Minister of Foreign Affairs.
Lazare Carnot	1753 – 1823	Organiser of victory for the first revolutionary armies. Member of the provisional government in July 1815.
Admiral Sir George Cockburn	1772 – 1853	Burned Washington in the war of 1812, supervised Napoleon's journey to St Helena.
Benjamin Constant	1767 – 1830	Liberal theorist and novelist.
Marshal Davout	1770 – 1820	Most loyal and successful of Napoleon's marshals, he abandoned him after the second abdication.
Admiral Denis Decrès	1761 – 1820	Fought at the Nile, became a time-serving Minister of Marine.
Fleury de Chaboulon	1779 – 1835	Aide and administrator.
Lord Eldon	1757 – 1832	Lord Chancellor
Lord Ellenborough	1750 – 1818	Lord Chief Justice

Joseph Fouché	1763 – 1820	Politician and Spymaster.
General Gourgaud	1781 – 1852	Ambitious aide who insisted on going with the St Helena party.
Lord Holland	1773 – 1840	Whig leader and a sympathiser with Napoleon.
Lady Holland	1770 – 1845	Notable Whig hostess.
Admiral Sir Henry Hotham	1773 – 1835	Maitland's superior officer.
Marquis de Jaucourt		Royalist politician.
Admiral Lord Keith	1746 – 1823	Commander-in-chief at Plymouth.
King of Rome (Napoleon II)	1811 – 1832	Napoleon's infant son and heir.
Emmanuel Las Cases	1776 – 1832	Napoleon's secretary and scribe.
Marquis de Lafayette	1757 – 1834	Liberal revolutionary and aide to George Washington.
Count Lanjuinais	1753 – 1827	Liberal president of the Chamber.
Count Lavalette	1769 – 1830	Minister of Posts and a trusted administrator, noted for a last-minute escape from prison.
General Lallemand	1774 – 1839	Strong Bonapartist negotiator on *Bellerophon*, founder of an exiled farmer-soldier project in Texas.
Lord Liverpool	1776 – 1828	Prime Minister after 1812, saw the fall of the Bastille.

Capel Lofft	1751 – 1825	Anti-slavery, pro-Bonapartist and radical activist.
Marshal Macdonald	1765 – 1840	Son of a Jacobite who aided the escape of Bonnie Prince Charlie. Encouraged Napoleon's first abdication, became an adviser to Louis XVIII.
Captain Frederick Maitland	1777 – 1839	Commander of *Bellerophon*
Empress Marie-Louise	1791 – 1847	Daughter of the Emperor of Austria, second wife of Napoleon.
Lord Melville	1771 – 1851	First Lord of the Admiralty
Prince Metternich	1775 – 1859	Austrian statesman who dominated the Congress of Vienna and created the Holy Alliance.
Count Montholon	1783 – 1855	An aide who took his wife and child to St Helena, sometimes taxed with murder of Napoleon.
Captain Ponée	1775 – 1863	Bonapartist, commanded *Méduse* at Rochefort.
Captain Philibert	1774 – 1824	Commanded *La Saale* at Rochefort. Suspected of royalist sympathies.
Comte de Régnaud	1761 – 1819	Lawyer, sometime Attorney-General, who as Minister of State first proposed Napoleon's abdication on 20 June 1815.
General Savary	1774 – 1833	Minster of Police
Prince Talleyrand	1754 – 1838	Diplomatist and intriguer.

Countess Maria Walewska	1789 – 1827	The most loyal of Napoleon's mistresses she visited him on Elba and asked to join him on St Helena.
Duke of Wellington	1760 – 1840	Victor at Waterloo

and, of course:

Napoleon Bonaparte	1769 – 1821	Victor at Toulon 1793, Italy 1796, overthrew Directory in 1799, became Consul, self-proclaimed emperor in 1804. Victories over Austria and Prussia. Defeat at Moscow 1812. Forced to abdicate in 1814 and exiled to Elba. Escaped from Elba April 1815. Hundred Days rule in Paris. Defeated at Waterloo June 1815. Exiled to St Helena. Died there 1821.

Waterloo: rendezvous with destiny

What will History say? What will Posterity think? I love power... I love it as a musician loves his violin... I love it in order to extract from it sounds, chords and harmonies. I love it as an artist.

Napoleon Bonaparte

His career is the most extraordinary that has occured for one thousand years... He was certainly a great, an extraordinary man, nearly as extraordinary in his qualities as in his career.

Talleyrand to Lord Holland

Prologue

In a memorable poem Thomas Hardy described how fate had brought the *Titanic* and the iceberg into a dreadful embrace. A similarly convergent course brought Napoleon Bonaparte and HMS *Bellerophon* together in a moment of destiny on 15 July 1815 in the Basque Roads, off Rochefort on the west coast of France.

At noon on Sunday 18 June 1815 Napoleon stood near the inn called La Belle Alliance, which looked across a shallow valley of ripening corn to a ridge he knew as Mont St Jean – though the British would always call it Waterloo.

To the right and left of Napoleon stood an army of 120,000 men who had marched up the Brussels road for a final settling of accounts with the allied armies which had beaten him a year before and sent him into exile on the island of Elba. There were five army corps, lead by his old commanders who had rallied to him in March 1815 when he escaped, returned to France and drove out the restored Bourbon king. Across the valley he would see the mixed force of English, Hanoverian, Dutch and Belgian troops amounting to a poorly organised and doubtfully reliable army of ninety thousand men commanded by the Duke of Wellington, here encountered face to face for the first time. Off to the right, about four miles away across broken country, were some hundred and twenty thousand Prussians commanded by Marshal Blucher. The Russians and the Austrians (who had also advanced at the call of the Congress of Vienna to capture the 'outlaw' Napoleon) had failed to reach the battleground in time, the Russians and Austrians having too far to come. The Prussian army, moreover, was also delayed and disorganised on 18 June, because it had been badly mauled by General Grouchy at the bloody battle of Ligny two days before. Since it was Napoleon's battle plan to strike at the junction of allied armies confronting him, he could be reasonably sure that he could drive a wedge between Wellington and Blucher and then destroy their forces piecemeal.

As the ground dried after heavy overnight rain Napoleon waited to give the order to advance. Six hours later, after a catastrophic rout, matched only in the long career of victories (which had made him master of Europe) by his ruinous retreat from Moscow in 1812, Napoleon and his aides were fleeing the battlefield, closely pursued by Prussian hussars he was sure would hang or shoot him if they caught him.

On that day *HMS Bellerophon* was already stationed in the rock-and-shoal-beset waters of the Basque Roads, the complicated estuary of the Charente. She had been placed there all through June as one of a squadron of British ships. Commanded by Rear-Admiral Sir Henry Hotham, they had sailed from Plymouth on 24 May as part of the British blockading tactics which had been so persistent throughout the French wars. Now as the alert sounded by Napoleon's escape from Elba, the Channel fleet was being hastily reassembled – possibly to serve in a new war or, perhaps, to seize him if he should be defeated and forced to flee from France.

Launched in 1786 *Bellerophon* was a 74-gun first-rate, one of the classic line-of-battle ships that Nelson commanded at the Nile and at Trafalgar. She had been dismasted and shattered in these engagements and although patched about and restored, her fighting days were done at the end of the Napoleonic war. When her captain, Frederick Lewis Maitland, took her out to sea in this new emergency she still had a noble bearing but she was crank and ageing, unfit for long voyages, and when she came home in July 1815 it was to face a sad destiny. She would eventually be broken up in a Devon yard, but for the next twenty years she would serve as a hulk anchored in the Thames. While she was to bring Napoleon to serve out his days as a prisoner on the remote island of St Helena, she was herself to survive as a prison ship for convicts awaiting transportation.

This book is the story of that strangely symbolic encounter.

1

Vanquished

Sunday 18 June 1815. At eight in the evening the sun was setting through the reek of powder smoke that lay across the battlefield of Waterloo. In the last hour Napoleon's Grande Armée had suddenly been broken, outflanked and driven off in a confusion that left at least 25,000 dead and wounded behind it. Unwilling to risk capture, unable to rally a sufficient force to make a stand, Napoleon turned his back on the gaggle of stragglers and deserters who were being cut down by the savage sabre-swishing patrols of Prussian cavalry. They swept across the shattered formations that had reeled back brokenly from the last desperate attack up the slope to the redcoat centre of Wellington's army. After a last look at some reserve battalions of the Guard which still held their squares Napoleon climbed into his carriage, and it carried him away along the choked turnpike that led back into France.

* * *

Waterloo is the most discussed battle in history and each new book brings its own explanation of why Napoleon lost a battle he should (and nearly did) win, and speculations. What might have happened if he had smashed through Wellington's thin and final defence, might it still have been merely a stopgap victory against the advancing allies or might it have been dramatic enough to persuade the temporising Austrians and lagging Russians that a bad peace was a better option than the cost of a good war?

So far as Napoleon was concerned, however, the explanations were obvious before he left the field. His original plan was to drive up the Charleroi-Brussels road and push a wedge between Wellington and Blucher and deal with each in turn – a tactic which left Marshal Ney to drive on through Wellington's scrambled defence at Quatre Bras and hurry his still-forming army back in disorder into the Forest of Soignes in front of Brussels. Ney, however, did not press his tactical victory at Quatre Bras, nor did he make a coherent move to his right to keep between the British and the

Egypt, Moscow, Leipzig... once again Napoleon deserts his army

Prussians and enable Napoleon to profit most from his tactical triumph over Blucher at Ligny on 16 June. Ney's hesitation, in fact, gave Wellington time to draw back to a predetermined line along the south-facing ridge at Mont St Jean, just in front of the village called Waterloo. The second share of blame went to Marshal Grouchy, who still had a strong mass of manoeuvre after Ligny but used it to chase the Prussians in the wrong direction, thus depriving Napoleon of the whole right wing of his army, which would have been sufficient both to hold back the Prussians who were rolling up his right flank and to give him the additional regiments he needed to make sure that the last-breath charge of the Guard reserve succeeded. Ney was blamed again for the third great mistake, the two futile force-wasting attacks on Wellington's right wing – the first the hours of attack on the outpost citadel of the farm buildings at Hougoumont, which brought the French to a stop at immense cost when a few batteries of artillery would have blown Hougoumont apart in less than an hour. Ney then compounded his error by throwing thousands of hussars, curaisseurs

In flight from the Prussians at Genappe

and dragoons in rolling attacks round the British squares on the ridge – without an artillery and infantry mix. Even exhausted and depleted British squares could not be broken by cavalry alone. Ney was brave, a man of hot-headed bravado indeed, but this failure to control this phase of the battle, where Napoleon had unwisely left him in charge despite the failure at Quatre Bras, was to cost Napoleon the battle – and his throne. It was also to cost Ney his life when weeks later the royalists tried and shot him for his double treachery.

* * *

Beaten back to Paris

While Napoleon repeated variations on these complaints for the rest of his life, he never spoke about his own failures on the field – the distraction and discomfort of his urinary condition which kept him well back from the best point to command the battle (five of Wellington's suite were casualties, none of Napoleon's); his reluctance to commit his reserves and the impulse to squander them when it was too late; above all, his failure to make contingency plans for any kind of defensive stand across the road to Paris if things went wrong. The situation along that road was not a retreat but a disaster. In the dark barely 4,000 Prussian cavalry were driving at will through more than 40,000 panic-stricken Frenchmen, many of whom had thrown away their weapons when they were convinced that they had been betrayed.

The situation in the small town of Genappes epitomised their plight. It took Napoleon and his staff the best part of an hour to work their way through a scrambling mob to reach the small eight-foot wide bridge over the little river Dyle: since that stream was only three feet deep, escape would have been easy if the soldiers had remained cool and disciplined. Instead, the chaos forced Napoleon to abandon his carriage at one end of the village as Prussian troops cut through the crowd at the other; while he hurried off on a borrowed horse the looters made a splendid haul. In the coach they found a gold dinner service (ready for the triumphal banquet in Brussels?), silver pisspots, Napoleon's medals, a fine dress uniform and, blowing away to be trampled in the mud, the leaflets printed with a triumphant proclamation ready to be distributed as the victor drove Wellington out of Brussels and reclaimed Belgium as part of his Empire. 'We have his hat,' the Austrian leader Metternich wrote afterwards to his daughter, 'I hope we shall soon have the rest of him.'

Napoleon's flight was in fact as near-run a thing as the battle, as Wellington afterwards described it. By the time the Emperor and his suite got clear of Genappes, riding past the ghostly-white stripped bodies the peasants had left unburied after the fighting round Quatre Bras, they were again caught up in a melée. Deserting looters were breaking into the supply wagons lined along the road of advance; they found enough wine and brandy to create violent chaos, and they had also fallen upon the coach containing the treasury – a million francs in gold and silver coins, banknotes, jewellery. Napoleon had good and experienced officers with him; his brother Jerome (who had contributed to the mistakes in the fight for Hougoumont), generals Bertrand, Drouot, Flahaut, de la Bedoyère, and Gourgaud. Yet none of them seemed capable of organising elementary discipline, let alone an effective stand. It was six o'clock in the evening, after nearly twenty-four hours on the road, that Napoleon's party came to the first place clear enough of the spreading demoralisation to consider reforming usable groups of disciplined soldiery. They were at Philippeville, a fortified border town fifty miles south of Brussels, where other senior officers were coming in to report, some with units still in good order.

* * *

It was here that Napoleon had to make the first of a series of choices about his future role. He had been concerned about the political situation in Paris before he left for the front, and he had left his older brother Joseph (sometime King of Naples) and Marshal Davout (the best general among those who had reverted to him) to keep the politicians in line; Davout, in particular, was badly missed at Waterloo, and he was still too far away back in Paris to be put in charge of a defensive rally.

From a room in the Hotel du Lion d'Or, where he was resting and bringing together a viable staff, Napoleon wrote two letters. One was a deceptively confident report to his Council of Ministers, giving a carefully misleading account of the battle. The other to Joseph, was more honest, but larded with optimistic phrases of defiance. Counting heads (though without any assessment of the quality or condition of the troops involved) Napoleon totted up a total of 150,000 effectives at his disposal. These were to come from the contingents surviving from Waterloo and from the reasonably preserved mauled 40,000 still somewhere with Grouchy and presumably making their way towards the road. He felt he could find another 100,000 fit to fight from the local militia and national guard units, and even comb out another 50,000 from the depots. The fantasy grew with the numbers. He might raise a further 100,000 by calling in the current class of conscripts, arm them with muskets captured from the enemy, seize carriage-horses to drag guns and supply wagons ... and to cap all these figments of his imagination, he would launch a new *levée en masse* among Bonapartist sympathisers in the south and south-east of France. Exhaustion and anxiety were taking their toll of his ability to balance his reason and his impulses. He no doubt expected Joseph to pass on these fantasies, propping them up with phrases to rally the politicians who should give France 'time to do its duty', because the Prussians would be so afraid of the peasantry that they would be slow to advance, because the Austrians always took their time to move their armies. There was a final assurance. 'Everything can still be repaired again ... I trust the deputies will realise that it is their duty at this great circumstance to stand by me to save France.' To such head counting Napoleon was to add, next time he proposed to go on fighting to defend Paris, the garrisons in the half-dozen fortresses on the Franco-Belgian frontier, which could indeed have held out for some weeks and had already begun to play a harassing role on the flanks of the British and Prussian armies as they moved towards Paris.

The obvious military plan would be concentrate on Laon, about halfway to Paris, in an area where Napoleon had fought some surprisingly effective battles in the defence of Paris the year before – disposing armies that were then in no way superior to what he hoped now to assemble. While Napoleon had defeated the allies in the field he had failed to cover his back in Paris, and had been betrayed there before he could move back into the capital.

Whatever he might say about rousing the political fervour of the French in a great patriotic stand, he knew he had not really consolidated his position in Paris before he left for the Belgian battlefields. The temptation to get back there and shake the politicians into a superficially loyal compliance was strong. But the only organised part of French society that was consistently loyal to him was the army, and while he still commanded it he could, at one and the same time, use it as his instrument of power at home and as a powerful deterrent against allied forces advancing too far and too rapaciously into France. His advisers argued on both sides of the question. He was inclined to stay at Laon; but in 1814 he had stayed on at the head of the army and let the political intrigues go on unchecked. Now, his inclination was again to stay with the army but, in his own words, he was 'persuaded to act foolishly' and he set off for Paris, fudging the issue by saying that he would return to the army after he had spent a few days putting things to rights in the capital.

* * *

It was another overnight journey. Early in the morning of Wednesday 21 June he reached the Elysée palace. He complained that he had eaten nothing for three days. He was tired, dirty with road dust; he was agitated and depressed, deluding himself with the belief that he could get the better of the political battle, teasing himself with the opposite fear that he might fail to carry the government with him and – he must be believed that this was a genuine motive in all his decisions in this critical week – that blood might once again be shed in the streets of Paris. Every time he was reminded of his coup in Brumaire 1799, when 'a whiff of grapeshot' had brought him the hold on France he held for more than fifteen years, he

Napoleon escapes from Elba to the *Inconstant*

would shake his head, speak of a possible clash between his supporters in the army and the faubourgs, on the one hand, and the royalists and the liberal opposition on the other, and back away from that sanguinary prospect. He had thought he could come back from Elba and appeal to the widespread French desire for peace and stability. The fact that not a shot was fired between his landing place and Paris was reassuring. He told General Malet, one of his closest advisers, that it was 'in my best interest to live quietly and use the remainder of my days repairing the evils brought on France by twenty years of war ending in invasion... The misfortunes of our motherland have robbed me of my retirement.' The claims that he had been misunderstood, misrepresented, even cheated by his enemies, became so common that this habitual self-justification as a response to setback raises doubts, then and now, about his intermittent grasp on reality. In the years of recollections that he later dictated on St Helena, nothing was ever his fault. No sooner had he arrived from Elba, after his escape in March 1815, than he was asserting that he had been driven to break his treaty promises by the failure of the victorious allies to pay his pension, and then by their conspiracy to seize him and carry him off to an African island. He even insisted, despite their lack of good faith, that they might have been willing to tolerate him back on the throne of his empire if only his enemies, Wellington and Lord Castlereagh (the British Foreign Secretary) did not stir them up and once more subsidise a war against him.

The counterpart of frustrated hostility is torpor, and after Waterloo the swings of mood between impulse and indecision marked most of Napoleon's responses to the crisis into which defeat had plunged him. What was to be done? It was now too late for peace, probably too late to bring the war to an early end by moving aside to make his son Napoleon II, too late in fact for any kind of settlement with the Vienna coalition. On 25 March the allies had declared that any kind of agreement must 'place him beyond the possibility of disturbing for the future, the tranquillity and general peace... the rights, the liberty and the independence of the nations.' As someone was soon to remind him in Paris, the blood of too many thousand men was now smeared across his professions of good intent. After all, he was the cause of the battle that had become the crowning disaster of his military career.

2

The Politics of Paris

The Hundred Days. Napoleon's brief spell of power between his escape from Elba and his flight from Waterloo began and ended in high drama, but the days between saw a remarkable series of improvisations. He had pushed away the nobles, the priests and the placeholders who had swarmed back in the wake of the Bourbons. He had stopped the return of properties to the émigré owners who had come to reclaim them – a very strong point with his peasant supporters. He had cut back on censorship, abolished the slave trade, treated royalists and other critics with moderation; he had even made a treaty with the persistently irredentist rebels in the western Vendée. Above all, but more ominously for a country that was beginning to prefer peace and stability to glory and upheaval, he had stopped the demoralising disruption of the army – his central arm of power – and set about rebuilding it, rearming and supplying it, and despatching it in a new order of battle to confront the enemies on his borders. Much though he made of his plans for peace and constitutional progress Paris was once again full of boots and bayonets as well as fine words and aspirations.

The momentum that had come with him on the long fast march across France on his way back from Elba was fading. It was a saying in Paris that people were more pleased to see the back of the Bourbon bodyguards than the front of Napoleon's column marching into the city to reinstate him, for all the breathtaking way he had reclaimed his throne without a shot fired or a man lost. Lazare Carnot, who had helped him build the great armies of revolutionary France, was only one of those close to him who began to feel that he was trying to do too many things at once. When Napoleon told him 'my policy needs a gleaming flash' Carnot did not dispute the point, saying to himself that the Emperor had become 'vacillating and hesitant... instead of acting he talks, he asks everyone's advice... gloomy, distracted, sleepy.' Napoleon's difficulties are understandable. His personal energies and moods apart, he was trying to rule a country that had been destabilised by war, occupation, dynastic upheaval and economic difficulties. It had also been politically destabilised by the rise and fall of different elites, changing social expectations, and all the desertions, deals and fantasy solutions to problems that whirled along in a kaleidoscope that flickered without rules. So much was done in the Hundred Days, and yet so little had been settled.

* * *

There was a further problem facing Napoleon – a challenge which he was ill-equipped by his talents or his experience to meet effectively. His experience of government was by and through an army; his style of command was regimental; his colleagues and subsidiaries were men who had come up through the ranks and on battlefields far from France. Such a system no longer fitted the situation he inherited in the Hundred Days. A new and increasingly powerful class was emerging; merchants, bankers, lawyers, journalists, professionals and 'notabilities' of all kinds, a middle bourgeoisie who had done well from the revolution and the empire but now had new interests and aspirations and new political attitudes to embody them. This class not only wanted peace abroad; it also wanted security at home. It had two fears. It was afraid of the sterile, Jesuitical and reactionary baggage that the Bourbons carried with them in and out of exile, afraid of censorship, justifiably afraid indeed of a 'white terror' if Napoleon brought defeat upon France. There was an equally strong anxiety about a *jacquerie*, yet another rising of Jacobins and Bonapartists from the faubourgs and in the still unsettled countryside, yet another radical regime imposed with the support of the Bonapartist army. Napoleon glimpsed what was happening but he could not judge the rate of change. Political problems demanded political solutions and there were now ambitious politicians to propose them. The ideas and achievements of the American revolution and the teachings of its ideologues – Tom Paine, Thomas Jefferson and Benjamin Franklin – had found their echoes in France. Some form of democracy had become unavoidable if not inevitable, and Napoleon's main asset among these political ingénues was the fact that the enemies on his borders were the reactionary monarchies who loathed the new nationalism, the new democracies, new economies which were breaking out of archaic near-feudalism. To the extent that Napoleon could grasp this change, and run with it, he could present himself as an epitome of a new kind of government. The question, in the summer of 1815, was not whether he had the understanding, the will and the political skills to engineer such a change. It was whether he could persuade this resurgent class that his change of mind was anything more than a timely conjuring trick.

* * *

Under pressure of time and events Napoleon had to act swiftly, at least to make a start on political change though rearmament and the deployment of his army were his main preoccupations. To that end he devised two large constitutional demonstrations. The first was a grandiose event of imperial jollification. The rally of the *Champs de Mai*, on 1 June, was something between a Roman feast and a repeat coronation. While the soldiers marched again behind their eagles, the Paris masses ate and danced, and the emperor and his brothers appeared in gold and silver coronation robes, got themselves blessed by archbishops, and – without explicit references to the petty kingdoms to which Napoleon had once appointed them and they had now lost – gave a poor and pretentious impression of democratic monarchs.

The second genuflexion to the democratic ideal had more substance. It was a revised constitution, called the Additional Act, proclaimed by Napoleon on 22 April. It was a remarkable document, full of the humane aspirations of the Enlightenment and the ideas of popular sovereignty. It had been drafted, for the most part, by the foremost liberal of his day, Benjamin Constant, a former opponent of Bourbons and Bonapartists alike, who found the document's commitment to rights and liberties radical enough to satisfy both his principles and his pride. The new legislature was to have an Upper House, peers nominated by the emperor; and an elected Chamber, whose 639 deputies were to be chosen by electoral colleges made up of liberal aristocrats and landowners, wealthy merchants, bankers, lawyers and other professionals and 'notabilities'.

The first election, held in the euphoric gap between the *Champs de Mai* and Napoleon's departure to the war, produced the freak result of a low poll of 7,669 electors from a constituency of 50,000. Only 60 of those returned were obvious Bonapartists; some 500 were liberals of various convictions, and among the remainder were a scattering of monarchists, former republicans and Jacobins. There was no mandate for any specific persons or policies, but even more obviously there was no vote of confidence for Napoleon himself; and the sceptical mood was given point by the Chamber's failure to elect Napoleon's brother Lucien as its president, choosing instead Count Jean-Denis Lanjuinais, a Breton who was a strong liberal and anti-Bonapartist. Across the Channel radical democrats in the House of Commons were much affected by such reforms which apparently afforded liberties and powers far beyond those overtly derived from the unwritten constitution of the United Kingdom. This sudden shift towards democratic principles was to play its part in persuading Whigs and radicals in Britain to look more favourably on Napoleon, despite his role in provoking yet another war.

The unexpected sound of a public voice, endowed with the means to express itself, showed that the problem of conceding a system of elections is that it may well be turned against its creator. Count Molé, one of Napoleon's Council of Ministers, made the point. 'In politics there is nothing worse than adopting principles without drawing logical inferences from them. Sooner or later they are thrown up in one's face...' Napoleon was to discover very quickly that this was exactly what happened to him.

Among the crowds of newcomers in the Palais Bourbon, who had to be drilled and directed into some kind of cohesion, were some veteran liberals with experience and reputation, generally regarded as lucky eccentrics who had somehow managed to survive the tortuous shifts of French politics since the knife fell on the neck of Louis XVI. Chief among these was the Marquis de Lafayette, a wealthy nobleman, distinguished for having served as an aide to George Washington in the American War of Independence, for having been the founder of the National Guard in 1797, and designing the tricolour. He had been the most consistent liberal through all the vicissitudes for twenty-five years and he now put himself at the head of the liberal factions in the Chamber who proposed to limit Napoleon's power, and shift as much of it as possible into their own hands; to seek a reasonable end to an unfortunate and damaging war; and to solve the dynastic question in a way that removed Napoleon without replacing him with a Bourbon king who had already shown his incompetence in the previous year.

* * *

If Lafayette was to be the stalking horse in this campaign, the stalker was the most deviously powerful man in France, who had already stage-managed the creation of the Chamber and the necessary elections. Joseph Fouché (the Duc d'Otranto to use the rank Napoleon gave him) was a notable regicide who had voted to guillotine Louis XVI, had been a notorious colleague of Robespierre in the Terror, and had managed to extract himself from this dangerously exposed position to begin his climb up the backstairs of power.

The fact that Napoleon could neither do with Fouché nor do without him confirmed Fouché's reputation as the ultimate survivor. 'I should have had him hanged,' Napoleon reflected more than once in his memoirs on St Helena, but in June 1815 it was Fouché and not Napoleon who had the life and death of the Bonaparte dynasty in his hands. It was the climax to an extraordinary career. His formal success over the years had come from his role as Minister of Police for much of Napoleon's reign. His great informal power came from his network of influence – his police spies, his political agents, his contacts with the confidential men of other European governments, whether or not France was at war with them. All such intrigues made him a man of mystery, of duplicity and disloyalty, though disloyalty was a relative term in the country that had passed through such convulsions that 'loyalty to what?' and 'loyalty to whom?' were often unanswerable questions. His skills were such that he somehow turned such handicaps of character into assets for political bargaining. He was a possibilist, a man who could distinguish between reality and pipedreams, very capable, a remorseless maker of plots and plans. He saw it as his task to make French politics work, and at this stage in his life, to make them work in a moderate way which would have been inconceivable in his younger days as a terrorist. He did not mind if he was not trusted; he knew he was feared; and what he wanted most was to be effective. He had a policeman's instinct for order, and he had learned the lesson that in the long run – and he had survived in the long run – repression begets counter-repression, that moderation begets security, that constitutionalism and reasonable liberties were better policies than another bout of Bonapartism for the France that was now at last emerging from the traumas of revolution and war.

Such abilities and such a range of information gave Fouché the foresight which permits prediction. When he had first talked to Napoleon on his return from Elba he had seen at once what was going to happen despite the emperor's new democratic clothes. 'He is cured of nothing and returns as much a despot, as eager for conquests, in fact as mad as ever... Europe will fall on him... all will be finished in four months.' It was a gloomy but accurate forecast, which Fouché followed by saying that the Bourbons were bound to return, and that the best hope was that they might be more tolerant and competent. In four or five sentences, Fouché had written the script for the summer of 1815.

* * *

Fouché's great advantage was that because he had the initiative and because he was patient, he was probably the only important figure in French politics who knew just what he wanted, and what he might be able to get by careful calculation of percentages at each turn of affairs. He was brilliant at setting events in train without revealing where he proposed to lead them. His role in the Chamber is probably the best illustration of the point. Once the Additional Act was passed he gave the Chamber the shape he needed for its purpose, organised its business to do just what he wanted. He persuaded a reluctant Napoleon to hold elections and he so arranged things that – again contrary to Napoleon's intention – the ministers could, like members of the British Cabinet, have the right to speak and thus influence decisions directly. These changes made, he began to shuffle the cliques and factions that emerged to serve his own purposes without declaring them. Even before Napoleon had left for the battlefields of the north Fouché had managed to make the Chamber's support for the venture contingent upon success, or forfeit in defeat. This was done so discreetly that even if Napoleon realised what was happening he could do nothing about it. A sense, if not positive knowledge, of this situation is enough to account for Napoleon's anxiety to regain Paris after the battle, rushing on from Philippeville to Laon without any attempt to rally his shattered army.

Such grand designs were always underpinned by detail, often so well concealed that even today, as one would expect from a master of subversion and surveillance, there is more guesswork than evidence about Fouché's operations. A particular case in point is his relationship with the Duke of Wellington. It is clear that they had similar views about the future of France after the fall of Napoleon: they both distrusted the Bourbons, they both were only prepared to shoehorn them back in office on commitments about moderation (which included the appointment of Fouché in any government which took office once Paris fell); and there is no secret now about the covert exchanges between them all through June 1815. But no one is able to confirm or deny Fouché's later claim that he sent Napoleon's plan of campaign to Wellington two nights before the fighting began. One can only say that some such action would explain the Duke's confidence in his

Swinging the Congress off balance

dealings with Fouché and the unrelenting pressure he put upon Louis XVIII to make Fouché his Minister of Police as soon as he got to Paris.

* * *

All such domestic machinations, moreover, were accompanied by furtive correspondence with foreign powers, most particularly with Lord Castlereagh, the Foreign Secretary, and Prince Metternich, the powerful statesman of the Austrian empire – the two men who were the movers and shakers of the allied diplomacy centred upon the Congress of Vienna. The key French figure in foreign affairs was the third of the important players in the game of setting snares for Bonaparte – Prince Talleyrand, another professional survivor, another defrocked clergyman who had become a collector of secular patronage and influence. It was said that Talleyrand served and betrayed every French regime for fifty years, from the revolution until the July monarchy of 1830. He was corrupt, devious, vengeful, greedy and dishonest, and yet made himself as indispensable in his own way as Fouché. Like Fouché, again, he was a pragmatist, somehow managing to arrange things so that what he considered best for France was best for him as well, and vice-versa. He had avoided being caught up in the disaster of the Terror by escaping to London and the United States, a stint of emigration in which his capacity for diplomatic intrigue gave him an ever-increasing role in European affairs. At the time of Napoleon's return to Paris he had given him nominal support but soon took himself off to Vienna, where he represented Louis XVIII at the Congress and became one of the architects of Napoleon's downfall. His immediate involvement in France before Waterloo was limited by distance; hurrying back again to join Louis on the road from Brussels to Paris he found new occasions for intrigue.

* * *

Talleyrand played a lesser role in the Parisian intrigues than his *de facto* allies Lafayette and Fouché, but he was at his most significant in the wider context. For the personal fate of Napoleon (they detested each other) was only one of three linked problems facing the victorious allies that summer – the ci-devant emperor, in fact had erupted into the complicated (even dangerous) diplomatic exercise of drawing a new map of Europe after a generation of war between the powers, and, at intervals, between them and Napoleon. His appearance, and the new war, made matters much more complicated, for there were new military costs and problems to add to those left over from his defeat a year earlier. Such issues as... how many soldiers should be settled in France and how should the proportions be divided among the occupying armies... where should the armies of occupation be stationed... who was to pay for them... what punitive indemnities could France pay... what territories should be taken back from territories that Louis XIV had seized beyond the 'natural' borders of France...?

All such questions and longer-term issues that affected the new maps had to be settled, partly according to the present balance of powers and partly according to contingent guesses about new alliances and hostile combinations that might arise. What allowances must be made for the relative wealth or military power or strategic advantages that might ensure from a given change? What was the best way to hold back the tides of nationalism and social change that Bonaparte had subversively sent sweeping across Europe (Italy was the most sensitive case in point)? Should the Tsar be given Poland in perpetuity? Could the King of Prussia be allowed to make his long-sought grab at Saxony? Most ominously for the future: should the three hundred odd petty principalities of Germany be rolled up together with Bavaria and Prussia to make a powerfully united Germany stretching from Poland to the French frontiers on the Rhine? Out of such a melée of ambition, greed and imperial hauteur had nearly come a new war in the winter of 1814; the seething antagonisms were barely patched up when the Congress delegates discovered that all the scripts had to be changed because the 'Corsican Ogre' had erupted into their proceedings as through a trapdoor. This was not something that they could risk happening yet again; and for all their differences (and with the encouragement of British gold) they were agreed that the sooner Napoleon's fate was settled, once and for all, the easier it would be to make a generally agreed and settled design. It would be for the future of France in the first place and then, whatever new rules might be agreed, for a new Europe, a Holy Alliance, which would be as much like the *ancien regime* as they could make it. And if all the perils of Bonapartism were to be kept out of Europe then Bonaparte himself must also be kept out too. Dead or Alive!

* * *

Immediately after the battle it was Blucher's cavalry patrols that were sent off after him. 'Blucher,' Wellington wrote after the victorious commanders had met at La Belle Alliance inn, 'Blucher wants to kill Napoleon but I advised him to have nothing to do with so foul a transaction.

He and I had too distinguished a part to become executioners of the sovereign.' The Austrians were saying nothing in public: Napoleon's separated wife was the emperor's daughter, the boy who might be Napoleon II was his grandson. The more vengeful royalists in France wanted a trial for treason. The Tsar of Russia, who was having séances of religious mania, might or might not recall his past attachment to Napoleon. Fouché was playing a cautious game, doing all he could to shuffle Napoleon away from any embarrassing outcome that might entail a trial, a sentence, even a firing squad for his former lord and master. The British, who had long been thinking that the best thing would be for Napoleon to end up on another yet more secure island home, thought it likely that his flight might eventually carry him to one of the waiting ships of the Royal Navy.

Meanwhile, as Lord Castlereagh was reputed to have said, when asked for his opinion: 'First catch your fox!' For the quarry had gone to ground in the Elysée Palace.

3

A Time for Decision

21 June: a bad start to midsummer day. A week ago Napoleon had left Paris in pomp, the master of his fate, clattering out to battle. He collapsed back into the city at five in the morning, after an exhausting ride back in the tattered livery of failure. Only Caulaincourt was there at the Elysée to meet him at this early hour. The Minister of Foreign Affairs had been a loyal and reliable colleague who had been the go-between in the negotiations to secure Napoleon reasonable terms for his abdication in 1814. Now he was here, a sombre omen of the ominous political situation that awaited Napoleon. His first words summed up everything. 'It would have been preferable for you not to have left the army,' he said dolefully, repeating the opinion of ministers who Joseph had called into an emergency meeting when he received the letter from Philippeville. 'It is that which ensures your power, your safety.'

That text set the tone for all the discussions that followed through this critical day. Could Napoleon survive, let alone prevail, without calling in the troops? Were there still sufficient men available for a police action to prop him up? Even so, if he did resort to the army, what kind of ruin might follow? Paris had suffered enough from the politics of the street in the past twenty years, and as Napoleon himself said, he had not returned to make blood run in the gutters again. Yet as his staff well knew, his great abilities were offset by his difficulties in coping flexibly with opposition – his reactions were shot through with instinct, grudges, suspicions, above all with a pattern of impulses that were ungovernable at one extreme and at the other, when he was thwarted, led to persisting moods of depression. Though his "take it or leave it" manner had so often carried the day when he was master of a diplomatic exchange or a battlefield, he had always found compromise difficult. In short, his personality served him ill in situations he could not control.

* * *

The mood in Paris, which Caulaincourt now tried to summarise, was extraordinarily volatile – there had been anxiety as well as excitement as Napoleon had driven headlong against Wellington and Blucher, enthusiasm as reports came in that Ney had forced the British back from Quatre Bras and that Grouchy had triumphed over the Prussians at Ligny. In fact, the rumours of a resounding victory ran so strongly that the Chamber found it tactically wise to send a message of congratulations that left Paris just as the gunfire was dying away at Waterloo.

Almost at once the tide of rumour set the other way. Joseph had shown the ministers the letter of nervy bravado from Philippeville, and disturbing gossip reached the Chamber just as other couriers were coming in with even worse news. The mood in the Chamber as it assembled on 21 June, while the party of ministers was gathering in the Elysée, was described by one visitor as a state of 'melancholy tumult', with 'men going in and out, disappearing and reappearing, talking to people of all kinds, who, like the deputies themselves, looked as though they had been bitten by tarantulas.'

* * *

Over at the Elysée it was clear that Napoleon was trying to get the situation into focus. Going straight to a bath he talked to one newcomer after another, compulsively, jerkily, like the spent man he was, telling Caulaincourt that he was going to call special meetings of both Chambers, describe the plight of the army. 'I will ask them to give me the means of saving the country. After that I will be off again, today or tomorrow.' Caulaincourt tried to stem the breathless flow of words with a damper of reality, telling him that there was 'great general agitation; deputies seem more hostile to you than ever before… the Chamber will not respond as you hope.' Napoleon was still in spate, repeating a mantra of intentions, still too shattered by his experience to be coherently logical. 'I have no army left, I have nothing but fugitives… I can find men but how can I arm them? But all can yet be restored… The deputies will support me. I think you misjudge them… If we join forces everything can be put right.' He picked out for blame the liberal leaders in the Chamber. 'Lanjuinais, Lafayette and the others don't want me. I'm a nuisance to them. My presence here keeps them under control.' In his bath he rattled on to Lavalette, who as Minister of Posts handled the regime's communications, because he too had reported that the mood of the Chamber was against the emperor. Abusing Ney and Grouchy for their failures, blaming the defeat on panic and desertions, he carried on his tirade with the latest arrival, Marshal Davout, the Minister of War, who had arrived early for the ministerial meeting called for ten o'clock. Napoleon had scarcely drawn breath when they were joined by his brothers Joseph and Lucien.

Joseph, who had been talking with Lanjuinais, who was the president of the Chamber and no great friend to Napoleon, gloomily confirmed what the ministers were saying about the hostile mood of the deputies. The youngest brother, Lucien, always the firebrand captivated by his own eloquence, admitted that matters were getting out of control, but insisted that drastic measures taken in time would do the trick: the army was the key to the survival of all the Bonapartists, not just the family but all those who had worked their way to wealth and influence. The morning had begun with an immediate crisis whose momentum would carry through the day, leaving little space for a considered appraisal of the situation.

* * *

All twelve ministers and aides were assembled by ten o'clock, but it was difficult to make a start. Some were too embarrassed to speak out, some had no idea how to make up their minds, some were too depressed to focus on such a desperate situation, but they had to listen through a frank report of the lost battle. It was left to Napoleon to take the lead. 'Our misfortunes are great... if, instead of taking drastic measures we spend our time arguing... then all is lost. ...I must have extraordinary powers and a temporary dictatorship... I could seize such powers, but it would be useful and more truly national if they were given to me by the Chamber.' The suspicion that in an emergency Napoleon would rescind the so recently granted powers of the Chamber was making the deputies very uneasy.

This was exactly the situation that Fouché had anticipated and proposed to exploit through pulling the strings which controlled the inexperienced factions among the deputies. He later described his tactics. To the anxious liberals – he called them 'the unquiet, mistrustful' deputies – his message was that Napoleon was 'becoming perfectly insane; he is decided on dissolving the Chamber and seizing the dictatorship.' To the Bonapartists in the Chamber, increasingly anxious about the deteriorating military situation and afraid that Napoleon might not triumph over what Fouché called 'the ferment against the Emperor', Fouché began to promote the idea of saving the dynasty by making his heir Napoleon II under a regency of the absent queen Marie-Louise.

Fouché's case was in fact being made by the debate in the Council of Ministers. Lazare Carnot, who had rallied the armies to save the Revolution twenty years ago, argued that Lucien was right, that Napoleon should call for a national rising to defend France, that the army should be regrouped south of the Loire, and that a vigorous counter-offensive should clear the enemy over the frontiers. Caulaincourt continued to insist that disaster loomed if the Chambers were not enlisted in the cause of national defence. Davout, as Minister of War in direct contact with the force falling back on Paris, wanted to save something from the wreck. It was necessary to control 'criminal or blind factions, whose intrigues and manoeuvres would hinder everything.' The Chambers should be prorogued, but to give a constitutional gloss to such a botched-up regime the deputies should be told to reassemble in some provincial town a fortnight later. It was probably Napoleon's indecisiveness at this point that persuaded Davout to change his mind and throw in his lot with the emerging peace party. His colleague Admiral David Decrès, Minister of the Navy since 1801, was to move to the same conclusion, but for the present he simply seemed confused and worried that the deputies were 'hostile... and might be led into every kind of excess.'

* * *

Now it was Fouché's turn. He came forward as the champion of moderation, criticising neither Napoleon nor the Chamber, saying it would be better if there was less hostile rhetoric and more good faith. There must have been a wry smile on his face as he said this in front of men who knew him so well. He had to temporise in time to prevent a rush of hasty and damaging decisions, and he had to avert an impulsive dissolution of the Chambers by Napoleon while he coached the deputies into the next scene of the constitutional drama. This measured tactic was nearly disrupted by Count Régnaud, one of the legal ministers whom Fouché had already persuaded to the view that in the long run abdication was inevitable. In the heat of the moment Régnaud blurted out what he believed Fouché wanted him to say. 'I am afraid that a great sacrifice is necessary,' and he did not mean an

Caught between two armies

unconstitutional dissolution of the Chambers. 'Speak frankly', Napoleon said, now the unpleasant truth was coming out. 'It's my abdication they want!' Régnaud stood his ground. If Napoleon did not offer to abdicate of his own accord, 'it is possible that the Chamber may insist on it.'

Lucien kept the debate moving after this distraction, answering for his brother. 'If the Chamber will not support the emperor he will do without its help... He must make himself dictator, declare martial law... call on all good patriots and Frenchmen.' Napoleon took the cue to move the talk back away from the one topic he most wished to avoid. He began a long tirade in the bravura style they had all come to know over the years.

'The nation did not appoint the deputies to overthrow me, but to support me... Whatever they do I shall always remain the idol of the people and the army. I have only to say a word to confound them all... national patriotism, hatred of the Bourbons and attachment to my person will offer us immense resources, our cause is by no means desperate.' Then came a repeat of the scheme restoring his fortunes that he had first sketched out at Laon – despite all the hassle and confusion it was another of the near-visions in which he seemed to sketch out his campaign plans, and he was to cling to it as his formula for retaining or regaining power. The great frontier fortresses could hold out for months and meanwhile they would draw off large numbers of allied troops to besiege them. Lyons and Toulon could be held. He could concentrate more than a hundred thousand troops round Laon, blocking the routes the allies must take to Paris, and disrupting their lines of supply; in any case, the British and Prussians had been badly mauled at Waterloo and Ligny, and had left a debilitating string of deserters and wounded along the roads behind them. The tactical advantage now lay with the French, once the army was brought back into shape, because Blucher and Wellington were taking different itineraries to Paris, at rates so different that combined action between them would be difficult, even unlikely, and he could therefore drive between them and tackle each in turn as he had so nearly done between Waterloo and Ligny.

This sudden recovery of energy, the way in which this scenario was rousing the pessimists – all the ingredients of Bonapartism appealed to men whose careers had been animated by it – alarmed Fouché, who said afterwards: 'That devil of a man really frightened me that morning. As I listened to him I thought it was all going to begin over again; but fortunately it was not beginning again.' While Napoleon talked on about martial law, about moving the government to Tours, about preparing to fight with two hundred cannon on the walls of Paris, Fouché waited with good reason, realising that the cronies who had come back from Waterloo were losing their grip on reality: they had moved on to discussing whether or not Napoleon should wear one uniform or another when he went across the river to address the Chamber. They had drifted on from policy to presentation. Fouché was also concerned about the impact this revival of confidence might have on the Chamber. Even while Napoleon was speaking he had managed to send a briefing note to his manipulators on the floor of the Chamber: even before he had heard what Napoleon had to say he had been alarmed by the combative temper of Carnot, Lucien and Davout. The next hours would be decisive.

* * *

The Chamber had come into session two hours early, at 12.15 and amid the excitement and rumour the stage had been set for Lafayette. At a caucus meeting on 20 June Lafayette had insisted that 'the Chamber must declare itself in permanent session... demand the abdication of the Emperor... in the case of refusal, to decree his deposition.' Lafayette had always seen himself as the foremost champion of liberty, and Fouché – invariably content to let others take the praise or blame for his initiatives – had encouraged Lafayette's useful vanity. Before the meeting of ministers began Fouché knew what to expect if they roused Napoleon to the foolish point of defying a Chamber in which he had no power. As if at signal, Lafayette claimed the rostrum, to move what seemed a matter of business, though it was as significant as similar occasions during the early days of the revolution, when Lafayette and others were making constitutional challenges to Louis XVI.

There was no melodrama about what was in fact a coup, a decisive shift of power. All Lafayette had to do was make a brief speech about 'the danger to the country,' refer to the alarming fact that 'sinister rumours... have unfortunately proved to be true... This is the time for all of us to rally round our ancient standard, the tricolour, the flag and symbol of '89, of Liberty, Equality and Public Order... to defend it against pretensions from without and upheavals from within.' Everyone knew what he meant, and there was 'tumultuous applause' for five procedural clauses, two of which were decisive. Article 1 declared that the independence of the country was threatened. Article 2 contained the core of the matter. 'The Chamber declares itself in permanent session. Any attempt to dissolve it is high treason. Whoever may be guilty of such an attempt is a traitor to the country, and may be summarily judged as such.' Flat words but menacing, in a country in which every adult could remember the Terror. Napoleon did not seem at all inclined to challenge them. 'I ought to have got rid of all those people before I left,' he said as the report of the resolution broke up the meeting of ministers. 'It's all over... They will be the ruin of France. Régnaud did not deceive me... I will abdicate if I must.'

Far from stabilising the situation the Council meeting had decided nothing, ending in more confusion than it had begun, and left the emperor in an overwrought and vacillating state which was to continue all this vital day. Even as the ministers left Napoleon kept Carnot and Régnaud back to take an official announcement across to the two Chambers. They were to tell the deputies and peers that 'after a signal victory the army had engaged in a great battle; that everything was going well; that the English were beaten; that we had captured six flags... when a panic was caused by mischief-makers; that the army was now reassembling... that I have come here to discuss matters with my ministers and the Chambers; and that I am at this moment taking the necessary measures to make secure the public safety.'

Such flamboyant mendacities had usually served Napoleon well in the past, when he had the power of decision in his hands and could misrepresent the facts as it suited him. Now a reality that he could neither recognise nor accept was overtaking him. As he sent the two ministers on their errand he did not realise that they were in effect taking away with them the baton of power.

* * *

It was only two weeks since the deputies had assembled, and none of them could have anticipated that a crisis would be upon them so soon. One day they were led to give patriotic support to the emperor, the next they were told to defy, in effect to discard him and become the government of France. Soon they were talking about a new government led by Lafayette defending the independence of a newfound liberal regime. Napoleon's stepdaughter, Queen Hortense – who had been the consort of his brother Louis as King of Belgium – was well-informed and forthright. Hortense thought that Lafayette and the Chamber which he now led had no idea of the implications of their resolution, and she commented that they were discussing 'the principles of political freedom as though armed Europe were advancing to enforce this ideal rather than its converse.' Nothing could be less likely.

Until another clause was implemented (Article 4: 'The National Guard is to be armed and called out to guarantee the liberty, prosperity and tranquillity of the capital') the Chambers did not even have the means to restrain the marauding crowds of Bonapartist militiamen and the masses of the faubourgs, let alone get the army to do what it wanted or persuade the oncoming allies to respect their newfound democratic independence. Napoleon himself did not know whether or not to take the liberals seriously. He undoubtedly did not take Lafayette seriously, saying later that he was 'man without talents either civil or military... dominated by vague ill-digested and ill-conceived ideas of liberty;' and he was still blustering when he heard that the peers (all nominated personally by him) had voted for the same motion.

'I'll send a few companies of the Guards to deal with those rebels... If they press me too hard I'll throw them all in to the Seine.' In fact, whether pressed hard or gingerly, he had enough sense of reality to understand that in this crisis he probably lacked the will and the power to seek a military solution. 'I should have to use force,' he told Lucien as his brother begged him to assert himself. 'And where is the force to do it? There are not even any soldiers left in Paris.'

Tipping points are not precise in history, but they can often be traced out to a matter of hours or even to a single event. The situation in Paris that afternoon was what that expert on revolutions, Leon Trotsky, a century later called "dual power". It is a point where it is possible for both sides to act but neither can yet make the decisive moves. It may not even be clear what this move might be, in advance. In this case the Chamber could take no executive action because it had no means to hand to seize and detain Napoleon, while he had no means to stop Fouché entangling him in a web of hostile power. The experienced old loyalist Davout, who so often in the past used his troops to solve Napoleon's problems, saw what had happened and summed up the Chamber's dramatic decision in a short sentence. 'The resolution is unconstitutional,' he advised Napoleon, 'but it is an accomplished fact.'

* * *

The Chamber now moved on cautiously to the next stage in the crisis, the issue of abdication. Getting it talked about was one thing, bringing it to a decision was something else. For the moment Napoleon carried on as though the word and all that it involved had never been spoken. In fact he took one step back to the position it would have been sensible for him to take a few hours earlier. Lucien, at six pm, was empowered to address the Chamber as Napoleon's special representative. He was not a conciliatory orator; much given to rodomontade when he was addressing people well accustomed to this Bonapartist line of talk, who knew when to cheer at the right points; but those days had passed on 18 June and Lucien was trying to arouse an assembly that was hesitatingly hostile. It did not quickly realise that Lucien had come to offer a compromise of sorts, dressed up with patriotic flourishes. The emperor, Lucien told them, wanted a commission of five deputies and five peers to join the responsible ministers to work out measures for public safety. It was an offer that would have pacified the morning sessions but it got a rowdy reception as it passed through the agitated Chamber.

In fact, the deputies wanted to move on, and Antoine Jay (a deputy who lived in Fouché's house and was tutor to his children, and obviously his spokesman now) put the vital point. He bluntly asked Lucien and the other ministers present to admit frankly 'whether they think France can resist the armies of Europe,' and whether Napoleon's presence was not 'an invincible obstacle to negotiations and peace.' When none of the ministers answered Jay went on to say that 'public liberty would never be established in France under military leaders,' and he went on to make the point that Fouché was using to great effect as he lobbied around – that the allies had declared that they were at war with Napoleon and not with France, declaiming that further resistance would plunge the country into disaster. Turning to Lucien he said: 'Go back to your brother... tell him that the people's representatives expect a decision from him that will do him more honour in the future than all his victories. Within a day, perhaps within an hour, it will be too late.' He called for a quite different commission from that proposed. 'It should go at once to Napoleon and demand his abdication, and tell him that if he refuses the Assembly will pronounce his deposition.' Everyone present would have picked up the change in name: the Assembly had been the Jacobin name for what was now the Chamber, and there was also an ominous and uncomfortably nostalgic tone in the words 'the people's representatives.'

Lucien did his best to stop this slide into an irrevocable decision. Separating the emperor from the nation, he cried, would disrupt the unity of the country and plunge France into 'abasement and slavery... bringing disaster upon the state, breaking your oaths, and forever tarnishing our national pride.'

Lafayette broke into the peroration. 'You accuse us of failing in our duty to our honour and Napoleon. Have you forgotten what we have done for him? Have you forgotten that the bones of our children and our brothers everywhere bear witness to our fidelity... three million Frenchmen have perished for a man who still wants to go on fighting against all Europe today. We have done enough for him. Our present duty is to our country.' Lafayette was the only person who could say the unsayable, and his speech settled the matter.

The deputies, apparently surprised at their own boldness, still held back from the ultimate decision. Events had so crowded one upon another that perhaps they were not sure they were safe from some violent response. In the event, they compromised by accepting the idea of a joint commission of deputies and peers to join the ministers to discuss national safety. It was to begin its meetings immediately.

* * *

There was growing evidence that Napoleon must put down the deputies or give way to them – more of his advisers had moved to concede in the course of the day. Now Savary, the minister responsible for security, told Napoleon, 'you would hardly find anyone to march against them.' Even if Napoleon succeeded in dissolving the Chamber, he 'would be at a loss what to do.' Since 'these bewildered and enthusiastic minds deem themselves so sure of doing better by following their views, they should be taken at their word and left to shift for themselves.' Savary thought that there was such a state of excitement that it would be no surprise if they sent to demand an abdication.

Napoleon, however, seemed drained by the succession of meetings and was in no mood to take on another round of confrontations. Now, when his health was beginning to fail and he was exhausted by battle, by travel, by anger, he appeared to draw back from the eddies of pressure around him, as if he temporarily escaped into some other part of his personality.

At incongruous moments, sometimes when an important decision was urged upon him, he would lead off into reminiscences, into reflections on history, literature, even music and the theatre. He was a well-read man, quite reflective by nature, and the manner of an enlightened despot was congenial to him. He often recalled Frederick the Great's patronage of Voltaire, or compared himself to figures from classical history. This evening, of all evenings, he sent an invitation to Benjamin Constant to come and talk to him. Constant had long been his critic and an outspoken opponent of the empire; he had, however, been so impressed by Napoleon's newfound liberal pretensions that he had served as the main draftsman of the constitutional changes of the Hundred Days. Comparable though he was to Lafayette in public esteem, Napoleon found him an agreeable sounding-board for the thoughts that had been running through his daylong arguments with his usual coterie.

Constant kept a record of this astonishing valedictory evening. Napoleon began by questioning him. Did his opponents realise the consequences of his abdication? Did they really think that metaphysical axioms and declarations of rights and parliamentary eloquence would hold the army together once he was no longer the focus of its loyalties? How could anyone persuade himself that the invaders marching into France could be halted by high-sounding phrases? If France abandoned him, as he kept insisting, she would surrender herself, admit her weakness, acknowledge defeat and encourage the conqueror's audacity. 'It is not liberty that is deposing me but Waterloo,' he repeated: 'it is fear, a fear of which your enemies will take advantage.' In any case, he said dismissively, as if a wave of the hand was enough, 'the Chamber has no legal right or authority to demand my abdication.'

All these points made a fair summary of the situation as he saw it, but it was a twilight soliloquy that seemed to be directed more at the record than at the actual situation. He was, Constant noted, a military leader who was shying away from a military solution to his problems, an impulsive reaction from the dramatic means he had used in the past. The same hesitation showed in his comments on the crowds of his supporters marauding the streets to shout their support. 'You see,' he said to Constant, 'the voice of the country speaks through their mouths, and if I wish it, if I allow it, the Chamber will cease to exist in an hour.' He paused. 'No. it is too great a price to pay for one man's life. I did not return from Elba to drench Paris in blood!'

Constant realised that in spite of digressions of resentment and recrimination about the past, Napoleon had apparently made up his mind: the argument now was not about the principle but about the price. He still vacillated, which made things difficult for his supporters as well as his opponents, but Constant was convinced that the coming abdication would 'be the result neither of the advice of his friends, nor the threats of his enemies, but was due to his own dislike of extreme measures and even more of a spirit of lassitude and exhaustion.' He could distinguish between the bloodied ruin of Waterloo – the impersonal deaths of the 25,000 Frenchmen he had left behind in Flanders – and the kind of vindictive personal savagery he had known in his revolutionary youth. He did not need to be reminded of the Terror. One of the better motives of his rise to power had been to take the guillotine out of French politics. He would have agreed with the dictum of Winston Churchill, almost a century later: 'grass grows quickly over the battlefield but over the scaffold, never!'

As he left the Elysée after one of the most revealing conversations in these days of crisis Constant concluded that Napoleon had 'greatly abused his unique opportunities and that he had misjudged the growing power of the middleclass, which had been docile so long that he believed he could always dominate it while despising it.' It was this new power that had ensnared him.

* * *

Next day would bring the foregone conclusion to such thoughts. Napoleon's favourite marching song had been *How Happy One Is In The Bosom Of The Family* and this evening there was an ironic truth to it. Before dinner his stepdaughter Hortense de Beauharnais had arrived in some distress, in the hope of consoling and possibly helping him. He seems not to have discussed his plans at the casual family dinner.

He did leave a summary of his feelings that evening, but only later when he was reflecting on the past on St Helena. His conclusions were much the same as those he had reached in the talk with Constant. Would anyone know what the 'doubt and anxiety' had cost him? He had seen that he could try to save the country by violence or by surrender to political pressure. 'He was left alone, he had to give in, and once the deed was done, it was done... the other course demanded unusual strength... create great criminals and severe punishments.' It would have needed a Terror, as in 1793, to save the empire by putting a stop to defection. He had so fused his own fate with the fate of France that he was probably unable to conjure up a positive vision of the country's future without him.

Napoleon had managed to distinguish between personal ruin and public disaster, distinction enough when it came to the sticking point, but his comments over the next few days suggest they kept coming together in his mind in the aftershock. In fact, in spite of the glimpses of might-have-beens, the deed was done as he fled from Waterloo, and all the argument that followed was about his fate, not the fate of France.

* * *

The issue was not yet quite so settled in the parallel meeting of the Chamber's commission with Joseph and Lucien as the emperor's proxies. Lucien continued to press the lost cause, to rant about rousing the army to a victory over the invaders, to claim that only his brother could accomplish this feat. Some of the ministers tried to keep the discussion away from talk about Napoleon's personal future and concentrate – as the terms of reference actually proposed – on public order and safety. It was Lafayette who kept insisting that the most necessary decision was the abdication, which was not mentioned in the draft. Lucien gave him the vital prompt line, saying that if the ministers had thought that Napoleon's departure was necessary for the defence of France they would have been the first to propose it. That verbal trick cost him the game. 'I adopt that idea and convert it into a motion,' said Lafayette. 'I suggest we go to the emperor and tell him;' Jean-Jacques Cambacêrès, the Minister of Justice who was in the chair, said he could not call a vote on such an *ad hoc* proposition.

Further talk went on into the small hours. It was next proposed that a commission should be appointed to negotiate with the allies. The summary contained a good deal of persiflage about 'universal rights of all nationalities' and vague phrases about measures to strengthen the armed forces and 'contain and repress the enemies within the country' but these were more principles than commitments. There was still no specific reference to abdication. Fouché protested against face-saving formulae that meant nothing. 'We must settle this today,' he said grimly at three o'clock in the morning as the commissioners wound up their stressful day, a day in which everything had been discussed and nothing had been decided.

4

A Crisis of Fits and Starts

The crisis came on stream in the third morning after Napoleon's return: there was no longer any doubt about the way it was running. The Chamber was already meeting when Napoleon roused himself to read the report of the commission of ministers, peers and deputies that had been prepared overnight. Despite what he had said to Constant the previous evening he had not reconciled himself to reality. In fact, the motion which Lafayette had proposed was to prove just as decisive as the meeting of the Constituent Assembly in 1789, which had been the moment at which the Revolution began, and outbursts of irritation and regret would make no difference. 'They think they'll save themselves by ruining me,' Napoleon grumbled on, 'but they'll discover they're mistaken' – a piece of bravado that Lucien was foolish enough to echo in the Chamber that morning, talking about coming with 'a battalion of the Guards.' There was still some anxiety on this point. Some deputies were so aware of Napoleon's propensity to lash out when cornered that they still opposed an enforced abdication: one said afterwards that he was relieved to wake that morning and find that there had been no arrests overnight. But while Napoleon was stranded between denial and defeat, his entourage was no longer in doubt. Those who mattered – Joseph, Caulaincourt and Savary – were convinced he no longer had any choice. It had to be abdication, which would be imposed if not voluntary. Napoleon was discovering that a lot of powers must slip painfully away from an emperor before he realises as well as his opponents that he has no clothes. The time had come for the symbolic acts that would mark the end of his regime.

* * *

They proved remarkably low key for such a significant event in the life of such a significant man. After a rowdy discussion about the commission's report, the moderate proposal that Napoleon should be invited rather than forced to resign was carried. It had not been enough for Napoleon to send a message saying that he agreed to the appointment of armistic commissioners, and that he would make every sacrifice to save the country. Anyone who had watched Napoleon's career would have been worried in case he suddenly changed his mind and used the army to stage a repetition the coup of Brumaire 1799, as Lucien kept suggesting. The matter had to be settled before he could change his mind. So General Solignac (who had served Napoleon well in the past) and four other deputies set off to the Elysée. The compromise between the hardliners and the hesitant had now come down to the condition that the emperor should be given an hour of grace to consider his reply. Meanwhile Davout made an attempt to describe the parlous military situation to deputies whose minds were elsewhere. 'They wouldn't listen to me,' he complained when he got back to the Elysée.

While Davout was speaking things had not gone well across the river. Régnaud had already reported the rising temper of the deputies and Napoleon's temper too was roused as he read the proposal brought by Solignac. He was defiant again. 'Since they want to force me, I will not abdicate. The Chamber are all Jacobins and ambitious men whom I ought to have denounced… But it's still not too late.' Lucien was making a final plea for dissolution of the Chamber, reminding Napoleon that on the night of 18th Brumaire in 1799 his seizure of power had not been legal but it had been justified. While Napoleon was flattered to recall that turning point in his rise to power, the memory did not persuade him. 'To-day, the law is entirely on our side, but I must not use it.'

That was the last gasp of protest. He suddenly sobered. 'Very well,' he said. 'Let it be as they wish. The future will show if their way has served France better.' He turned to Fouché, who had watched this scene impassively. 'Write and tell those good people to keep calm – they'll get what they want.' It was this message from Fouché that broke the expected news to the Chamber. Next, he called Lucien up to the table, and in the histrionic style he always used in sending orders at the height of a battle, he struck a posture and said: 'Write.'

It was a wordy declaration in the circumstances, as Soliganac's hour of grace was running out. When he had embarked on the war of 'national independence', he dictated, he had counted on the united support that could have brought success. After this over-modest and evasive statement of fact he admitted that 'Circumstances seem to me to have changed. I offer myself as a sacrifice to the hatred of France's enemies.' This was a form of words that he had used in his previous abdication, and it came with

NAPOLEON BONAPARTE.

CHEF DE BRIGANDS;

at his Post of Honour.

Some Frenchmen thought this the Post of Honour he deserved

another repetition, this one proclaiming his small son, the King of Rome, as Napoleon II and calling for a regency.

The Chamber was to take no more notice of this regency proposal than it had done a year ago. In any case, the boy was a virtual prisoner of his grandfather, Emperor Francis, in Vienna, and his mother, Marie Louise, was off in the Swiss Alps gallivanting with an Austrian staff officer. The only sentence that had some pertinence was the equally futile hope that the victorious allies would 'prove sincere in their declaration that their quarrel is only with me personally.' Fouché was going to make use of this point in trying to persuade both the Chambers and the allies that the Bonaparte dynasty should and could continue. It had some short-lived domestic value, but it got nowhere with the allies. In fact Wellington was about to tell Fouché that this proviso was no longer valid, that it had become void as soon as the French army was engaged and the fighting began.

For the moment a scrawled signature gave a semblance of reality to the occasion. At this point any nod would have been as good as a wink. Copies were hastily made but before Carnot could carry them over to the Palais Bourbon the adjutant of the National Guard rushed in to say he could not be responsible for public order if the Chamber was kept waiting any longer.

Abdications are rarely occasions of dignified agreement. By their nature they are usually played by the rules of catch-as-catch-can.

* * *

Matters were now in limbo. It was one thing to extract a signature from a reluctant emperor, but the political and administrative consequences were not dealt with so easily. Napoleon believed that new constitutional arrangements would be made to establish a regency for his son as Napoleon II. Not so. The act of abdication was taken to Lanjuinais, who read it to the Chamber with a few florid and insincere phrases about the grandeur of the emperor's sacrifice. The deputies ignored the reference to the King of Rome and went on to take the first steps towards a provisional government, to be controlled by an executive committee consisting of three deputies and two peers.

Fouché was the obvious choice as president of the commission – certainly in his own scheme of things. He had some trouble preventing the choice of Lafayette and Lanjuinais as members; the leaders of the liberal faction would certainly have been inflexible about the Bourbon restoration that Fouché now thought almost inevitable. He flattered the two men as being more suitable in other posts – head of the National Guard and president of the National Assembly now being metamorphosed out of the present Chamber. Only Carnot, the obstinate old-time republican, might create difficulties. For the next two weeks this commission would be the government of France. It would make the decisions about Napoleon's future, about the armistice, and about the restoration of the Bourbons or some alternative to them.

Things had not gone so smoothly with the peers. Caulaincourt was a sensible nomination, and would give status to the commission, and the second peer was Quinette, like Fouché an old regicide who would follow his lead. The peers had been roused by a sudden intervention from Marshal Ney. Like a demonic upstart from the ghostly chaos of Waterloo, he made a sensational speech about Napoleon's mistakes, panic and underestimation of Wellington and his army. As many of the peers were generals this gave a new emphasis to the act of abdication which was being read to them. At the same time it shadowed Lucien's last attempt to save something from the wreckage. Saying that civil war must be avoided at all cost Lucien called for the succession of Napoleon II, to maintain the continuity of the dynasty. Amidst the uproar some of Napoleon's supporters tried to support a proposal for a regency, but it was talked out in a procedural clutter. Lucien received a derisory vote as the peers voted for the commission.

* * *

That day, Napoleon himself had the last word. Lanjuinais led a deputation from the Chamber to announce the acceptance of the abdication, and to utter some vagaries about the nation's gratitude. Napoleon, however, was not the man to usher them out with polite thanks. He took the chance to point out that the abdication left 'the state without a leader, without political guidance. The time spent in overthrowing me would have been better employed in putting France in a condition to crush the enemy... take care lest your hopes prove false; this is the danger.' After he 'commended' his son to France Lanjuinais said vaguely that 'the sovereign's wishes concerning his son would be conveyed to the Assembly.' When a similar deputation arrived from the peers to receive the same response, Napoleon's advocacy of a regency was more explicit, even threatening. 'I have only abdicated in favour of my son; if the Chambers do not proclaim him, my abdication will be null and void. I will reclaim all my rights... After the step you are now taking, the Bourbons will be brought back... You will soon be shedding tears of regret.'

Since he pressed the point of the regency it was not possible simply to ignore it. There were circumstances, indeed, in which Fouché would have taken up the idea and run with it – given time he might even have accepted it as a better solution than the return of the Bourbons. But events now pressed too closely for the question to be moved on to the agenda of the provisional government which was now being formed. What Fouché did, in fact, was characteristic; to get some credit for apparently endorsing the idea, and more credit for ensuring it was dismissed. His henchman, Jacques Manuel, whose allegiance to Fouché was well-known because he edited *L'Independent* for him, rose in the Chamber next day to propose 'that Napoleon II had become the emperor of the French as a result of the abdication of Napoleon I' in conformity to the Constitution. The same motion proposed a provisional government 'to give the nation the guarantee needed for their liberty and repose, by means of an administration possessing the entire confidence of the people.'

The ends were being neatly tied up. The first part of the motion was ignored, the second was implemented. Two days later, the now-formed executive committee 'in the name of the French people' published a footnote to the succession affair, with a typical twist of Fouché's ingenuity. Blandly pointing out that Napoleon II had not yet been recognised as sovereign by any power 'we cannot negotiate with foreign nations in his name.' In that case, it claimed that it was 'its duty to act in the name of the French people, in order to deprive the enemy of any pretext for refusing negotiations.' Thus, maintaining the fiction of a possible succession, Fouché was now in practice the ruler of France.

* * *

There was to be no dramatic conclusion to Napoleon's tenure of the Elysée. He was free to speak, he could receive guests, he was not formally put under house arrest; he even had time and opportunity now to reflect on his future. He spoke afterwards of the sense of anti-climax. 'I knew I could no longer be sure of ultimate success: I had not the confidence of the old days... no longer attended by that good fortune that had once loaded me with favours.' He was now confronted by 'a harsh destiny, always prompt to avenge any advantages I managed to snatch from it by force.' He was a man of power and glory no more. Now the substance of those years had been taken from him he could devote his remaining years to cultivating its legend. What he now said and did, as he himself confessed, was for the record of history.

5

Who Governs?

It had been relatively easy to dethrone Napoleon. After all, those most concerned had been through the process a year before, and if practice had not made perfect at least there were lessons to be learned from the process. One was to decide about the fate of Napoleon himself, in the short run and as a long term answer to a problem whose previous solution had been a costly failure. Once again there would be two stages in the process to get him away from Paris, and to despatch him to a place where he no longer presented a standing threat 'to the tranquillity of Europe'. A related issue was the search for a new regime which could provide a competent and acceptable successor to the empire. That would not be easy. The Bourbons had moved in as Napoleon was taken off to Elba, and their year in power had been such scandalous failure that popular dislike of it may have been as much responsible for Napoleon's dramatic return as any enthusiasm for him and his brand of politics.

France could not afford to go through such a shuttlecock process again, with war and two allied occupations in a twelve month, political instability, economic stress – even the harrowing experience of revenge. So the most pressing question in Paris as June gave way to July was what kind of caretakers were needed to deal with the transfer of power, and what kind of answers they would offer to the difficulties of the transition.

By the evening of 24 June the paperwork was done. Napoleon had signed, and now sat in the Elysée awaiting his marching orders. The two Chambers had passed the necessary motions, and Fouché was anxious to move on. The debate in the peers, where the Bonapartist generals Flahaut and de la Bedoyère had stirred up some support for Lucien's plea to continue the dynasty showed that there might still be a move to call Napoleon II to Paris, or at least to set up a regency for that purpose. It was the task of Manuel to keep the idea of a regency as a floating abstraction that never came to the vote. Fouché described his role to the royalist Pasquier. 'I told him... it was absolutely necessary, at any price, to prevent the

A hostile French view of his destiny

child's rights from being recognised. He told me to rest easy.' Provided that the deputies could be eased into leaving the initiative (and the decisions) to the executive committee, and content themselves with the debater's joy of constitution-drafting,' Fouché could use his effective power to get on with the business without much argument, to stage a replay of the turnover in 1814, and to do his best to avoid repeating its mistakes.

* * *

To move on, however, was easier said than done. Fouché controlled the executive committee, which functioned for the time being as 'the voice of the people' in a tenuous relationship with the Chambers, and if they represented the 'people' Fouché was for the interim its unchallenged spokesman. He had managed to survive so much, and he now brought the arts of survival to find peace and stability in a France that was both war-torn and peace-torn. In the whirl of partisan conflict that threatened to destroy France he sought peace through appeasement, and the times had provided him with the necessary diplomatic foil. Prince Talleyrand came from minor nobility, so he too knew how to survive, from a start as a debauched bishop to a capacity in foreign affairs that took him into as many governments as Fouché, equally unprincipled, equally effective.

Their objective was the same, with a shade of difference. Talleyrand saw himself as the architect of a Bourbon restoration in a restored France, with Louis XVIII accepted again as an equal by the allied sovereigns, and France combining with Austria and Great Britain to resist Prussia's eager domination of Central Europe. This purpose greatly appealed to Castlereagh, who equally saw a restored royalist France as the ally Britain could count on in the new Holy Alliance that was emerging from Vienna. That was not really Fouché's concern. Personally Fouché would have preferred any government but the royalists. He knew their faults only too well. He had seen at firsthand the mistakes and excesses of the Bourbons when they came back from years of exile after Napoleon's first abdication; he was the best informed man in France about the tide of public resentment that had flowed against them; and would have preferred the new head of state to be the Duke of Orleans (the only moderate Bourbon) in some kind of a regency for Napoleon II. He was also realistic enough to know that neither was possible – though he had to get through a few difficult days until the Chambers could be brought to accept reality. Where he differed from Talleyrand was in his estimate of how much reality the Chambers would accept, for there would have been chaos if the installation of Louis XVIII had been put to them *tout court*. What he was hoping to do was to use this period of uncertainty to extract reasonable terms from Louis XVIII, to hold off the white terror which might sweep into France on the bayonets of the allied armies. There were men close to Louis who had their programme of purges planned, death warrants drafted, the dangerous drastic dissolution of the army put in hand once more. There were twenty years of scores to be paid off. The Bourbons were said to forget nothing, but learn nothing. Fouché was trying to teach them some of the virtues of moderation. He was helped by the fact that Lord Liverpool and other members of the British government had themselves been uneasy about the Bourbons: after all, Louis had lived for years only thirty miles outside London, and the royalist émigrés were familiars and fellow-conspirators against Napoleon. It was Wellington, however, who played the decisive role. He was to be the puppet-master in introducing Louis back to Paris, and – though he disliked Fouché – he needed an ally to accomplish this affair without a riot or a military farrago. Therefore he and Fouché had to strike a secret bargain to mutual advantage. As far as Fouché was concerned the Duke had to understand that he had to keep up appearances by putting up a case against the Duke's requirements, thereby giving people the impression that he was fending off even worse terms. Both men clearly understood the tactics, because both sought the same end to the game.

* * *

Marshal Macdonald was a key contact for Fouché in this complicated process of go-betweens, some of whom were being used to good purpose while others, like emissaries chosen from the liberal faction in the Assembly, were deployed as a distraction. Macdonald had played a leading role in the cabal of marshals who had brought about Napoleon's abdication in 1814, and he was now a close adviser to Louis XVIII as he tried to pick his way back to Paris through the web of military and political intrigue. The marshal had discreetly returned to Paris after the recent abdication to meet a group of royalists who were anxious to make a move before a new government could rally around the image (if not the person) of Napoleon II. He was anxious to defuse schemes for a premature royalist movement, and in this opinion he was effectively supported by Vitrolles, who had been the leader of the covert royalist organisation during the Hundred Days and unwisely released after his arrest. Vitrolles, who had just seen Fouché, said that the political entrepreneur was acting in the Bourbon interest and that he should be allowed to advance it in his own way and at his own pace. The next day Macdonald himself saw Fouché in a mixed company of generals and politicians who, he said, talked 'such nonsense' that at last Fouché said, 'Never mind them; they are a set of fools.' Macdonald was to report Fouché's private assurance of loyalty to the King, and he was told to stress that if Fouché 'had played a part in recent events it was only to serve him better. He urged me to impress upon him the advisability of coming quickly.' Macdonald was then sent on to impress his old comrade-in-arms, Davout.

* * *

Between the problem of Napoleon and the restoration of Louis there was a link which tied their fortunes together and it was fragile enough to be Fouché's most immediate concern. The army was certainly in a chaotic state, but there were substantial parts of it which were still in good order, notwithstanding defeats and desertions, and some of them were still fighting, especially in the east. More could, and Bonapartist enthusiasm meant that more would answer a rallying call to keep the allies at bay: this is what Napoleon was saying and kept saying for the next week, and as long as he was in a position to make such a call there was a risk of chaos if not civil war. Nobody but the allies would benefit from the disruption. At the same time, to declare Louis king and bring him back in to Paris in triumph could well be the spark to ignite a soldierly outburst, ill-organised perhaps, unfocussed, a military jacquerie that could achieve nothing but disaster. Somehow, in the short time since Napoleon lost command of the army, Davout had to bring some cohesion back to it.

He was the steadiest of all the marshals, so reliable that Napoleon had counted on him to hold the centre steady in Paris while he marched off on his gamble at Waterloo. His long record of battles won and sieges sustained was unequalled, and he was trusted by his generals and his troops alike. He was not, however, one of the marshals who shared their politics with the emperor. His loyalty was patriotic, expressed through the army – to maintain its coherence, its reputation, its ability to protect the national interests of France. He could effectively have thrown in his lot with an adventurous foray by Napoleon, for he alone knew best where his divisions were, in what condition, and how they could be matched up to face the advancing allies. Both Wellington and Blucher were anxious about such a counter-stroke as they approached Paris, their units widely-dispersed, strung out over vulnerable lines of poor communications and supplies. But there was one factor in this complicated situation which Wellington recognised and Davout probably recognised as well. If the French people as well as the army turned against the allies, as Napoleon proposed, the allied march could have been halted outside Paris at the price of making the country ungovernable.

'It would have been ridiculous to suppose that the allies would have been in possession of Paris in a fortnight after one battle,' the Duke remarked, 'if the French people in general had not been so favourably disposed... if the disposition of the inhabitants of the country had led them to oppose the allies.' That may well have been true but Davout as Minister of War still had to make up his mind what to do with the army that was still in being, with major units still able to fight under generals angry at the betrayal of Napoleon, with the rank and file now a mix of fervent Bonapartists, defeatists and deserters, with defence works still going on around the walls of Paris. Time was too short for things to be left to sort themselves out. Without an immediate decision to hold the army together and take a new oath of allegiance, the government itself could not hold together, and there would be no way to negotiate an armistice let alone the orderly surrender that would be a necessary condition of terms of peace.

* * *

It was not easy for Davout to come to that decision, let alone to manage it against patchy opposition and demoralisation. His argument may have been strengthened by Savary's repeated insistence that Napoleon was actually in danger, and should move away from Paris. Certainly Napoleon would have taken Davout's argument seriously. Davout described his change of affiliation in a letter to Fouché on 27 June, urging haste, because the executive committee was still hesitating about its attitude to Louis. 'There is no time to lose in adopting the proposition I made yesterday: we must proclaim Louis XVIII... I have conquered my prejudices, my ideas; the most irresistible necessity and the most sincere conviction have determined me to believe that there is no other way to save our country.' It was a concession that gave Fouché power to move on.

Fouché of course agreed. The delay was in part due to the time it was taking to explore and strike deals. He was using royalist intermediaries to seek some guarantees from Louis about his own political future, and he was not a man to lose a trick through playing a card too soon. He was annoyed at the 'bungling lot' at the exile court in Ghent who had no agent in Paris with whom he could deal directly. Replying to Davout that same day Fouché explained the reasons for caution. He feared that 'poorly calculated conduct' would mean recognising Louis before any commitment on his part,' thus allowing his unconditional entry into Paris. The matter was then discussed by a meeting of the ministers, where there was still hesitation. With Davout's support he persuaded them that 'to avoid the greatest misfortunes we must rally to the king while obtaining from him a certain number of essential guarantees.'

At this point Fouché's case was disrupted by a confusing report from two more envoys who had been sent out to contact Blucher. He had refused to receive them but they came away with an impression that he did not care who occupied the French throne. (Every signal from Blucher's headquarters at this time made fiery demands for Napoleon's arrest, rather than offering support for the Bourbons he disliked.) Before the meeting ended Fouché managed to get the ministers to agree on the names of four commissioners to be sent formally to seek an armistice from Wellington; but doubts remained. Next day a group of deputies called on Fouché to ask plainly if he was working for a Bourbon restoration, and whether talk of conditions was simply a device to pacify the doubters in the Chambers. They were of course right, but Fouché gave proof that he was still a champion for the rights of the French people, showing a letter he was sending to Wellington with the armistice delegates. The French people were working on their 'social compact', it said: once this was completed and signed by the sovereign called to replace Napoleon, then that sovereign 'will receive the crown and sceptre from the people.' This mendacious subterfuge more than satisfied the restive deputies, who had it read to the Chambers as proof that a new sovereign would not be imposed without their consent.

Fouché probably expected difficulties of this kind in such a confused situation, where anxiety and rumour were as common as principle, and he sent an urgent secret message to Wellington to reassure him that the doubters were under control. The messenger was a half-English, half-Italian Colonel named Macirone who had been an ADC to Murat,

(Napoleon's sometime cavalry general, his brother-in-law, a King of Naples) and, in Fouché's words 'his man of trust'. Besides the letter Fouché had shown the deputies he also carried a secret addendum from an English agent named Marshall, whom Fouché kept by him for such purposes, saying he wrote with Fouché's authority. 'He wishes to know what the allies want and what are their intentions. He is for the king. You may have utmost confidence in him.' While Fouché was being obliged by recalcitrant deputies to drag his feet on the issue of a Bourbon restoration, he was desperate to get some commitment from Wellington. His first priority was to avoid a disastrous battle outside Paris, and because Blucher's columns were two days nearer than Wellington, he needed Wellington to restrain his rampaging ally. To that end he was offering the bait of an early welcome to the Bourbons, if he could be helped to manage it.

Wellington's reply at least was blunt. It may have brought the deputies more speedily to the conclusion that Fouché sought as being the only option. 'Tell them,' Wellington wrote, 'that they had better immediately proclaim the king. I cannot treat till then, nor on any other condition. The king is here at hand, let them send their submission.'

Fouché now had formal confirmation that all other options about Napoleon's successor were closed – there could be no question of Blucher or the Austrians or the Russians offering or accepting any alternative. Armistice negotiations with them were going to be about the person of Napoleon, not the person of his successor.

* * *

Here Fouché had a different difficulty. The liberal politicians with whom he had to deal were not keen to welcome Louis, and they were reluctant to part with Napoleon without any settlement of his future, to accept what the consequences of the abdication might be for him personally. Except for the most militant royalists, mostly émigrés, nobody wanted to see him arrested and tried: or to hand him over to Blucher to be shot out of hand. The idea of exile, even forcible deportation, was now being canvassed in much the same way the possibility of abdication had been the focus of talk in the past week. Fouché had been thinking of some such solution for over a year, but he was reluctant to incur the public odium of driving Napoleon out of the country with ignominy. His aim was to make it seem that Napoleon had gone into voluntary exile – about as voluntary as his abdication, perhaps, but a dignified agreement would keep up appearances. When the delegation was sent to Wellington its instructions included an insistence on 'the safety and the inviolability of the emperor Napoleon, out of the territory of France.' Fouché was determined that, nominally at least, Napoleon should have the choice of his ultimate destination and the means to get there. This tactic would work only if Napoleon cooperated, while Fouché covertly made the ground rules to give himself flexibility as the situation changed from one day to the next. The first move was to shake Napoleon out of the Elysée, where there were too many rough crowds of street people calling out their support, and where he had free access to sympathisers who might be turned into conspirators. Who was to be given that task?

The answer was Davout.

6

Where Next?

In the afternoon of 24 June Davout came to see Napoleon at the Elysée. It was an uncomfortable meeting for both men, who had known each other and worked closely together for a dozen years. More to the point, there had been trust between them, and Davout had not been one of the turncoat marshals who only the year before had welcomed the Bourbons and shipped Napoleon off to Elba. Now, however, came the painful cutting of old ties. Davout came to say that earlier in the day there had been a demand in the Chamber for Napoleon to leave Paris, since his continued presence would be 'nothing now but a pretext for troubles and a source of public danger.'

For an impatient man, long used to command but now a defeated soldier and a humiliated emperor, Napoleon was keeping his tirades brief and under control in this difficult period, and his reply to Davout seems to have been a variant on the line of protest which he was taking through the crisis. He could rally the army, he insisted, he could put himself at the head of a great movement of protest against the Bourbons, he could disperse the loud-mouthed braggarts among the deputies... they were dragging France into ruin... Davout heard him out. Napoleon finished with a shrug of the shoulders. 'So they want me to go. It will cost me nothing more than anything else would. Fouché deceives everyone, and will be deceived himself in the end, and get caught in his own net. He can fool the Chamber, but the allies will ultimately fool him. There was no more to say. Notice to quit had been served by Davout with a bow. They did not shake hands before they parted in this sad end to a long partnership.

* * *

Napoleon knew what was coming and had been preparing for it. In the course of a visit from Hortense, he had talked to her about the possibility of retiring to her palatial house at Malmaison, an hour west of Paris, which had been the home of her mother Josephine, the divorced and late wife of Napoleon. This large estate, with splendid gardens, could quickly be reopened to accommodate Hortense herself, Napoleon, his mother and brother, a sizeable staff and servants, even visitors. It was a house that Napoleon liked. It was well provided, comfortable, full of memories of good times spent there in the past; and he said he could well settle there. But, probably, he said, that would not be permitted. 'If they won't let me stay in France, where do they want me to go? To England? My life there would be ridiculous, and uneasy too. Even if I kept quiet they wouldn't believe it. Every fog would be suspected of tempting me to the coast.' With good reason, Malmaison was chosen as a temporary refuge while other possibilities were discussed.

* * *

Napoleon enjoyed planning. Both as a general and a politician he was given to calling for maps, papers, reports, and juggling them with speculations – some that produced remarkable results, others that were or proved to be fantasies. Even now he was dipping into some of the great range of geography, travel and history books in his excellent library, talking with visitors about places where they had lived or he thought he might go.

When it came to the point, however, he was receiving two sets of advice. Some of his staff favoured the notion of living in Britain. Las Cases, who was making himself a close adviser and was to become his amanuensis on St Helena, had spent years of exile in England and for a time in the United States, because of his earlier royalist opinions: Fanny Bertrand, the outspoken wife of General Bertrand, the Master of the Household who served as Napoleon's chief-of-staff, was Irish and desperately wanted to settle herself and her children back in Britain. General Gourgaud was for England too, and Caulaincourt, always a moderate diplomat who had no intention of going into exile, thought London an acceptable necessity. Other members of the suite spoke strongly for asylum in the United States. Savary, the Minister of Police when Fouché was otherwise employed, was urgent to get away from Europe, as was General Lallemand who had been wounded at Waterloo. Both men were right in fearing that if the Bourbons caught them they would be tried on charges of treason. And there were family influences as well. Lucien, who had spent some comfortable years as a prisoner of war in a country house in England, gave a warm account of those years, though for political reasons he preferred the United States. He had, in fact, been on his way to America when a British ship had captured him at sea. Hortense, anxious that some decision be made, was sure America would be a congenial destination. Finally, there was the sober brother Joseph, who was the warmest for an American solution. A strong reason for his opinion was that, like Lallemand and Lucien, he thought that once in America Napoleon might be able to repair his damaged fortunes in American politics or some kind of military post, perhaps rally a Bonapartist emigration or profit from the hostility between Washington and London. After all, the Americans and British were still winding up the distracting but not greatly significant war that began in 1812.

* * *

Suggestions of an American asylum were thus founded on well-informed opinions. Napoleon had been interested in the United States ever since he was a military cadet writing his geography lessons. He had lived through thirty years in which even royalist France had supported the American War of Independence, and where more recently there had been the close political links between two countries that had come from their common experience of popular revolutions that had swept away monarchist regimes. There had even been larger and more complex dealings about the French colony of Louisiana, which comprised a quarter of the land area of the later United States. First, there was an abandoned plan to make it into an enlarged French colony in the New World; and then, in an extraordinary deal, there was the epoch-making sale of the territory to Thomas Jefferson. It was the key to the American expansion to the west. The notion of America as a land of opportunities was already so strong, indeed, that many of Napoleon's followers were to flee to America, and their experience showed various ways in which he might have been occupied had he managed to get there – from landowner and farmer to politician and soldier. The United States already had the reputation of an open and welcoming society for immigrants, and the vision of this distant, democratic and increasingly powerful country had a continuing appeal to Napoleon. There was even family contact – his brother Jerome had spent years in Baltimore, married there and had been summoned home in disgrace. He therefore had good reasons for his repeated assertion that he hoped to find refuge in America: it was not an ill-informed pipedream. He talked of it as a place where he might be comfortable, secure, honoured even, certainly welcome. He was always interested and well-read in science and mechanics, as well as geography – even as he filled in time at Malmaison he was reading Alexander Humboldt's *Voyage to the New Continent*, and one of his visitors was the celebrated mathematician Gaspard Monge, to whom he lamented that he could not take him as a companion on an expedition of discovery in the New World. He even had visions of a life as a gentleman farmer scientist – Jefferson and Franklin were role models. One of his favoured recollections when he was in this mood was the successful work of the scientists he had taken on his invasion of Egypt. There was even talk of a possible role for Napoleon in American public life, and a cautious glance at the demands for experienced European soldiers to help in the revolutionary wars now being waged in the Spanish colonies in Latin America. He was never narrow-minded in his speculations, and in this instance he was certainly encouraged by a memory of Fouché's suggestion a year ago of a possible refuge in the United States, when there had been a possibility that the suspicious allies might try to move him away from Elba – which, as events proved, was dangerously near to Europe.

* * *

There was, therefore, thought and expectation about America as a refuge of last resort. While Napoleon was still in the Elysée he sent Bertrand to see Denis Decrès, the former admiral who was staying on as Fouché's Minister of Marine, to find out what American ships there might be in the Channel or Atlantic ports of France. Specifically, he was to ask Decrès to assign to him the use of two frigates that were at anchor off the historic naval port of Rochefort, where the muddy river Charente opened out into a wide estuary with three possible exits to the Atlantic. Even through the years of the British blockade of the French coast it had been a usual port of departure for the West Indies and America. This was the first move in what was to become a game of cat-and-mouse with these two frigates. They were certainly the right ships in the right place at the right time, if all went well. *La Saale* and *La Méduse* were fairly new, well equipped and fast, large enough to accommodate Napoleon and his staff between them, and they could quickly be made ready for sea. The question that was to be asked repeatedly in the next ten days was whether the provisional government had any serious intention of letting them thus set sail. It is not even clear how they came to be in Rochefort and available just when they might be needed. It may have been an accident, but there have been suggestions that Napoleon had previously and covertly placed them there as some kind of insurance against failure in Paris, or, as it turns out, at Waterloo. Stronger suspicions suggest that Fouché was to use them to set a trap: if Napoleon took the bait and went aboard one of them he could be held there at a distance from Paris while his ultimate fate was determined; or, as a prime opportunist, Fouché could ensure that ships from the blockading Royal Navy were kept informed where they might find Napoleon. French historians opt for some such trap, though no specific evidence is offered for such a conspiracy. Fouché certainly knew that blockading warships were already off the mouth of the Charente, the Loire and Gironde too, and had been there keeping a speculative watch for three weeks before Waterloo. Such a configuration – secret contacts with Wellington, via him and or Castlereagh and the Admiralty, the British ability to send fast messages to the coast by the speedy telegraph system and to ships at sea by despatch boats, the chances for Decrès to send changing instructions to the frigates; the Rochefort solution was full of complications. Even if there was no deliberate plan to ensnare the fleeing emperor, all these discontinuities and delays meant that Fouché could change his intentions from day to day, as the situation developed.

Fouché's prime agent in all this was Decrès, who might have had a lingering feeling that he should help Napoleon in adversity, but also knew that he had no power to decide anything without reference to Fouché. He was a steady if not brilliant bureaucrat, gruff, insecure, noted for his difficulty in reaching troublesome decisions, who had fought at the Nile and for the last ten years had been the political head of a navy in slow decline from the defeats at Trafalgar. As it happens, he had served in the 'fireship' battle at Rochefort in 1809. Now he was in a position that was uncomfortable for a worried man.

At this moment there were many such careerists in Paris, in the army and navy, and in the provincial administration, who had switched their loyalty from the tricolour to the white Bourbon flag in the summer of 1814, had switched it back again in April 1815, and were now wondering when to go back to their flagpoles. They faced an immediate question about their careers, and were looking to the provisional government for an answer. Their more serious anxiety was about the returning Bourbons who had unleashed a purge that came close to a 'white terror' when they returned from exile a year ago, and there was now a justified fear of another such bout of revenge forcing a choice between loyalty and self-interest. Even Fouché, controlling so much, so skilled at survival, was at risk. A prime motive, indeed an explicit motive in his negotiations with Wellington was to secure his position in whatever government Louis XVIII was going to form if he was reinstated.

In this situation it undoubtedly suited Fouché to proceed as if the provisional government was doing all it could to assist the departing emperor to an acceptable destination. On 26 June Decrès had sent orders that the frigates were to be stocked up as if the head of state were going aboard. Decrès, moreover, sent instructions to the captains that Napoleon was to be received with honour and every comfort, provided with anything he wished. These orders are too substantial and precise to be regarded as more window-dressing; they clearly came from a man who believed that this was to be a bona-fide departure, who must have assumed that this was also Fouché's intention at the outset. Certainly there is nothing to suggest that Fouché was in a punitive mood: he would have wished to encourage Napoleon to leave Paris, to leave France, this would have been the most attractive solution on offer. There is, however, reason to suspect that Fouché was equally keen to keep Napoleon within reach while his negotiations with Wellington were proceeding, and a pause at Malmaison would enable him to keep Napoleon in play, so to speak, to be able to hasten, slow or prevent Napoleon making his way to the sea, as it suited his restricting purpose. There was another consideration, too. As long as Napoleon's attention could be focused on the frigates, the prospect would distract him from any consideration of other, or less desirable outlets for his energy.

Does this explain, in some respects, the ensuring equivocations about the frigates? Decrès of course had referred Bertrand's original request for the *Saale* and the *Méduse* to Fouché. When Bertrand came back to the Ministry of Marine next day he was again told to wait for an answer. Fouché must have known that by this time British ships were lying on and off the Atlantic coast, even that there were vessels off Rochefort specifically; and he would also have been aware that it would be very difficult (since France was still, in a complicated way, at war with Britain) for any French warships to run through the British blockade without risking a devastating engagement. That is why safe-conducts from the British were needed to ensure a permitted passage. Napoleon or his naval advisers would have been equally aware of this requirement, as well as the need for French passports to leave the country. He would also have known that Fouché was already issuing passports for some of his senior collaborators who were threatened by the Bourbons and needed to get clear of France before the incoming government was installed. If he attempted to leave the country without such papers he might be captured, for treason if the Bourbons caught him, as a prisoner of war if he fell into the hands of the British, or even as the 'outlaw' so designated by the allies at the Congress of Vienna. A conventional 'escape' was also a doubtful option. Even if it had been possible – and some kind of escape was feasible – Napoleon might well have regarded it as beneath his dignity to flee like an absconding financier or even as a smuggler; and, in any case, without papers it would have been impossible to get other members of his party away (wives and children included) and everyone would have been at risk in a flight which might end in an exchange of gunfire.

* * *

It is here that Fouché's role became uncertain. It is hard to reconcile all the arrangements with the frigates – the provisioning, the arming, the instructions that Napoleon was to be treated as a distinguished passenger with every comfort – with a double game about the safe-conducts. Yet he must have known that it was going to be difficult if not impossible to obtain them from Wellington. Difficult, because it was at best unlikely that Wellington would concede them without referring the matter to London, which would have meant a turn-around time of four to five days. Impossible, perhaps, because the British were probably determined to prevent Napoleon leaving France and would ensure he was kept to hand until his future was settled. Fouché may have hoped that a free passage for Napoleon might be part of a package deal with Wellington which dealt generally with capitulation and the surrender of Paris, which would enable Wellington to get what he wanted – the reinstatement of the Bourbons without trouble. Yet such a settlement was unlikely: the British were determined to make sure Napoleon was never again in a position (as they repeatedly put it) 'to disturb the tranquillity of Europe.' In which case, if Fouché – for old times' sake or any other reason – wished to save Napoleon's neck it would have to be done by sleight of hand. That is a possible interpretation of the fandango of orders, counter-orders and negotiations, but the conventional view in France is that it was all a trap to place Napoleon eventually in British hands.

Whatever the speculation had been Wellington's answer was immediate and final. 'I have no authority from my government to give safe-conduct to Napoleon Bonaparte.' As for Napoleon's protestations that he sought only a peaceful retirement, first paraded a year ago when he was being dethroned and sent to Elba, the Duke was equally scathing about this change for the better. 'You tell me he has abdicated. I knew that a year ago.' And then, cornered, Fouché tried another tack. He suggested that he might hold Napoleon and hand him over to the British or the Austrians if that was a condition of a favourable armistice. That idea, too, was rejected by the Duke. All that Fouché could be sure about at this point was that he should get Napoleon out of Paris as soon as possible, but keep him within reach as a bargaining counter.

* * *

Napoleon had come to the same conclusion. Even before Davout had arrived with his marching orders he had felt cribbed, cabined and confined, and increasingly uneasy in the Elysée. On 24 June, the day on which Bertrand had first raised the matter of the frigates, Napoleon had already been told by Hortense that she would receive him at Malmaison, on the other side of Paris from the advancing allied armies and on the road that led to the Atlantic coast. She had become increasingly uneasy about the way he talked more and more to less effect. Noting that he did not even have a competent bodyguard she thought he would be safer at Malmaison. While his valet Marchand arranged the collection of valuables and personal effects – such as the portraits of Marie-Louise and their son – were all added it amounted to a substantial collection of movables to be carried on to Malmaison. When he had decided what to keep and leave Napoleon had a last conversation with Lazare Carnot, who was one of the few great names surviving from the first wars of the Revolution and was now one of the five members of the provisional government. He had been elected in the hope he would be some sort of liberal check on the machinations of Fouché. 'he was a friendly and ingenuous man, readily influenced and misled,' Napoleon said. He was the only member of the new temporary regime to make a farewell visit to the Elysée for old times' sake, and to add his mite of advice.

'Don't go to England,' he insisted. 'You will be insulted by prize fighters.' After this curious allusion to the English sport of bare-knuckle pugilism, Carnot said he was sure the best thing Napoleon could do was to seek asylum in America. 'From there you will be able to make your enemies tremble... your presence in a free country will be a support to national opinion.' Unwittingly Carnot had put his finger on the main reason why Lord Liverpool did not want to see Napoleon cross the Atlantic without condition and without restraint.

As Carnot left, Napoleon sent another request for the frigates. Then, avoiding the clamouring crowds in the streets, he went out through the garden gate, mounted a plain coach, drove past the labourers still completing the Arc de Triomphe at the top of the Champs Elysée, and left Paris for the last time.

7

Malmaison

Malmaison was the first stop on a journey whose means and ends were uncertain. It was Napoleon's choice, but it was not a free choice: though he was aware that he was now moving into a genteel form of house arrest, where else could he go? At least the house was familiar, and very comfortable, though it had been standing empty and had been quickly refurbished for the occasion. 'Whoever would have thought to see the emperor of France a prisoner in Malmaison!' Hortense said, as she put herself out to make him feel at home. A fine country chateau, with the impressive gardens that Josephine had cleverly and extravagantly laid out, it was not really a suitable place for a state prisoner, whether to detain or protect him. Still it was refreshingly attractive, and secluded from the noisy crowds of street Bonapartists who had demonstrated outside the Elysée. He had spacious apartments, rooms for his staff, and a convenient place to entertain visitors; above all it was a place where Napoleon could maintain the mode and manner of imperial style. This mattered a great deal to him, especially now he was a dethroned head of state and a defeated commander-in-chief. He valued his imperial presence no matter how small the stage on which it could be displayed, preferring, it was said, marks of respect to affection. To put it bluntly, his lackeys wore livery to the last and his entourage kept up the protocols of court – as they had done in his comic-opera regime on Elba, and were to do on the British ships where he was detained, and in the final performance over the years on St Helena.

* * *

The key personage in this decline from the classical glory of his palaces to the pathetic pretences of exile was Bertrand, the grand-marshal of the palace, an efficient military martinet, who had taken over the position in 1813, had adapted himself to the restricted scale of the household on Elba, was now doing his best to manage with the dislocations and stresses of the pathetic journey into exile, and would stay with Napoleon until the last on St Helena. It was a difficult task which he performed with a precise and rigorous loyalty to the emperor, making sure the rules were kept, the means provided, and personal dignity maintained. He was not just a manager, responsible for the staff, for the provisioning and the organisation of the household, the carriages, and the complicated movements from one location to the next. He also represented Napoleon in making arrangements and served as a confidential adviser. His wife Fanny had become almost as important a person in the entourage. Her family, wealthy planters in the West Indies, were related to Josephine; her father was an émigré Irish general who had been murdered by his own cavalrymen in the revolutionary wars, Fanny Bertrand valued her British connection so much that, at this moment, she wanted the stressful journey into exile to end in Britain, where she would have preferred to live with her three children. She was attractive, flighty, outspoken in argument, jealous in support of her husband's standing. With the Montholons and their one child the Bertrands had pledged themselves to Napoleon and in turn were much considered by him.

It is fair to say that Napoleon could not have weathered the changing storms of his late career without Bertrand, and without his valet Marchand. A young man, he had come to Napoleon late in his imperial phase and stayed to be at his deathbed; even to remain loyal to the Bonaparte dynasty for another forty years. He was Napoleon's most trusted intimate, and his memoirs are among the most valuable and creditworthy of all those written, or ghost-written, by others with close private access to Napoleon. Scarcely a valet, more a welcome and competent companion, he was the domestic counterpart to Bertrand's formal role and they had a working partnership which saw the entourage through the hard years of Napoleon's decline.

* * *

There were others at Malmaison who were also staying on, taking the ultimate steps in loyalty when that no longer brought the shower of titles, pensions, properties and sinecures with which Napoleon had rewarded his family and close associates in the years of glory. Where were they now, the Bonapartist nobility who had come up through the ranks, benefited by the Revolution, and reaped the rewards of assisting and flattering the Emperor in the triumphant days of his empire? Some had fallen away at the first abdication, in 1814; some had failed to rally in 1815, most of the remainder were turning away in the current disaster, claiming their loyalty was to the state and not its failing master. Decrès put it frankly when he later told the maritime prefect of Rochefort, Casimir Bonnefoux, 'honours pass, the country is immortal.'

Such a comforting gloss on desertion. It did not apply to Emmanuel Las Cases, who made himself a spokesman for Napoleon, spending much of

Malmaison was Napoleon's favourite palace

his last years in his daily company and writing the *Memorials* which are the largest if not the most reliable record of Napoleon's retrospect of his thoughts and experiences. It did not apply to Gourgaud, a trusted and ambitious younger general who had saved the Emperor's life in a battle and stayed on to be one of his closest aides. Nor to Montholon, a more irresponsible careerist trying to rise by holding Napoleon's coat-tails, who was a troublesome member of the household who eventually came down in the world to poverty if not disgrace. And there were others who were not to make the final choice for the St Helena party, but were nonetheless faithful knights of the Bonapartist circle – de la Bedoyère, the young colonel who had led the first unit to desert to him on his return from Elba, had been one of the last to leave Waterloo, and was soon to be shot by the Bourbons for treason. Savary, currently head of the national gendarmerie, had played box-and-cox with Fouché as Minister of Police and was so hated by the Bourbons that he had no safe place away from Napoleon's side; François Lallemand, a general, was one of two fiercely Bonapartist brothers, and equally at risk; so, too, Lavallette, the Minister of Posts who ran Napoleon's communication system. Spacing out this inner group was a cluster of aides and equerries who were for the most part eager to continue the fight and were undoubtedly important to Napoleon's personal convenience and safety.

Around this suite there was an astonishing corona of servants, keeping up the ease and style of an imperial entourage. For them, little had changed except their location. The almanac showed that in the Tuileries there had been a domestic staff of more than one hundred footmen, pages, chambermaids, a retinue of arcane domestic occupations. A surprising number of these flunkeys had been brought along from Paris, to form a comfort zone around their master. Thirty-seven had left on the departure from the Elysée, twenty were asked or chose to stay on to Rochefort, and more than half the remainder continued into a loyal exile. There were chamberlains, waiters, valets, footmen, pages, a chef and cook assistants, grooms, stable boys, watchmen, even a lamplighter and a lavatory attendant.

Bertrand and Marchand between them had brought quantities of chattels, valuable and domestic, to provide the equipment for this working model of an imperial court. They had permission to move the hundreds of silver and gilt place settings, the crested Sèvres porcelain services from the Elysée and they transported the Tuileries sets as well. There was so much silver and gold that it provided a cashable asset in time of need; but it was so little needed in the event that some of it was still crated on St Helena at the time of Napoleon's death. When the whole stock was being packed for onward travel from Malmaison, it required more than fifty leather trunks and packing cases, many of these having compartments specific to silver and porcelain services, table furniture such as épergnes, tureens, clocks, wineglasses, and large quantities of table linen, bed linen, even twenty-four sets of curtains, a great many books, maps and scientific instruments, silk screens, stools and mattresses, family chattels, medicines and bath salts. To round out such a collection of amenities came more practical

possessions – sporting guns, horse pistols, swords, sets of bridles and saddles
– and out there in the stables were the imperial coach, coupes, berlines,
calèches, to carry the household on its way. There was no furniture: special
permission was required for that and removal wagons brought it on in their
slow way later. The transport of all this impedimenta to the coast was to
prove an embarrassment to Napoleon's freedom of movement, specifically
as he waited at Rochefort for its delayed arrival. To have it all packed and
waiting, and fifteen carriages ready to hand, was only part of the burden
that Bertrand and Marchand were carrying in the uncertain days at
Malmaison. Even if Napoleon was relatively modest in his personal fortune,
he had no intention of falling into a scrimping retirement.

* * *

There was an important if uncovenanted addition to the household a few
hours after Napoleon had arrived at Malmaison. This was General Nicolas
Becker, who had been appointed as commander of a small unit with
ambiguous orders. The general, who had served Napoleon until 1809, and
was currently in charge of parliamentary security and a liberal member of
the Chamber himself, was a good and considerate choice. It was years
later, he recalled, that it was revealed to him that Fouché and Davout were
regularly in touch with the royalist government. He had at first been assured
that he was appointed in order to save the emperor and protect him. He
was agreeable, even-tempered, and respectful to Napoleon even when he
disagreed with him or had to pass on unpalatable orders. He was to be
Napoleon's minder until he left the country, cast in the difficult role of
answering to Fouché and Davout and yet ensuring that Napoleon neither
came to any harm nor caused any.

'The honour of France,' Davout wrote, as a Minister of War who
had no other form of reference for his authority, 'demands that care should
be taken for his personal safety and the respect due to him.' So far so
good. The implication of the ambiguous words that followed was not
so pleasant. 'The interests of the country require that malicious persons
shall be prevented from using his name to excite a disturbance.' Becker,
in short, was there to make sure that Napoleon did not succumb to any
dangerous impulse or invitation to set himself up as some kind of freelance leader of an army defending France against the invaders. In the
current crisis that must still have seemed to Fouché and his colleagues

to be possible, even likely, and such a coup was as much to be feared as the chance that Napoleon would fall into the hands of the Prussians before he could be spirited away out of their reach. For this purpose, some three hundred grenadiers and chasseurs were stationed in the barracks at nearby Reuil, a troop of cavalry (the government in Paris knew that Blucher's search parties were getting closer) guarded the house, and a large force of gendarmes was set to patrol the seven hundred hectares of the grounds.

Davout knew the way Napoleon thought well enough to guess at some of the ideas that would chase through his impatient mind. Like Fouché, he also had ample experience of Napoleon's capacity for deceit when it suited him, and it might now suit him to 'excite' the febrile opinions of the army. Davout was right. Napoleon had only been in Malmaison for a day when he drafted what purported to be a farewell proclamation to the army, which he proposed to publish in the *Moniteur*, the official newspaper. 'Soldiers!' it began, 'a few more efforts and the coalition will be dissolved. Napoleon will recognise you by the blow you strike. Save the honour, the independence of the French nation!' It is understandable why, given the strange mood of the army, this appeal never saw print. Defeatism and what Wellington called 'the revolutionary spirit,' competed for the support of the large units which were still fighting, or in a position to do so. Both the Duke and Fouché continued to be afraid that Napoleon might make another dramatic performance like his unforeseen eruption from Elba: there was still no armistice; there were still Bonapartist generals in the field and there was mutinous defiance of the Bourbons among their men. It was already beginning to seem that an eventual peace treaty might bring harsh terms to an occupied and pillaged France. While there was a sad and increasing hope for peace throughout France – that seemed to be a widespread feeling – there might be a response to Napoleon's claim that better terms could be obtained by fighting on, and that he was the only man who could lead such a struggle. He was still a major piece on a board where all the moves were uncertain.

* * *

The mood at Malmaison was curiously erratic, as Fouché and Napoleon matched prevarications: part of the problem was simply a matter of disrupted communications. While letters and reports went to and fro, the situation was changing; and if Napoleon himself did not have much to do, the provisional government had so many problems on its hands that few decisions had time to mature before they were overtaken by events. Fouché simply could not make up his mind he wanted to do about Napoleon, what he was able to do, and what might turn out to be the result – there was no way to ensure that what was proposed was actually carried out. The demands that the allies were making, and the role that Napoleon's fate played in Fouché's responses, meant at best delays and overall a great deal of muddle.

It also meant that the days of Napoleon and his retinue seemed purposeless, a tedium punctuated by visitors, by messages from Paris, and by a lot of talk among the house party. The future was obviously the main subject, its hopes, fears and possibilities being canvassed in so many combinations. Napoleon seems to have played a socratic role in these conversations, asking questions, listening, seldom showing his own hand in anything but general terms. Lucien and some of the younger aides undoubtedly talked about the possibilities of fighting on, or of retreating to exile to rally forces for a comeback, but Napoleon would not have considered this subject suitable for sociable chatter. A more typical subject was the discussions about America. The entourage seemed to take the idea of America seriously. 'He is going to the United States, where we shall all join him,' Lucien wrote to his sister, Pauline. A young aide, probably Fleury du Chaboulon, asked about the prospects of America. Napoleon said he thought the United States might give him land, 'or I'll buy it and cultivate it. I shall end as man began. I shall live on the produce of my fields and flocks.' The answer was typical of the mock-modesty which alternated with grandiose visions in his table talk. It did, however, lead on to an interesting speculation.

'Do you think the English will leave you in peace to cultivate your fields? They will force the Americans to send you away from their country, even if they do not turn you over.'

'Then I will go to Europe.'

'And the English fleet?'

The questioner was obviously familiar with the way Napoleon glossed over awkward points, and was pressing him. This time he got a prescient reply.

'If I can't elude them they will take me. Their government is useless but they are a great nation, noble and generous. They will treat me as I ought to be treated.'

Napoleon was a good logician, a trait he had often turned to advantage in his campaigns.

Three weeks later, as the situation developed, Castlereagh was thinking on exactly the same lines, writing to the Prime Minister speculating about what should be done if Napoleon should make a successful break for the United States. This was typical of the way planning and communications kept being overtaken by events. In such circumstances, Castlereagh wrote, 'the allies should call on the Americans to arrest and surrender Bonaparte to them. Such an appeal could do no harm, and at the same time I should expect little to come of it. I do not see how the president of his own authority would take such a step, and the utmost our influence might accomplish would be his removal from the United States.' This speculation casts a doubtful light on the theory that Fouché and Castlereagh had already jointly conceived a trap for Napoleon: if they had done so, at this point, the Foreign Secretary would not have been writing in such exploratory terms. It does show, however, that expectations of this kind could have influenced Wellington in his point-blank refusal of safe-conducts, just as they must have prompted the cautionary instructions to 'seize and detain' Napoleon that the Admiralty had sent out to its captains early in July.

* * *

Fouché's uncertainty is revealed by the succession of orders which came to Napoleon from the provisional government direct or through Decrès, still at the Ministry of Marine. In what appeared to be a decisive ruling on 26 June the provisional government stated that the frigates were empowered to sail for the United States, that facilities and an escort would be provided to take Napoleon to join them and that, their task accomplished, the frigates should return to France. The catch was in Article V. 'The frigates shall not leave the roadstead at Rochefort until the passes have arrived.' Put in context, there was an urgent need to send Napoleon on his way, out of reach of the advancing Prussians, but not so much on his way that he slipped wholly out of reach. The limiting condition meant that once abroad one of the frigates Napoleon could be held as a virtual prisoner, indefinitely, until a further decision about his fate was made. For this reason Savary disputed the condition with Fouché, who brushed his objections aside with some flippancy, saying that he wanted to make sure that every precaution was taken for Napoleon's safety. He did not wish to be blamed if there was any confusion: that was why he was sticking to the issue of the safe-conducts. Neither Savary nor, subsequently, Napoleon was deceived – the only conclusion that could be drawn from this piece of double dealing was that Fouché wanted to hurry him away from Paris – there was a genuine security risk from the Prussians – but was by no means disposed to let him, the erstwhile emperor, get clean away. He might still be required as a pawn in the continuing negotiations.

The need for haste was certainly underlined by a letter from Fouché to Decrès on 27 June. The enemy was 'fast approaching': Napoleon must be persuaded to leave 'as we could not be answerable' if he was caught. Suddenly, the rules were changed, no doubt to encourage the emperor to depart, for Article V was now rescinded. If Napoleon could get himself down to Rochefort and persuade one of the captains to take the risk of sailing without a pass, well, that was his decision. Decrès, moreover, had come to Malmaison with a comprehensive set of orders for Captain Philibert of *La Saale* and Captain Ponée of *La Méduse*. They were to treat Napoleon 'with all the consideration and respect which is due to his situation and to the crown which once encircled his head.' The sailing orders were comprehensive, setting out what powers were given to this distinguished passenger and his suite, how the frigates must sail within twenty-four hours, what they were to do if they encountered British ships – the frigate on which Napoleon was not aboard was to interpose itself and draw the enemy fire 'and give the one conveying him the means of effecting his escape;' and arrangements for arrival in the United States. To conclude this encouraging set of orders, the officers and crews were to ensure that the departing emperor enjoyed 'the safeguard of the loyalty of the French people.' Napoleon could not have asked for more, down to the last injunction, 'that the frigates should set sail as soon as possible.'

Unless Fouché and Decrès were engaged in an unnecessarily complicated deceit, these instructions must be taken at face value. There was no need to rouse Napoleon's hopes with such detail: the urgent necessity for haste was now so self-evident that it did not require dishonest decorating with such explicit orders. In any case Fouché still had the means to modify or cancel them. And that is exactly what he did, within a few hours. It suddenly became essential for him to retain Napoleon on a leash after all; and a new courier was despatched with yet another set of orders. The situation had changed dramatically before Decrès had even returned from Malmaison. Once again Napoleon was told he would require a safe-conduct.

The reason for this volte face was an urgent despatch from Lafayette who was out at Blucher's headquarters trying to secure a ceasefire. He was, he said with evident regret, 'loath to repeat that one of the great difficulties would be the person of the emperor... the powers will demand guarantees and precautions against his reappearance on the scene... his escape, before the conclusion of negotiations, would be considered as an indication of bad faith on our part and could materially compromise the safety of France.' Fouché was resolute about the implications of this sudden veto: he now wrote to Decrès that 'the welfare of the state' required that Napoleon must be kept waiting at Rochefort 'until his fate and that of his family should be regulated in a definitive manner.' The decision to re-impose the conditional delay was not ameliorated by softer words about employing every means to ensure that 'this negotiation may turn out to his satisfaction.'

Decrès left no doubts about the matter. Napoleon was now instructed to go on board one of the frigates but they should not sail until the passports from Paris had arrived. Meanwhile, Decrès added, introducing a new aspect of the problem, he was going to ask Fouché if, on arriving at the Aix roadstead, Napoleon could be 'immediately conveyed to England on board a frigate or any other vessel.' Decrès, thanks to the telegraph, would know what British ships were on blockade watch off the mouth of the Charente, and he was now giving a broad hint that the insistence on remaining on one of the French frigates might be eased if Napoleon wished to evade that condition by going over to a British ship. This is the first hint of such a move.

More instructions followed. This time from Davout, responsible for the role of General Becker, who was again insisting that it was urgent for Napoleon to leave Malmaison. If he chose to ignore the latest messages then it would be Becker's duty 'to exercise the strictest surveillance, both with a view to prevent His Majesty from leaving Malmaison, and of guarding against any attempt on his life.' To that end (which may also have been prompted by anxiety about the consequences if a Prussian patrol should seize Napoleon) the Malmaison guards were being put on alert. That order had scarcely been received and put into effect when yet another letter from Davout told Becker he was to stay close to Napoleon as long as he was at Rochefort, and that the passports would be sent to him there. The growing sense of urgency, even of doubt and uncertainty, like the repeated emphasis on Napoleon's personal safety, show how anxious Fouché and

Davout had become as the Prussians hooked round toward Versailles and Malmaison. Roadblocks were set up, bridges by which the Prussians might cross the Seine were destroyed. If Napoleon were to fall into the hands of the Prussians it would tear apart the delicate web of negotiations linking Fouché and Wellington in the decision about the threatened emperor's future. It would not have suited Fouché at all if he had suddenly found his main bargaining asset tipped into the Prussian camp.

* * *

The triangulation of relations between Wellington, Blucher and Fouché was indeed causing difficulties for reasons other than the personal fate of Napoleon. A ragged line of trust had enabled the two military commanders to scrape through the crisis at Waterloo, but their relations were deteriorating thereafter. Wellington was afraid the Prussians were getting out of control, would go on a destructive rampage in Paris, riot with loot and rape through the French villages as they advanced, recalling old resentments at their defeats and occupation by the French in the past ten years. They were clearly less interested in how the country was to be governed in this aftermath of victory than in what they could get out of it. Blucher was simply not interested in the future of the Bourbons; his hostility to them was as nothing to his desire to seize and execute Napoleon. He was prepared to humour Wellington's distaste for murdering a defeated enemy, but he saw no reason to make concessions to the Bourbons, whose restoration he regarded as part of a British scheme to use the Bourbons as puppets through whom Britain could manipulate France as a check on Prussian aspirations for the domination of Europe.

All these stresses came out in the exchanges between the two commanders. Gneisenau, Blucher's chief of staff who had been reluctant to save Wellington at Waterloo, wrote one letter after another to Baron Muffling, who was his liaison officer with Wellington. All those missives were demanding summary treatment for Napoleon, one snide comment saying that if Wellington had 'parliamentary reasons' for being lily-livered about the matter it was because the Whig opposition would have been infuriated by a summary execution. So he should turn Napoleon over to the Prussians to do the work he shirked. A day or two later Blucher cynically offered another reason why Wellington was so hesitant. The English were hedging because they were under an implicit obligation to Bonaparte, whose wars had given a spurt to British trade and industry, accelerating their rise to its 'greatness, prosperity and wealth.' The unfortunate Prussians, said Blucher pleading mock self-pity, had been fought over and 'impoverished by the war.'

While Napoleon could have had no direct knowledge of these differences between the allies he had much experience of such diplomatic stresses, and was well aware of the tactical division between the two armies and their objectives. The same would have been true for Fouché, whose efforts were being directed towards a settlement with the Bourbons – a purpose for which Wellington's help was essential – and a reasonable agreement about Napoleon's future. In both respects he needed the British to ward off and mollify the Prussians: the peace terms with Berlin would be draconian enough without France being left exposed to the full force of Prussian revenge. For Fouché, sending contradictory messages to Napoleon was only a relatively trivial aspect of this tortuous situation.

* * *

Napoleon knew, or could guess enough about what was happening, and he sent a firm protest against the changed arrangements. He despatched this to Davout, in consultation with Becker, saying he renounced the journey to the coast because of the risks to his own safety. It was his increasing opinion that once on a frigate he might well be a virtual prisoner, since Philibert and Ponée would not be permitted to sail until 'the arrival of the safe-conducts to go to America, which will probably be refused.' Whatever the embarrassment might be to Fouché he proposed to 'await his arrest at Malmaison until a decision on his fate has been made by the Duke of Wellington.' Two more days of standoff had ended in the same stalemate.

In a last attempt to break out of this sinister paradox, in which every day's delay reduced his chances of getting away, Napoleon now sent a personal emissary to Davout. This was his aide General Flahaut, the natural son of Talleyrand, and the lover of Hortense and he had been a conspirator in the escape from Elba. Flahaut was to insist that the release of the frigates, with or without the passports, was the condition of departure from Malmaison, and he seems to have pressed the case to the point of insubordination. Giving as good as he got to Davout's intransigence, he managed to prick the conscience of Napoleon's old comrade-in-arms, now embarrassed by his change of loyalty and reacting with blunt anger.

'Bonaparte doesn't want to leave but we must certainly get rid of him. It prejudices our negotiations. If he hopes we will take him back he is wrong. We want no more of him and if he doesn't leave at once I shall have him arrested. I will arrest him myself.' Flahaut derided Davout as a renegade, contrasted his own loyalty with Davout's defection, resigned his general's commission on the spot and went back to tell Napoleon he had achieved nothing.

On 29 June Fouché changed his mind again. The Prussian cavalry had now circled so far round Paris that the road leading out to Malmaison had to be barricaded at Neuilly and Becker was sent orders to blow the bridge at Chatou if that was necessary. This sense of urgency might explain the gruff tone of Davout's remarks to Flahaut. Davout, now speaking for Fouché, sent yet another changed order to Decrès, stating that 'because of the long delay since the safe-conducts were requested, and because of the fears about Napoleon's safety resulting from the present situation,' Article V was suspended once again. 'The frigates will therefore be at Napoleon's disposal. There is now no obstacle to his departure. The interests of the state, and his own, make it imperative that he should leave at once.' Decrès was instructed to ride through the night to Malmaison, taking whatever orders that might be needed to release the frigates and instruct the captains to receive Napoleon on board.

Even if this panicky order meant that there was now no French restriction on sailing without the safe-conducts, Napoleon realised that should he manage to reach Rochefort it now looked as though everything he did there would have to be at his own risk, without any laissez-passer to get him through the British blockade. If the frigates did sail they would have to make a run for it and might even have to fight their way out. This was not an inviting prospect. One obvious interpretation of this sudden release, Napoleon decided, was that Fouché had decided to hustle him into a trap. Be that as it may, with Prussian cavalry almost within an hour's gallop there was nothing he could do but set out for Rochefort and see the situation for himself.

8

Last Chance

Napoleon's future might well have been different if he had been sharp enough to ignore the temptation of Malmaison after he abdicated and gone straight on down to Rochefort, or some other port. The British had relatively few ships watching for fugitives or the movement of naval and merchant ships leaving the long coastline from Cherbourg to Bordeaux. In the time frittered away at Malmaison Napoleon could certainly have reached the sea and found some means of sailing away. The prospects of success would have been fair, if not good, even if the British captains had some prior knowledge of his destination or even good guesses about it. But he had chosen to delay, partly because he was keen to stay within reach of Paris while the confused situation might offer him some chance of a comeback, partly because he had a large retinue to consider, and moving them in a hurry would have been as problematic as trying to find a ship or ships to accommodate them; and partly because he felt a hurried flight with one or two companions would be undignified. Scurrying out of the country as 'contraband' was the way he put it, and that would not have been an acceptable entry into history – a consideration that was never far from his thoughts in these last weeks in France. There was, finally, a risk he was not prepared to take. Travelling in disguise, without official approval or an escort, he might have been arrested on the way by police or military patrols, or even murdered by bandits. This current instability of purpose meant that he had hung on at Malmaison until he was actually forced to quit in a rush. There was nothing more to be gained by delay – except the very last idea that had occurred to him.

Becker must go to Paris for a final throw of the dice.

* * *

All through his career Napoleon had gambled on surprises, on doing what was unexpected, even improbable, and at this crisis in his fortunes this old campaigner's itch was tickled by a glimpse of an opportunity. He had never put the escape from Elba far out of his mind; it was such a heart-warming example of what self-confidence and ingenuity could achieve that he often reverted to it when asking his staff to trust him.

How could one forget the way in which he had evaded the blockading frigates, set off with a few hundred men from his Guard, and marched hundreds of kilometres across France without a shot being fired either for or against him. Perhaps nothing like that could be done again. He was aware that the mood in France had changed, that the people had been depressed by the butcher's bill for the casualties at Waterloo, that they were beginning to ask – as Lafayette had asked in the crucial debate in the Chamber – why the lives of so many should be spent to promote the ambitions of one man? Even old Bonapartists were becoming eager for peace, and, despite the gravity of the situation and the exactions of the Prussians, many were unlikely to respond to a rallying call as they had done a year ago. 'I must wait until the voices of the people, the soldiers and the Chambers recall me,' Napoleon said in a mood of resignation at Malmaison.

Yet... the word was never very far from his thoughts until he was finally seized and detained, yet... his fancy that one last glorious improvisation was possible was strengthened by the sound of cannon over at St Denis, by battalions of French troops on the march cheering as they passed Malmaison, by every report of the anger provoked by the marauding Prussians and the fears what they might do when they entered Paris. 'I could throw myself upon the mercy of my soldiers,' he insisted. 'My appearance would excite the army and they would blow the enemy to pieces.' When Napoleon was gripped by this kind of impulsive belief in himself people close to him knew that he was likely to convince himself into believing what he said. All of them were familiar with some unforgettable examples of this trait. Sometimes it had led to extraordinary triumphs, and as often as not to failures and even disasters. He had, after all, deserted his men in Egypt, at Moscow, Leipzig and Waterloo, though it was the successes he chose to remember.

Now this reckless state of mind, which did not brook much contradiction, was prompting an undeclared, undiscussed and unlikely venture. He interrupted his preparations for departure, went to his bedroom and returned dressed in his full uniform as a colonel in the chasseurs, sword and all. Becker, as much concerned as he was astonished, was given no chance to argue. He was told to go to Paris and report to Fouché and Davout that the greatest of French generals wanted to take command of the army and crush the enemy outside Paris. That done, the honour and the territory of France saved, he declared, he would resign his commission and settle abroad. Bravado was only one element in this muddle of intentions; a fear that his final overthrow was otherwise at hand was another. A brilliant coup would snatch a crowning glory out of the scrap-iron of defeat.

Once Becker had left for Paris the preparations for leaving for Rochefort were suspended; Napoleon and his young staff officers turned them into a readiness for a campaign. One can envisage Napoleon, in his characteristic way, rousing his supporters with rhetorical and often unfounded questions. Well, there were about 100,000 troops and 500 guns which could be marshalled for the defence of Paris, were there not? How tired and disorganised Blucher's 60,000 men must be? So many? Surely nearer 40,000, strung out alone the line of march, spread out for looting? And the wounded? And had Wellington even so many to hand? He would have seen his Dutch and Belgian troops stay at home, after Waterloo, his Hanoverians returning to the English king's personal fiefdom, some of his better troops left besieging the unsurrendered frontier fortresses? The Duke would have trouble with his supplies, with the wounded; what replacements would he have received for his losses? And neither Blucher nor Wellington would be expecting a counter-stroke, would they? Wellington had said he was humbugged at Waterloo. Very well, he could be humbugged again. All such guesses hardened Napoleon's conviction, and militated against the more depressing conclusions about the state of the French army. True there had been heavy losses at Ligny and Waterloo, that much of the French army was defeated and demoralised, that some generals were preparing to demobilise even if others were still holding out and eager for leadership – the two generals commanding the western departments were in a combative mood, with fresh troops; Grouchy, with disciplined and competent units, was pulling back with his men buoyed by the victory at Ligny, and no wish to disband. Davout was telling the generals generally that they should hold on.

Conjugating all these factors, none of which was verifiable by him at even a day or two's notice, Napoleon had turned to the maps spread on the dining-room table, and concluded that this gamble too would succeed – if only the provisional government would let him take it.

Hindsight suggests that he indeed had a good case. Davout was in fact considering this possibility at the same time. There might well have been a battle, even an indecisive battle which would halt the allied advance; a series of engagements might induce war-weary allies to offer reasonable terms; a rising of this kind, if it did not degenerate into widespread and disastrous civil war, could well have made a Bourbon restoration unsustainable. Fouché and his colleagues were capable of making their own calculations and deciding that all these escapades were far more likely to end in expensive and disastrous ruin than to snatch a victory from the jaws of defeat. Even if they succeeded in whole or in part they would be left with a triumphant Napoleon. It would be them, not him, looking for a ship to leave the country.

* * *

All this explains Fouché's grim greeting when Becker presented himself to the provisional government and delivered the fantastic message he carried. 'Is he really making fun of us?' Fouché asked Becker incredulously. Wasn't Becker neglecting his duties, leaving his post and failing in the order to keep Napoleon under close surveillance? Might Napoleon have taken the chance to slip away in Becker's absence? Driven by anxiety and anger Fouché sent a chastened Becker back with a note he had scribbled out while they talked. Napoleon was told that he 'must leave without delay. The Prussians are now marching on Versailles.'

Did Napoleon not realise that the provisional government could no longer guard his personal safety? 'The front – such as it was – had begun to collapse, and Napoleon's presence was not merely embarrassing, but dangerous for the provisional government and himself.

The first words Becker heard as he rode back into the stable yard at Malmaison came from an excited aide. 'The emperor is going to rejoin the army.' People were milling about the stables at Malmaison inspecting saddles, weapons, horses – Bonaparte's own horse was ready for mounting. Boxes of food and ammunition were being broken out, and a messenger was already on the road to summon the garrison at Reuil. Napoleon might well have said that he had more men available there than the vestigial companies he had carried across to Antibes from Elba.

It is hard to understand how Napoleon could have placed such hopes on Becker's mission that he had allowed his young officers to turn Malmaison into a parody of a campaign headquarters. Becker thought the scene one of such unjustified expectation that a shake of his head when he returned was enough to silence the hubbub into disappointed silence.

Incognito: Napoleon leaves Malmaison in disguise

All waited for Napoleon's reaction. For once he did not react to Fouché's dismissive note with a rant about lost opportunities and what he could still do to retrieve them. He said, sadly, 'these men do not understand either the state of affairs or public feeling if they resist my offer.' For once his pendulum of decision swung quickly and decisively. 'I now have no alternative but to leave. Give orders for my departure.'

* * *

While the packing was resumed and all the entourage who would be leaving were making their final preparations Napoleon fitted his actions to his words. He went to his room, changed back into simple civilian clothes, the incognito guise he had been told to assume – a round hat, brown coat and blue breeches. Then began the long business of farewell, gifts, messages; a good many staff were being left behind, and provision had to be made for them. They would not see Napoleon again, and they knew their lives would now be less exciting, less pleasant, less comfortable without his presence and his patronage. There was a sad, stoic parting with his formidable mother, whose large family he had done so much to promote. There was an emotional farewell, too, with Hortense who would miss him, for they were genuinely attached, and she was in tears as she offered him a valuable belt of diamonds as security for an even rainier day.

Once again the caravan was on the move. All those goods and chattels, those trunks and numbered packing cases, had to be loaded again into the convoy of coaches and wagons which would eventually follow the retinue down the road to the west. The party was divided to limit the demand for horses on staging-posts. Napoleon, Becker, Bertrand and Savary were to go by Tours, Gourgaud and Marchand would follow them. Las Cases and his son, the Montholon family, various aides, the supply wagons, the chests of arms, would go by Orleans. Madame Bertrand, Lallemand and Joseph Bonaparte would follow from Paris the next day. There was no hint of any kind of interference with these departures; with their postillions and servants they were safe enough against anything but armed troops.

The sudden decision to leave in the early evening may well have been prompted by the news that the Prussians were getting even more dangerously near. A Major de Colomb, with a troop of the 8th Prussian hussars, could have reached Malmaison at midnight. They stopped at Montesson, five miles away, to be told that their mission was futile. The emperor had already left.

9

Delays and Difficulties

Napoleon had been one of the great travellers of his time. Though he was still only forty-six he had sailed to Egypt, he had taken the Grande Armée on the long march to Moscow in 1812, and through his years as consul and then emperor his coach journeys had stitched the map from Paris to Madrid, to Warsaw, Berlin and Vienna. He had a campaigner's routine, special travel equipment – a portable library, a special bed – and a physique strong enough to go from one campaign to another, from one capital to the next. Some of his rides were memorable if not comfortable to recall: the retreat from Moscow, the flight from Waterloo, the depressing crossing of France on his way to exile on Elba. He was now heading west on what was to be the last of them. No glory this time, no glittering bevy of officers and escorts, no welcoming dignitaries at the head of welcoming crowds. There was little to lift his spirits on the road to Rochefort, no certainty about his reception, no idea of what delays and difficulties would be found at the end of it.

Rochefort, of course, he knew. He had visited it in 1808, on a tour of inspection, and proposed some improvements to its fortifications. His government had put in hand the draining of the marshes. It was a fine baroque town, stone houses, laid out in a classical grid to the orders of Louis XIV, who made it a premier Atlantic port along with Brest and Cherbourg. It had excellent facilities for building and repairing – over five hundred warships had come from its yards – and its arsenal remains a model of its kind. It had, however, been in decline, as the French navy suffered defeat at and decline after Trafalgar. While Rochefort itself was protected in a loop of the Charente, some way back from its estuary, the river empties into a large roadstead, with three passages between the islands of Ré and Oléron that lead out into the Atlantic. Apart from the difficulty of navigating the shoals and rocks of these channels, the Basque Roads, as this expanse of water is generally known, had one serious disadvantage in the days of sail. That was the prevailing and frequent wind from the Atlantic, together with a strong tide that sets right up to Rochefort, making it easy to enter and hard to leave through the roadstead. In April 1809 a British fleet, led by Admiral Gambier and given its punch by the adventurous Cochrane, found a group of French warships and a merchant convoy waiting to sail for the Antilles. Unable to manoeuvre to bring them to battle the British took advantage of the onshore wind and sent in fireships, creating a panic which left four ships destroyed, others damaged and run ashore, and a lasting memory of the destructive *brulots*.

Apart from this disaster Rochefort had suffered all through the Napoleonic wars from the constraints that the long years of the British blockade put on the economy of the port. It had once been a valuable focus of trade across the Atlantic, especially with the French colonies in Canada and the West Indies, but its prosperous days were over. French boats had to be blockade runners; neutral boats, especially Americans, preferred the ports on the Gironde, especially Bordeaux and Royan. A few naval ships still used the roadstead, though they anchored some way off the coast near the small oyster-rich port of Fouras, a few kilometres north-west of Rochefort, where a finger of land curves round and points out to the fortified Ile d'Aix, one of a set of forts which dominated the whole stretch of water. At the time Napoleon arrived there were few significant vessels, just the two frigates, *La Saale* and *La Méduse*, the brig *l'Epervier* and a corvette that does not seem to have been ready for sea.

It is a curious feature of such an important port that the town should have no view of its anchorages. Almost all the coast is flat marshland, without any high points to give a view; it must have been difficult to operate the telegraph system which linked the town to Paris in the frequent conditions of mist and rain. Most of the coastline of the islands shows up as dark blue lines upon the horizon, Oléron lying to the south and Ré to the north of Basque Roads; small islands and forts on sandbanks punctuating the great spread of tidal water.

Napoleon may have chosen Rochefort as a preferred destination for his journey from Paris but boarding a ship there and making its way out to the open sea was not easy in any circumstances, especially when wind and tide were foul; a disputed departure could be risky, even dangerous by comparison with Bordeaux, or Le Havre, or with Royan at the mouth of the Gironde some kilometres south. Yet it was the port which Napoleon had chosen from the first, and a destination in which he persisted through all the complicated dealings with Fouché and Decrès. There are casual references to alternative ports, mostly by his brother Joseph who had already chartered an American vessel moored at Royan, but that apart no other port was formally considered by Napoleon or his advisers. This insistence on Rochefort, and on the two frigates anchored there, suggest that Napoleon may have had prior knowledge of this possible means of escape; and the fact that he was not greatly surprised by the close blockade of the Royal Navy gives at least a hint that the course of his journey into exile might have been predetermined. Had he all along believed that of all possible captors the British would prove the most responsible and considerate? Indeed, he said as much on several occasions. No doubt he would have been pleased to go scot-free to the United States, but that was a chance that could be combined with his dealings with the British. And so it was to turn out: in the event the delays and debates that marked his passage from Paris, through Malmaison and down to Rochefort, made little difference. After a few close shaves – the Prussian patrol, later the Bourbon police – he ultimately ended where he might have intended all along.

* * *

Napoleon was no doubt aware of the logistic problems ahead as his coach rumbled out of Malmaison, but he was no longer making an imperial progress through his realm and he had to take things as they came. Time pressed, communications were poor, and he could not have had any detailed knowledge of the situation at Rochefort. Could he count on the neutrality rather than the hostility of the port authorities? Would the frigate captains be sympathetic, or had they been given secret orders to delay or even to detain him? How would the local population receive him? Would the royalist and Catholic sentiments of the area – after all, this had been one of the centres of the counter-revolution in the Vendée – inhibit the crowds that were accustomed to greet him with shouts of support, as the citizens of the faubourgs had done in Paris? And there were the most significant questions which only time could answer. How near had the British blockade come to closing the port to any departing vessel? How many ships, and what kind of ships would be there to bottle up the frigates in the Basque Roads? And what were the chances of evading them? In what weather conditions would that be possible? True, it was almost July, but the Atlantic weather was notoriously variable and a west wind would block any escape attempt. He would know that even if all went well, even if Fouché was genuinely willing to let him go, he was taking a gamble on his own life as risky as any he had taken as a politician or a commander in the field.

* * *

For a start, however, he had to get himself and his retinue down to Rochefort, and there were uncomfortable reminders of what had happened in 1814. Like that journey which had started at Fontainebleau and crossed France to take him to a British warship to be ferried to Elba, he was again setting out from a royal chateau and driving through France to a different coast where, for all he knew, another British warship might be waiting to receive him. He was not a prisoner, but he was not quite a free man, and the collapse of his fortunes would have been poignantly marked when he paused briefly at Versailles to recall days spent there with his late wife Josephine, and possibly his living but separated empress Marie-Louise. The shades of former greatness fell across his first stop. Rambouillet was the summer lodge of French kings, set in a vast forest about thirty kilometres from Malmaison. He spent a long night there, lingering, it was said, as if he hoped to be overtaken by a courier with news to his advantage, and then left at 11 am having chosen some maps and books from the library.

It was a hot journey on to Tours, but there had been occasional consoling cheers from little crowds who heard the cortège was on the way, and it was midnight when the prefect of Tours came out to greet him and reassure him about his safety. So, with this assurance, the party rolled on through the night, reaching Poitiers at noon. From there Napoleon sent a letter to Casimir Bonnefoux, the maritime prefect at Rochefort, asking about the availability of the frigates. Then the party went on to Niort. Hundreds of kilometres had narrowed down the remaining distance.

At Niort there was a warm welcome, as the prefect Busche moved him from the scruffy Boule d'Or to stay in the prefecture. Here a local regiment as well as the citizens turned out to celebrate his arrival, and the presence of Bonapartist hussar officers seems to have set off another relapse into a fantasy of a comeback. He listened while he was urged to make common cause with two generals, Lamarque and Clausel – in command of the Vendée and the Gironde – and when Lallemand and Joseph arrived there seems to have been yet another informal council of war about this distracting idea of rehabilitating himself with the army. In response to Joseph's report that an American ship was available in the Gironde estuary Gourgaud was sent ahead to find out whether a small boat could put out from the Charente to meet the American brig, but nothing came of the idea.

Napoleon had first to hear the bad news. Bonnefoux was diplomatically unwell and had sent Querengal, the Rochefort harbourmaster, to make his apologies and deliver a disturbing note to Becker. It said that English ships were blocking off the channels out from Rochefort, that it would be 'extremely dangerous for our frigates and those on board to try to force a passage' and that it would be necessary to wait for a favourable moment to get away – if, indeed, the frigates could break out at all. This gloomy report, which certainly put an unjustifiably pessimistic gloss on the facts, may have been a delaying move by Bonnefoux, who certainly didn't wish to be implicated in a rush to board the frigates and sail away that could well end in disaster. At this moment, in fact, the chances of getting away were better than they would become over the next week. This news from Bonnefoux and the prompting of the military enthusiasts was enough to make Napoleon hanker back to the policy he had abandoned on the last frantic afternoon at Malmaison.

* * *

It was now 2 July and Becker wrote a letter in Napoleon's name to the provisional government, saying that the emperor was 'very tired and extremely worried about the state of France,' and that the government 'were in too great a hurry to remove him from Paris.' Napoleon claimed he could 'exercise a considerable influence in politics by supporting the government's negotiations with an army for which his name would have served as a rallying-point.' Napoleon then introduced an important new idea into the debate about the frigates. Following up the report that 'the English squadron has redoubled its vigilance since 29 June, making it impossible for the ships to get away,' he asked Decrès to do something which picked up a passing reference that Decrès had made to embarking on a British ship. He now wanted Decrès specifically to authorise the captain of the frigate he was to board to 'communicate with the officer commanding the English squadron, if extraordinary circumstances should make this step necessary.'

This letter written by Becker but inspired by Napoleon is the first specific reference to the idea of a negotiated surrender to the British, and Napoleon added a strong justification for it. This act would not merely safeguard his personal safety: it would spare France the 'sorrow and shame' of seeing Napoleon 'taken from his last refuge and handed over unconditionally to his enemies.' What did this opaque statement mean? It seemed still to assume that there would be no safe-conducts waiting at Rochefort. Since Napoleon would be going to fend for himself once he reached the coast, it also foresaw the risk that he might board a frigate and be told by the captain that, safe-conducts or no safe-conducts, he could not sail, could not even be permitted contact with the British vessels without an explicit order from Decrès. And what did Napoleon mean about being 'handed over unconditionally to his enemies?' Was that likely to happen at Rochefort? And why had this phrase not appeared in any of the previous exchanges with Paris?

Though there had been an air of cheerfulness about the reception at Niort Napoleon was still unsettled. As Becker's letter was being drafted a two-day-old rumour came in from Paris, saying there had been a great battle against the allies outside the capital, and Napoleon hastened to add a footnote wishing the army well, repeating his forlorn offer of help. 'if, in this situation, the English blockade prevents the frigates getting away, the emperor is at your service, as a general whose sole desire is to be of use to his country.' It was a slender hope that Fouché and his colleagues would accept a proposal they had rejected more than once, and Napoleon himself – though he still played with the idea – was as doubtful about it as they were. When all the talk at Niort was said and done Napoleon reluctantly came back to what he had said since his first day at the Elysée. He could not embark on an adventure which would plunge the country into civil war; and Fouché could ignore the implied threat since he was sure that Napoleon could not make the offer seriously for more than an hour or so of reckless impulse. That night at Niort, where Joseph had turned up, his spirits were high; there was a party at the prefecture where a military band played marching songs and crowds sang and danced in the streets.

The caravan moved off at dawn crossing miles of the dreary marshes of the Charentais until it arrived at the gate of Rochefort at eight in the morning. Napoleon was greeted by a somewhat shamefaced Bonnefoux, who had to confess to an 'indisposition' that revealed more about the uncertain state of his mind than the state of his health. In 1814 he had raised the white flag to welcome the late king's brother returning from long exile; in 1815, with Napoleon returning from exile, he had to hoist the tricolour again, and he was now having to tread warily through the morass of complications into which Napoleon's arrival was dragging him. Bonnefoux was no partisan. He was yet another bureaucrat with an instinct for survival, and bearing Napoleon no ill-will; he even showed a sneaking sympathy with him at critical moments. Nevertheless he had orders from Paris he had to obey as best he could, and he undoubtedly knew that within a few days he would be hoisting the Bourbon flag again. Napoleon had in fact arrived on the day that Paris capitulated.

* * *

If Napoleon had expected to move straight on board one of the frigates he was disappointed. The situation was too confused for such a simple solution. After this exhausting journey he lapsed into apathy and disappointment. He could not move straight to one of the frigates, and it was hard to decide whether the reasons were true or deceitful. The orders for Bonnefoux and the captains were certainly ambiguous and outdated, the information about the hovering British ships was patchy, and Napoleon's official party was divided. Personal problems about self-preservation or career prospects were clouding the judgements about the best choice of his advisers for their leader. True, they were told the frigates were there, even if they could not be seen from Rochefort let alone boarded without a coach journey up the coast and about a kilometre's sail in a small boat to reach them. But what did the captains think about the situation, and what secret orders had they received with strict instructions not to reveal them? And did they share the now common anxiety about taking decisions that might cost them their posts, or worse?

It was certain, however, that the frigates were good, well-found and fast, a 38 and a 42 gun vessel, as good as or better than their British counterparts. *La Saale* was commanded by Captain Henri Philibert, who had more than twenty years of service around the world to give him experience and also to make him cautious about doing anything irresponsible – that meant he would not disobey or even try to second-guess Decrès.

He was also said to have royalist sympathies and carried the fleur-de-lys on his cabin windows. François Ponée, who captained *La Méduse*, had spent much of his career in the West Indies, was fully accomplished in Atlantic voyages, and he seemed to be eager to help Napoleon on his way and take risks in doing so. When they came in to join the discussion in the prefecture Philibert took his stand on the question of the safe-conducts: he seemed to be unaware of the on-and-off nature of these instructions, said he could not sail until they arrived, and spoke for both captains about the

La Méduse went from Rochefort to be a famous wreck in 1816

difficulty of evading the British squadron and the need for unusually favourable weather if there was to be any chance of doing so.

The context of this gloomy professional opinion was a meeting with Napoleon, Bertrand, Savary, Bonnefoux and Becker, who were later joined by the sympathetic Pierre Martin, a former admiral and maritime prefect who had been retired after the fireship fiasco in 1809. Martin was eager to help and brought his considerable knowledge of the Basque Roads into the discussion. It was a beginning to a running argument that went on for days. Accepting for the moment that the frigates were not operationally available, Napoleon and his advisers had to look for and consider alternatives. What other ships might be available? How could they be reached, let alone deployed? Could they cater for the whole party, which would amount to more than fifty men, women and children by the time all the coaches rolled in, or would they only be able to take Napoleon and two or three cronies? Where would they be, how could they be seen, how suitable would they be for a long voyage, how trustworthy would their captains prove in a possible confrontation with the British ships? Within hours of arrival Napoleon's party was facing a long list of unconsidered difficulties.

* * *

Meanwhile, as if in proof of good faith, the two captains were proceeding to water and provision their ships as Decrès had instructed when the frigates were first offered. They were preparing to treat Napoleon with every honour and comfort, as if he were still a head of state. The logbook of *La Saale* carried a long inventory of the supplies being taken on – enough for a voyage of at least four months. There were two calves, two goats for milk, stocks of ham and pork, five hundred eggs, three hundred bottles of Bordeaux wine, sixty bottles of champagne; sugar, flour, butter, preserves and delicacies. The *Méduse*, too, was preparing for passengers, though no one had been told how many members of the household might be expected to accompany Napoleon. All this could be taken as evidence of good intentions, at least that Decrès had been acting in good faith when these initial orders were drafted; and the captains declared they could be ready for sea in twenty-four hours if they were released or, as Philibert repeated, the safe-conducts arrived.

These preparations were matched by Napoleon's organisation of his retinue for travel – a necessary task since they could not all be crammed into two ships for a long voyage, and some sort of provision had to be planned for those who must necessarily be left behind. At this stage the senior staff positions were those arranged before leaving Malmaison. Bertrand, of course, as ever with so much responsibility that it is surprising how he managed to cope with the staff, his colleagues and the emperor. Gourgaud, Savary, Montholon, Lallemand, Planat and Resigny would be aides; Las Cases, invaluable as the best English speaker, would be chamberlain and his son a page; then, led by Marchand, there followed the long train of domestics. The persisting demands of imperial domesticity were apparently one of the practical reasons for Napoleon's distracted moods; it seemed as though his reputation for audacity was being corroded into procrastination. Long afterwards Montholon recalled these fits of hesitation; staying at Rochefort for five days – until 8 July – was 'a mystery that I have never succeeded in fathoming.'

Some of these days were certainly taken up with discussion of what should be done if the frigates were obliged to remain at anchor. Even if Napoleon showed no great enthusiasm for other options for escape, always being quick to dismiss proposals that he considered inappropriate to his dignity or, more reasonably, if they left out of account the train of people who had followed him thus far. There was a real problem of numbers – even when footmen, and grooms and ushers had been dismissed, Bertrand was going to have a hard time head-counting to match the accommodation that might be on offer on the frigates and, as events turned out, any smaller vessel that could carry the persons and effects of the household. It is, however, unlikely that these uncertainties were the prime cause of delays that would prove fatal to the fugitive's hopes. There is no record of secret messages – that was in the nature of things – and Napoleon would not have had access to the telegraph which could quickly carry coded messages from Paris to the Rochefort officials or move any important signals in reply. It is conceivable that his procrastination at Rochefort was still due in part to the possibility of the much looked for and not altogether improbable recall to lead the army again. He had seemed to be looking out for such a message all the way down from Paris. He might still be hoping for it.

10

Means of Escape

Napoleon must have had only the sketchiest idea of what was happening in Paris while he was on the road. There were stale newspapers to read, and rumours that came along with them, but the only mention of couriers catching up with him are those dealing with letters from and to the provisional government. Napoleon was having to make guesses from such messages as the journey proceeded, trying to explain the double-shuffling of Fouché's intentions, and make more guesses about what he should do about them. He could get only fragmentary and out-of-date news about the military situation, and it is doubtful whether he had any coherent account of the day-to-day crisis that was occupying Fouché's attention in this vital week.

It began on Saturday 1 July. On that day Blucher's advanced troops had reached Versailles and were across the Orleans road, but two Prussian regiments were badly cut up in a surprise attack by the Bonapartist cavalry general Exelmans. It was a local success, but not the only one, as half a dozen fortresses held out between Waterloo and Paris. It was enough, however, to encourage those fellow generals who were still not ready to surrender, and added to the problems facing Davout, who was now in overall command of the army. The Minister of War had received a blunt rejection of his sixth request for an armistice to the local Prussian commander, General Ziethen: nothing could be agreed, he was told, until he surrendered both the army and Paris. Staying out at his headquarters at La Villette, Davout did not go into Paris to a meeting that Fouché had called for nine in the morning, where he presented a set of questions to an *ad hoc* group of ministers and some of the marshals who were in the city. It would be generous to call them the elder statesmen of this scratched-up and short-lived government. Fouché asked whether they thought the approaches to Paris could be held, whether the allies could still be resisted on all fronts, and how long the capital could hold out against a Prussian occupation. Since the meeting could not reach a conclusion the questions were then passed to a meeting of the Council of War, which Davout had convened out at his La Villette headquarters that evening and went on into the small hours. It had been attended by an impressive turnout of active and ranking generals – eighteen of them – and Davout sent their conclusions to Fouché.

No. Paris could not be defended with any degree of certainty. Yes, it was possible that a local defeat could be inflicted on the over-extended Prussian army, but such a victory would not achieve much unless it was followed up by the defeat of Wellington, and some substantial body of troops was got together to deal with the 250,000 army of Austrians and Russians which was just beginning to cross the Rhine on the south-east frontier. If a victory was so problematic, the meeting decided, defeat would be a disaster as the Prussians stormed into Paris without any agreement imposing restraint on them – the situation most to be feared. A few of the fiercest generals demurred, protesting that they and their men still had fight left in them, but this was the moment when Davout had to make up his mind for them all and for Fouché too. He had received an insulting letter from Blucher. It warned him to save the Parisians from the fate imposed upon the citizens of Hamburg by Davout's stubborn defence of the besieged city in 1814. Wellington had also written a personal letter saying he wished to avoid further bloodshed. 'Up to this point,' Davout wrote later, in words that seemed to concur with the terms in which Napoleon was still using to justify his return to the army, 'I was sure of beating the Prussians and throwing them back in disorder on the English before the English army would be in a position to help them' But the meeting, together with the latest reports from the fronts, had persuaded him, and he wrote to tell Fouché to get whatever terms the English and the Prussians would offer.

The reluctant conversion of Davout, a man who felt that his ultimate loyalty was to his army, was just what Fouché needed in his dealings with his government colleagues and the Chambers. He could cite the Council of War to justify sending fresh emissaries out to the Allies, formally asking for terms – an end to the fighting, the transfer of the army from Paris to south of the Loire, and an eventual but controlled occupation of Paris. At the same time he resorted to his clandestine means of seeking a deal, sending his personal intermediaries with letters to Wellington not shown to the government's peace commissioners. The first was a letter to cover himself, showing the Chambers, the army, and the royalists with whom he was secretly conniving, that it was in everybody's interest to close down the war as quickly as possible. 'The legal state of France,' he wrote in words that would please liberals such as Lafayette, 'is a government with the grandson of the emperor of Austria at its head.' That said, he also opposed Blucher's plan to march into the city without prior agreement. 'The increasing evils of war' that would follow such action, he insisted, would make reconciliation difficult. 'It is in the king's interest for everything to remain in suspense. What is more reasonable than to conclude an armistice?' At the same time, Fouché's representatives – the double agent Colonel Macirone and General Tromelin – were to present a handwritten message, which clearly summarised Fouché's difficulties. 'The army resists because it is apprehensive; reassure it and it will be loyal. The Chambers are opposed for the same reason; reassure each of them and you will have everyone's support. In order to be understood,' Fouché continued in a characteristic example of his stage management, 'some explanation is needed; consequently do not enter Paris for three days, so that everything may be made easy. The Chambers will be won over, will believe in their independence and will consent to everything.' Macirone was to add verbally that since Davout had been 'won over to the Bourbons' he needed only a promise of good treatment of the army for him to get it away from Paris to any point that may be assigned.' Once the army and the Chambers were separated, both would quickly agree to accept Fouché's proposals.

* * *

It was Castlereagh, above all, who knew – even more than Wellington – what complex roles Fouché had played; and he comprehensively described them to Lord Liverpool. 'The great service performed by Fouché,' he wrote, was that 'he had the merit of acting with great personal courage and address.' He had been 'opposed successively to the resentment of the Bonapartists, of the army and of the assemblies; with a majority against him in the executive government he succeeded in saving himself, dissolving them, and bringing in the King.' For all this, as well as the manner in which he had systematically outmanoeuvred Napoleon, it was essential that Fouché remained close to the King when the Bourbons returned to Paris.

He may have had an astonishing record of betrayal under Louis XVI, the Terror and the Directory, and was now to ensure the second betrayal of the Empire, but it was also an astonishing record of success.

* * *

Drummed out of Paris

While these exchanges went on both Wellington and Blucher began to move closer to the capital, but Wellington was still sufficiently concerned about the residual strength (and what he called the 'Bonapartist fervour') of the French army to hold off – any further action might be disruptive, even dangerous. If Napoleon was really sent away, and the French army could be persuaded to withdraw, south of the Loire, it would be better to halt, and he persuaded Blucher to do the same. 'It seems to me,' he told Blucher, 'that to attack Paris with the force that you and I have at present under our command would be to risk much and to expose ourselves unnecessarily to the possibility of serious losses.' It would be better to wait, let the National Guard maintain order in Paris and forego 'the useless glory of entering Paris at the head of our victorious armies.'

* * *

Blucher did not budge on this point of demonstrative vengeance. A letter putting Wellington's moderate views was scrawled all over with derisive comments by Gneisenau, and Blucher was making it clear that he proposed to ride down the Champs Elysées at the head of his troops. Wellington continued to remind him that the armies were exhausted and divided, and asked what would happen if they became dangerously overexposed and a French army marched up with Napoleon at its head. This led to new complaints from Blucher about the 'faint-heartedness' of the English, and an assertion that the Prussians would not waver in their demand for a 'heavy' occupation of France and swingeing reparations. If Napoleon had seen this exchange of letters, indeed, he could have used it to great effect to justify his own speculations and proposals. On the immediate question of an armistice, or at least its political terms, the two Commanders continued to stand by the allied policy which Metternich and the Russian Nesselrode had spelt out in a memorandum on 26 June. A copy of this document was now handed to General Tromelin to show Fouché what they had required, and still required, as the basis of a ceasefire.

There would be no truce before Napoleon's departure, and 'nothing must be allowed to halt the operations now going on.' They would not negotiate with Napoleon, or any other member of his family, 'would not recognise any authority set up by him, not even the Chambers which owe their existence to him… as far as the government which France is to have, this question will be postponed until later…' The statement that this matter had not been agreed between the commanders (Blucher was well aware that Wellington wanted to ease the Bourbons into Paris as much as Blucher wanted to take control of the city himself) was sufficiently ambiguous to be misconstrued by the liberal majority in the Chambers who still hoped to install Napoleon II. It was, however, a last gasp of people who hoped a constitutional government might somehow be squeezed in between Napoleon's fall and the arrival of Louis. Such a proposal could barely be expressed let alone voted, because Fouché was trying to manoeuvre them into capitulation. Helped by Fouché's assertion that Davout had the army under control Wellington now agreed to terms for an armistice. Fouché was permitted to add a few sweeteners for the benefit of the deputies: 'capitulation' became 'convention' and there were minor concessions to offset all those that the French had granted to get the document signed. Before it went to the Chambers it was given another push to approval, this time the disagreeable news that the means of defence for Paris were 'exhausted', and that if the agreement was not endorsed there was nothing to prevent the allies entering Paris by force, with the dreadful consequences every one of them could envisage.

* * *

For Fouché this settlement put some vital decisions on the agenda. The Chambers and the provisional government had to resign at once, remaining in office only long enough to ensure public tranquillity. The Bourbons, or at least Talleyrand on their behalf, had to accept certain constraints – a reaffirmation of the Constitutional Charter under which they had governed after the first restoration, formation of a new Chamber which would have common powers with the King to propose legislation, relaxation of press censorship, and above all a fairly extensive amnesty, excluding only those who had actually 'plotted' for Napoleon's return.

Being told that these were the best and only terms he could expect, Fouché now went out to see Talleyrand and Wellington at his Neuilly headquarters. Fouché made a last attempt to secure concessions that would make it easier to get the backing of the Chambers. One was the retention of the tricolour as the national flag. The other was an unqualified amnesty. Neither request was accepted. The tricolour was dismissed (with good reason) as the symbol of revolt, and Talleyrand insisted that it had been difficult for him to wring out even a limited amnesty from the vengeful Bourbons. That done, Fouché then named his price for all he had done to help the Bourbons. He knew they disliked him even when he was working with them or to their advantage, but Wellington – who had been having troubles of his own with them – now insisted that the Bourbons could not have managed without Fouché's adroit manoeuvres, and that for the time being they would still need his accomplishments as Minister of Justice. Even the hard-line Comte d'Artois, the King's brother, reported all the ways in which Fouché had assisted the royalists during the confused and difficult Hundred Days.

'Everyone joined in,' Chateaubriand wrote in his memoirs, 'the religious as well as the impious, virtue and vice, the royalist and the revolutionary, the foreigner and the Frenchman … They cried from all sides that without the proposed minister there would be no security for the King and no well-being for France.' There was no gainsaying the attitudes that this testimonial described. Fouché himself was arguing the valid point that a Bourbon government could not be formed, or would not last, without his presence. The strongest of all his arguments was the state of the Paris streets, with small demonstrations of support for Napoleon always threatening to build up into larger and more dangerous riots; and he was aware that in the first days of July it was possible that a substantial part of the army might refuse to disband. The pressure he put on Napoleon to take himself off was essentially a response to allied demands. Better than any other man he had reason to believe that, in these disturbed weeks and even more in the year or so ahead, a Bonapartist revival was not just a chimera conjured by Napoleon's resentment: the escape from Elba was too fresh in the minds of politicians and generals alike. On 2 July Blucher's chief of staff, Gneisenau, was alarmed at what he complained was Wellington's slack attitude towards another spell of Bourbon rule without strict and enduring controls. 'Who is going to stop Bonaparte, after having fled to America for two years, from coming back and causing new unrest?' It was all right for the English 'to be satisfied with the return of the Bourbons. Their islands are free from attack.'

So Fouché was in the new government and the new government was going to be installed before the arrival of a Prussian army bent on rapine and loot. The sense of being denied an overdue triumph, since one was denied after victory a year earlier, runs through all of Blucher's letters and orders. He could not stop the Bourbons, however, and it was left to Talleyrand to turn the defeat of Napoleon into a political resurrection of Louis XVIII. On the evening of 6 July, Talleyrand did what Wellington wanted. He took Fouché out to the King at Saint-Denis, where Louis had paused while he was waiting for the last touches to be put hurriedly to the necessary paperwork for his entry into Paris. There, in the stiff encounter characterised by the phrase describing 'Crime entering on the arm of Vice,' Fouché and Talleyrand were sworn in as members of the exile crowd who would accompany Louis into his capital and start to govern France again.

Next morning Fouché had to complete one more piece of business. To accommodate the incoming government he had to get rid of the old one. It was another of the close-run events that had marked his process ever since it began at Waterloo. While the deputies were meeting in the Palais Bourbon, as if there were no hostile armies waiting to get into Paris, they were discussing proposals for a new liberal constitution. Prussian troops had already arrived and were filtering into the gardens of the Tuileries where the members of the provisional government were about to dissolve at the instance of Fouché. The next day Louis was installed in Paris without any opposition or disturbance. Fouché had stage-managed the whole business from start to finish.

* * *

Lazare Carnot might share the anxiety of Gneisenau. 'The one fear of the allies both within the country and abroad,' he wrote as the French troops marched out of Paris as the Prussians marched in, 'is that Napoleon will ride once more, that he will return at the head of any army.' Napoleon might still be having such fantasies at Rochefort; the fact that he kept returning to the possibility of a breakout shows how difficult it was for him to accept the reality of his situation. He was like a man in a fugue, going through the motions of talking to other people without seriously reacting to what they are saying, or relating to what they proposed he should do. When he arrived at Rochefort, it is true he was exhausted, disappointed, worried – but he was familiar with such states of mind, and in the past he had shown a remarkable resilience when things were going wrong – an ability to recover himself and revive his energy for a fresh, perhaps a different start. It is this quality of response that seems to have atrophied. By the time he arrived in Rochefort; he may have been distracted by the argument about the frigates, which he found frustrating as the prospect of using them was tarnished by the repeated changes in the conditions on which he could use them; he was also uncertain how to react to the negative reports about their availability that the harbour-master had brought to him at Niort. In these circumstances it is surprising that he did not go out to the frigates immediately to see the situation for himself. He seems simply to have accepted what he was told on arrival – the prevailing winds were too foul to get the frigates out against it; there were problems with the strong tides; above all the British warships were blocking all three exits from the Charente. It is now clear that Bonnefoux exaggerated. Until 3 July there was only one frigate on blockade duty, and its commander repeatedly noted his concern that during this window of opportunity he lacked the ships to make his surveillance proof against an ingenious and determined attempt to get through it.

* * *

It was uncharacteristic of Napoleon to accept such a veto without challenging it, and for him to be so unresponsive when his advisers tried to interest him in other methods of escaping from France. They knew that time was pressing, that each day lost made successful escape more unlikely, and that covert operations designed in a hurry could well fail for lack of reliable people or circumstances which could be trusted. Still he procrastinated. They were also familiar with the fits of ill-health and depression which left him unfocused, indecisive. His changes of mood had become more marked since Waterloo and the abdication crisis. The delay at Rochefort was fatal to his hopes.

Lallemand, writing years later, was more explicit about the reasons for delay, blaming it on members of the suite who were close to Napoleon and wanted to persuade him to turn himself over to the British. 'They caused a deadly delay with their coolness and irresolution,' when they were confronted by alternative schemes for getting away,' he wrote. He also felt that there was no 'high political interest' and that Napoleon 'became much too indifferent as to his personal consideration' and left everything to his 'loyal advisers who, unfortunately, were not clear-sighted.' Lallemand exempted himself from 'the common error'.

At last a start was made on the problem of the frigates when Bonnefoux called a meeting of the port authorities for 4 July, including Napoleon and his party, ostensibly to discuss what could be done if it proved impossible to leave on one or both the frigates. The discussion seems to have been dominated by the views of Admiral Martin, who had been the port-admiral at the time of the 'fireship' raid in April 1807. He knew as much as any man about the waters at the mouth of the Charente, and when it became clear that there were continuing difficulties about the use of the frigates, he took the meeting on to consider another way of getting the emperor out to sea and on his way to America. This plan was to be quite well developed, and the naval advisers supported it, but it was only the best of a series of escape proposals which were being proposed and discarded up to the last night Napoleon spent on French soil.

* * *

The question of where, when and how Napoleon should leave France was answered in various and seldom convincing ways, but each of them was vitiated by a single, understandable and irreparable mistake, and it is possible that Napoleon had realised this and that it was the main reason for the depression which made him stay aloof from each idea, and led him to reject them all in succession. From the moment he left Malmaison he was burdened by a cortège of aides and followers whom he could not bring himself to abandon; they were to travel with him all the way to the coast, to go on in some numbers to England, and even into exile. It was simply that he felt an obligation to people who had rallied to him in his downfall. A more significant reason was that he could not shed the illusion of imperial grandeur, and the travelling court – like a band of strolling players – was needed to support that illusion, both for his own pride and for the impression it made on others. It was a gaggle of courtiers; Bertrand, the Grand Marshal of the Palace, managed them all, the chamberlains, footmen, pages, chambermaids and grooms, with all the paraphernalia that went with them. They were a fatal embarrassment to a fugitive who was trying to save his life in flight.

There were moments which dramatically illustrated the problem. The hectic confusion, described by Marchand, as the procession was mobilised to flee hurriedly from Malmaison was one such; the succession of departures and embarkations at Rochefort were three more examples. Later, getting all the aides – with arguments about status and role – off to England showed how desperately Napoleon needed a pathetic pomp to shore up his pretensions. This is why the frigates were needed; this is why safe-conducts were essential; and it is why, at Rochefort, it was really a waste of time, and a raising of false hopes, to consider alternative means of escape. If Napoleon had been willing to make off by himself, as he did in the calamitous retreat from Moscow when he left his dying army and fled to Paris, then it would have been quite possible, if not easy, for him to have got clear away to the United States. It is perhaps to his credit that he declined the opportunities.

* * *

The Baudin escape plan was the best example of all the schemes because it was the one which was best organised and most likely to succeed. Napoleon could accept the failure to board and sail away in the frigates, refusal of passports made it appear like an affair of state, a matter of negotiations which could be bruited about and make his enemies appear dishonourable and make Napoleon look cheated and ill-used. But going away in the darkness without a farewell, no melodramatic departure staged for future generations, was not his idea of an exit into history. As the pressure on him increased, the more unlikely it became that the juggling of the frigates would be permitted to work, the more appearances were maintained that it was going to work. There were discussions about the convergence of a suitable wind, the phases of the moon and the time of the tides; the ships were fully provisioned; the professional and political attitudes of the captains were discussed; there were dramatic changes in orders from Paris, and above all there were the safe-conducts. Napoleon knew very well that they were not coming, yet they played such a part in his drama that up to the first contact with the British ships Napoleon kept the demand for them in the forefront of his presentation. This is the context in which his response to repeated and unacceptable offers of help from outside friends and allies must be placed.

Charles Baudin was a celebrated seaman, who had explored the South Pacific in his ship the *Bayardère*, a corvette which with its companion ship *l'Indefatigable* was moored at Le Verdon, at the north-west of the Gironde estuary near Royan. He was a friend of Admiral Martin who had mentioned his name as a possible helper at the meeting on 4 July and was then authorised to contact him. The response could not have been more encouraging. Baudin's father had been a Jacobin, he himself was still a republican who had disliked Napoleon's imperial ambitions. He made that clear at the start of his letter, offering help, saying for the same reason he had 'opposed in will and deed his attempt to remount the throne because I considered it would be fatal to France and events have justified my forecast only too well.' But he was to be trusted. 'There is nothing I am not willing to do to spare our country the humiliation of seeing her sovereign fall into the hands of our most implacable foe.' In order to get Napoleon off to 'live in a free country' he proposed with the support of the American consul Henry Lee, that Napoleon should be embarked on either the *Pike* or the *Ludlow* 'American privateers of exceptional speed.' If there was an attempt to intercept the chosen vessel Baudin was prepared to go out with his two corvettes and 'bar the enemy's way'. So far so good. It was possible to make the journey from Rochefort, going out of the south passage between the coast and the Ile d'Oleron, landing, crossing about ten kilometres of the peninsula and joining Baudin at Le Verdon (it was only at the last minute, on 14 July, that the British warship *Patroclus* came into that mooring). The proposed journey over to the Gironde was practicable. Napoleon's brother Joseph made it twice, so did one of his aides, General Lallemand. The risk was that a night journey across a promontory where there were royalist sympathisers, gendarmes, informers, even bandits and smugglers, was a risk that Napoleon would not take. It was kept as an open possibility until he gave it final consideration on the eve of his departure for England. He would not go without some of his court ,and he could not go with them; he could not leave the rest of his retinue to fend for themselves; and, like other proposals of the kind, it was 'degrading', not 'dignified'.

* * *

The same adjectives could be applied to other furtive proposals, like Captain Besson's scheme, Napoleon insisting he would not leave the country like an 'absconding bankrupt'. Besson was a French officer married to the daughter of a Danish ship owner, whose vessel *Magdeline* was off La Rochelle, to the north. He had shipped a cargo of cognac (it is said it was purchased by Las Cases), and he proposed that Napoleon should be shipped out in a padded barrel fitted with breathing tubes and hidden among the cargo. Napoleon's objection to this was not just discomfort but the possible ignominy of discovery, in such a hiding place, which would make him liable to summary arrest and forfeit any claim to an honourable reception. Here again there was dalliance up to the end. Three days before Napoleon surrendered a group of young marine officers and men fitted out a pair of luggers which could take him and some aides out at night, slipping along the coast where British warships could not venture, and putting him on board the *Magdeline* waiting off St Martin-de- Ré. It was, once again, a possible flight in desperate circumstances, and it is claimed that some of Napoleon's baggage was actually loaded, but late at night he dismissed the plan. It was just as well he did; the security was bad and the young men were arrested by the port authorities in the dawn of the night they had proposed to sail.

Of all the proposed events the most sensible practicable and, ultimately attractive were the two attempts of his brother Joseph to get him to go to America and set up a new life there – the phrase was justified because that is exactly what Joseph did. He had advantages. He spoke English, he was wealthy, he was politically experienced, and he had good contacts. In this case, as an important figure in French freemasonry, he found himself given the use of a chartered American ship, the *Commerce*, on which he (and Napoleon if he wished) could depart incognito. There was the same difficulty that had been involved in the *Bayardère* proposal of the risky night crossing to Royan, for that was where Joseph's ship was anchored too; but Joseph paid no account to that. He was, indeed, prepared to make it easier for Napoleon by taking his place for the few hours necessary for him to get away.

Looking rather like Napoleon, Joseph suggested that he should stay in Napoleon's room claiming that he was unwell and housebound, a deception that would be kept up loyally by Marchand for sufficient time for Napoleon to reach Royan. Joseph was confident that he would not suffer any great penalty once the impersonation had worked. He was to have a very prosperous and successful life in New Jersey, in a house which became a focus of Bonapartist intrigue (Appendix III) to rescue Napoleon from St Helena.

* * *

So the schemes went on, with poor security. One reason to believe in them is that bits and pieces of news about them reached the British commander, making him anxious enough to intensify his surveillance and reposition his ships. He did not take them too seriously, however, with one exception. This was a desperate idea to use the frigates after all. The details are obscure, but they are part of the legend, perhaps part of the facts since the British commander had feared he had insufficient force to deal with it.

The two frigate captains were to do what they had been instructed to do, disregarding only the latest order from Decrès that they were not to do anything which endangered their ships. They had provisioned the frigates for a long voyage, armed up, and ready to sail. At this point they differed significantly. The junior, Captain Ponée, of the *Méduse* was a Bonapartist who was prepared to risk his career, even, perhaps the lives of himself and his crew, to get Napoleon away. His senior, Captain Philibert, was a stickler for orders – a sensible thing to be in those changing times – and who throughout these two weeks kept his mind narrowly on his duty, and on how obedience now would profit him with a future government. All along, as the correspondence with Paris and Bertrand showed, as in his dealing with Bonnefoux, Philibert was always prepared to sail if Napoleon could produce the necessary safe-conducts; even without them, but that instruction had been superseded by another telling him he must not risk his ships in an engagement with the British. He certainly was not going to run into an unnecessary flight with the Royal Navy. Given Philibert's unyielding stance, it is hard to see how Ponée's proposition could ever have been seriously considered. He wanted the two frigates to sail together, if they had the wind, and that he should use the *Méduse* to draw the British fire, while Philibert with Napoleon on board would pass by in the lee without risk. It was the sort of proposal that would have appealed to Napoleon, desperate though it was, and in other circumstances he might have tried to persuade Philibert to take a chance.

By now, however, time as well as the tide was running out, and Napoleon's fate loomed four miles down into the Basque Roads, and there was nothing the frigates could or would do to avert it. What was left to him was preparation for the new role he would have to play in exile. The faded imperial style would suit. He would be the fallen eagle, chained defiant and maligned to a distant, weather-beaten Atlantic rock, having given his all for a nation that would acclaim his destiny but would no longer have any part in it.

11

The Man who Captured Napoleon

Captain Frederick Lewis Maitland, who commanded *HMS Bellerophon*, brought his ship into the Basque Roads on 31 May. He already knew the quirks of the Rochefort channels – to the north was the Pertuis Breton, a narrow and rocky passage between the coast of Brittany and the Ile de Ré. The wider and deceptively open Pertuis d'Antioche, protected by forts on either side and the impressive Fort Boyard in the middle of the channel, was the normal way into the mouth of the Charente and Rochefort beyond. The risky passage over the shoals between the mainland and the Ile d'Oleron led out to the Pertuis Maumasson and to the coastline falling away to the south. Six years before Maitland had commanded one of the smaller ships in Admiral Gambier's fleet when Lord Cochrane launched the fireships that brought ruin at the east end of the roadstead on the French navy. Now luck and good judgment had carried Maitland into a position where, if the reports he was receiving were true, he had a chance of making his name as the man who captured Napoleon. He could equally be the man who, with bad luck and poor judgement, might miss this great chance, or at least so mishandle the affair that it would become a diplomatic and professional scandal.

He was, however, a senior, experienced and self-confident officer, who came from an aristocratic and service family on the Scottish Borders. At the age of thirty-eight he had seen service in the Mediterranean, the West Indies and, most recently, on the North Atlantic, convoying troop transports for the American war that was now petering to its end. Tallish, lean, tousle-haired, courteous and reserved, he had the talents required for the delicate situation in which he now found himself, though his unpractised French was to be a limitation. He was liked by his officers; his polyglot crew,

Captain Frederick Lewis Maitland

press-ganged over the long years of war, was the charge of his able first lieutenant, Andrew Mott, who was a devil for detail and ran a tight ship. But Maitland was still fairly new to the responsibility of this command, which had fallen to him suddenly. He had only been transferred to the *Bellerophon* in April, when Napoleon's escape from Elba had put the Royal Navy on alert at the very moment it was running down. Ships and officers had to be brought together hurriedly and despatched to what for many of them were familiar stations. For more than twenty years the Channel Fleet had trudged up and down in the blockade of the French coast that had helped to bring Napoleon's France to defeat. The blockade had been regular, professionally accomplished and monotonous work, punctuated by rare chases, skirmishes and battles, but all those years of it had left the ships that sailed out of Plymouth on 24 May with a legacy of skills and experience, their crews knowing all the tricks of the trade when it came to stopping and searching vessels entering or leaving French ports.

The orders for the blockading ships, as they spread down the French coast, came from Lord Keith, the admiral in command at Plymouth. Though his station was more than two hundred miles from London he had couriers constantly on the go, and he was receiving and sending more urgent messages by the telegraph that functioned by day in clear weather. The problems of communication with his patrolling vessels could not be solved so directly and easily. Ships had to be found at sea to receive their latest orders, or responses to questions that had been raised with Plymouth; those ships, in turn, had to use passing vessels or despatch-boats to get their reports to Lord Keith. This kind of difficulty meant that the officers concerned had, navy-style, to take a good deal of responsibility on themselves. Keith could not always wait for word from the Admiralty; a captain of a ship ten days sail away from England, as Maitland was on the *Bellerophon*, had to decide weighty issues for himself – and be prepared to face the consequences if a decision proved wrong in the event, or he failed correctly to interpret or anticipate government policy. This meant that every despatch had to be scrutinised both for what it said, and what it might imply, and captains knew that their reports would be parsed with equal care when they reached the commander-in-chief. They might turn out later to be evidence at a court-martial. Maitland had indeed some previous experience of this risk when he had been court-martialled (and acquitted) for wrecking a brig he commanded.

At the beginning of July Maitland received the first important signal of this whole affair, sent by Keith on 27 June. Maitland had already learned about Napoleon's defeat at Waterloo from a French ship captured off the mouth of the Charente, and now the Admiralty was spelling out the consequences. He had also received a mysterious message from Bordeaux (on thin paper rolled upon in a quill) warning that a defeated Napoleon might be heading that way, possibly to board the American ship *Susquehanna* out of Philadelphia. The next day Maitland received news from Keith to similar effect, quoting rumours that in the event of adverse fortune it was the intention of Bonaparte to escape to America. 'If he should embark on a small vessel from one of the numerous ports along the coast of France it may be scarcely possible to prevent his escape; but if he should wait until a frigate or a sloop of war can be fitted out for him... you may be enabled to watch and intercept her... you should take every precaution in your power with a view to his seizure and detention should he undertake to quit France by sea.'

This was the first phase of the operation now set in motion, since every naval vessel in the area would have received similar notice authorising them to implement the key words 'seizure' and 'detention'. What then? Sir John Croker, the powerful and prescient secretary of the Admiralty, was already looking ahead to consider what might be done if and when Napoleon actually fell into British hands. Events that two weeks earlier would have seemed optimistic speculation had now become an unexpected and urgent matter for the policy-makers in Whitehall. On 1 July, after reminding Lord Melville (First Lord of the Admiralty and a member of the powerful group at the heart of the Cabinet) that Wellington had already rejected an application for passports and safe-conducts for Napoleon and his entourage, Croker thought that some more illicit attempt at escape to be likely. Hence the search for Bonaparte should be intensified. If he was captured, Croker said emphatically, no communication with the shore should be permitted; the whole transaction should be kept a profound secret. The basic rules had thus been laid down. What might happen thereafter was still to be discussed.

* * *

There was as yet no news from Maitland which could be the basis of policy. Wellington was having to improvise his policies in his dealings with

Fouché, though he had daily contact with Lord Castlereagh, after the Foreign Secretary had moved to Paris on 6 July. Wellington's role was to get a capitulation and the acceptance of the Bourbons in Paris; and in the process he had to keep up the pressure on Fouché, who in turn was herding Napoleon towards the western coast of France. The Admiralty's role was so to dispose its ships to catch him when he arrived. Lord Liverpool, always having to make do with information that was days late, even a week or so, overtaken by events, was having to anticipate the way things would go. On 7 July he wrote to Castlereagh, 'What is to become of Bonaparte?' If he were to sail from Rochefort or Cherbourg, Liverpool continued, 'we have a good chance of laying hold of him... we shall keep him on board until the opinion of the allies has been taken. The easiest course would be to deliver him to the King of France, but then we must be quite certain that he would be tried and have no chance of escape.'

Wellington was worrying along the same lines. As late as 12 July he wrote to Castlereagh saying that the new French government 'will not, and does not seem to have sufficient authority to undertake, to charge themselves with... executing Bonaparte as a traitor.'

This is another argument against the idea of any agreed subterfuge between Fouché and the British. Liverpool had obviously been taking soundings in the Cabinet, consulting Lord Eldon, the Lord Chancellor, who apparently thought that in the end it would be the British who would have somehow to dispose of Bonaparte – this being 'in all respects, the least objectionable course'. Asking why so much importance should be attached to one man, Liverpool summed up the general opinion of the allies who had been pursuing him in this final attempt to settle his account. After thirteen years of supreme power, he wrote, Bonaparte 'has a title which belongs to no other man... no other man can play the same part that he has done, and is likely to play again.'

In a letter which crossed with one from Liverpool next day, Castlereagh said he had made the same point to Louis XVIII as Wellington and Blucher had been making to Fouché's provisional government. 'I conceived the policy towards France must be materially influenced by Bonaparte's being left at liberty to return again to the charge, when a new complot would be arranged.' Over the next few days, though London still had no definite news about Napoleon's whereabouts, the Cabinet considered a repertoire of possibilities, and reduced them to two, as Liverpool reported to Castlereagh on 15 July. If he was caught, and Louis 'did not feel strong enough to bring him to justice as a rebel, we are ready to take upon ourselves his custody as a person' rather than leaving it to any other ally. The Prime Minister did not favour the appointment of any joint allied commissioners to superintend the prisoner – a scheme that had been tried and failed on Elba and was now misguidedly revived by Castlereagh. 'The decisions should be vested entirely in ourselves, and we should be at liberty to fix the place of his confinement.' This might be somewhere in Britain (Castlereagh had suggested the formidable and isolated Fort George, near Inverness), Gibraltar, Malta, the Cape of Good Hope, even St Helena. Whatever destination was eventually chosen it should be a distance from Europe. The last sentence was telling. 'If we are to have the severe responsibilities for such a charge, it is but just that we should have the choice of the place of confinement, and a complete discretion as to the means to render that confinement effective.' These words, written hundreds of miles away, were in striking contrast to Napoleon's fancies and guesses about the nobility of British character: he had sadly miscalculated about the generosity of those whom he called 'his greatest and most generous enemy'.

Before the Cabinet could move from words to deeds Napoleon had first to be caught. Liverpool got the first news that Napoleon had made contact with the *Bellerophon* from Castlereagh in a despatch that he reopened just as the courier was about to leave. The exciting but bare facts had reached Paris in the evening of 17 July, two days after the event, and Castlereagh only had time (his phrase suggests that he was not quite sure the matter was finally decided) to insert an extra note telling Liverpool the news, adding 'You must make up your mind that you are now to be his gaoler'. The details would have to wait until Castlereagh learned where, and how, and by whom Napoleon had been 'seized'.

* * *

The answer to all those questions was the Royal Navy. While the Cabinet was speculating where Napoleon would appear, like a jack-in-a-box, Lord Keith, Rear-Admiral Sir Henry Hotham (commanding the British squadron off Brittany) and Captain Frederick Lewis Maitland (tucked into the estuary of the Charente) had managed it between them. Even before it seemed probable that Napoleon was heading for Rochefort the ships of Hotham's squadron had been spread to watch the exits from the Atlantic coast of France. Their captains were as well aware as Keith (who kept reminding them) of the risk that Napoleon might cut and run in a small boat, or at night, or in poor weather: with all their experience they knew how hard to it was to detect a particular blockade-runner, and even harder to tease out a particular person who might well be in disguise. They knew, Maitland especially, that their naval force was barely sufficient for the task. But they also knew something else. If Napoleon and a group of his officers were to make a dash for America, they would have to use an ocean-going ship, provisioned for a long voyage. If it was not an American privateer – working these waters because of the war with Britain, or a trader out of Boston or Baltimore, it would have to be one of the fast and well-built frigates which the French made so well. This narrowed the range of possibilities.

That is why Hotham's first orders in late May had been for his squadron to search the ports that might harbour such vessels. It was, indeed a sighting of the frigates anchored off Rochefort that had brought Maitland into the Basque Roads in the first instance; and having found them he was ordered to stay and watch them – which he did all through June. *Bellerophon's* logbook shows that he stayed on station because it was increasingly clear that Rochefort might be the port from which any Bonapartist adventure might be launched, not least an attempt by a defeated emperor to flee overseas. This was intelligent speculation which was well rewarded.

The squadron was deployed in an arc of over 300 miles, to the north and south of Maitland, from Brittany right round to Bordeaux. Hotham had positioned himself in *Superb* in Quiberon Bay. *Sheldrake* and *Opossum* were watching the Loire. *Phoebe*, *Larne* and *Endymion* were at the mouth of the Gironde. Then there was *Bellerophon*, the plug in the estuary of the Charente, anchored four to five miles out in the Pertuis d'Antioche. The smaller *Myrmidon*, *Slaney*, *Daphne* and *Cyrus* were available to block the others exits from Rochefort, to check rumours by coast watch, and generally to act as despatch boats for the squadron. The *Swiftsure* was north of Finistère. *Vengeur* was in the Channel a hundred miles west of Ushant, the *Glasgow* off Brest, with *Esk*, *Prometheus*, and *Ferret* close in to Ushant. The courses to America were being covered as best as possible.

If it were to come to bangs and blows in the Rochefort sector, there was no doubt that the *Billy Ruffian*, as she was nicknamed in the navy, would be more than a match for the frigates – her guns and trained fighting men were more than double what they could muster. After Waterloo, moreover, the formidable shore batteries would not bother *Bellerophon* unless she came in too close and seemed about to attack: the war was clearly petering out. Her log, and those of her satellites, bear witness to their state of readiness and the way they were kept up to the mark by movements and anchorings.

The problem, as Maitland was aware, lay in the fact that *Bellerophon* was old, storm-weary, carrying scars of the savaging and dismasting she had suffered in the great battles of the Nile and Trafalgar. She was still powerful, but lumbering, and a newer frigate that once got past her could outsail her in a day and lose her in a night. From the first Maitland was conjuring up and practicing tactics to deal with the frigates, given that he could not simply force his way in and blast them into blazing hulks. He thought he could deal with one quite easily, with two it would be 'difficult'. This concern about his 'lack of force' was mentioned several times in Maitland's own notes, and he felt it acutely when either *Myrmidon* or *Slaney*, or both, were away on a mission. *Myrmidon* was a smaller frigate, *Slaney* a sloop, but numbers would have counted in blocking an escape – all the more so if Napoleon should come out with two or more smaller vessels and it was unclear which should be the target. This was exactly the situation between 3 July and 5 July, when *Bellerophon* was alone in the roadstead, leaving a window of opportunity for an attempted escape; Napoleon, however, missed it. He was still in the prefecture at Rochefort talking up and down about what he should do.

It must be assumed that Maitland had sources of information ashore – royalists, perhaps agents landed from his own ships – but there is little mention of them apart from the mysterious Bordeaux message in a squill, and a few reports from fishermen or seamen on intercepted boats. The fact that he mentioned these examples suggests that he may not have been too well-informed: up to 9 July, for example, neither his log nor his own notes show whether he knew Napoleon was there ashore, on the frigates or on the Ile d'Aix. The information that came through the squadron appears to have been better. At least one of Hotham's despatches had affirmed that Napoleon's destination was Rochefort and that 'one of the frigates at the Ile d'Aix' could well be the intended means of escape. The trouble with Hotham's messages was the time-lag. In a letter dated 7 July Hotham was expressing the same concern as Maitland that *Bellerophon* might not have 'force enough to stop them both' and that Napoleon might well be aboard the one that got away. That notion was worrying Maitland less now his two smaller ships were back on station. The letter, however,

Bellerophon's successful blockade

put Maitland on notice about his duty, reminding him of the general and earlier instructions what to do if he did 'detain' Napoleon, going on to say that he must 'use the best means that can be adopted to intercept the fugitive, on whose captivity the repose of Europe appears to rest.'

These orders, carrying the hint of disciplinary overtones that any naval officer would recognise, were clear as far as they went, but they gave no guidance at all about the way Napoleon was to be treated once 'seized', apart from the repeated insistence that any vessel detaining him should keep him 'isolated' and proceed at once to a British port. It was the lack of more specific guidance that would prove so troublesome to Maitland and Hotham in the next two weeks. Neither had the training, experience or the kind of orders which would enable a sea-captain to face up to a ruler of such power and self-importance as Napoleon – a man of destiny who, in his turn, was faced with the novel situation of voluntarily treading the deck of a British man-of-war. True, he had been carried over to Elba on the *Undaunted* a year ago, but the terms on which he was placed there were formally agreed, and signed in a treaty, and did not have to be negotiated from scratch in the uncertain position of disadvantage in which Napoleon now found himself. In the versions of this encounter which Maitland wrote at the time, and later, there is a sense of baffled good intentions on his part eking out his minatory orders, of a decent feeling of embarrassment coping with a persisting doubt as to whether he was doing the right thing.

He lacked any preparation for this ominous task. When the sight of a sail coming out to *Bellerophon* roused the excitement of every officer and man, the best Maitland could do was to fall back on natural politeness, routine, and the King's Regulations which set out the parameters of duty and the consequence of disregarding them.

Wellington

Napoleon

Banging the Drum

Napoleon and his cronies: Fouché, Davout, Savary, Ney, Caulaincourt...

The tragic-comedy of surrender

"I climbed up twice without any help!"

The farewell to France

Bellerophon mobbed by sightseers

His carriage, bed, and chamberpot – a museum attraction

A Tory view of the Whig attitude

The jump to *Northumberland* : St Helena next

Paradise Lost

12

Journey's End

While Maitland was containing himself with expectant patience, and faltering ideas of clandestine escape continued to occupy Napoleon's naval and military aides, Bertrand, Becker and the emperor were still coping with the problem of the frigates. It was a paradoxical situation. The greater the pressure from Paris to urge Napoleon aboard, the more suspiciously reluctant he became. Would he have any power of command once he boarded *La Saale*? Was it entirely for Philibert to decide whether and when the frigates might sail? Or, perhaps, Philibert had secret and undisclosed orders? Did these include a specific instruction to prevent Napoleon 'parleying' with any British ship? And what control did Philibert have over the other and smaller boats – the brig *Epervier*, for instance, or the schooner *Sophie* or the tender *Mouche*? Who would have the final say on how many of the entourage could be embarked, and make any selection between them? Even Becker, the man authorised by the provisional government to be the go-between in such matters, could not answer the questions that Napoleon and Bertrand posed. The situation was further confused by the fact that Bonnefoux had his own chain of orders from Paris, and it was difficult to distinguish between his official and his private opinions. It seems that he was continually in doubt about what, sensibly, properly, officially he should say.

The week had been spent in talks that had come to nothing – the only last minute novelty had been a visit from Joseph Bonaparte, still unsuccessfully trying to persuade his brother to go with him on a dash for Philadelphia. But procrastination was no longer possible. On 8 July the provisional government was to resign and from now on the orders from Paris would come from new Bourbon officials. That morning Becker, asked for his opinion, and recognising that time was fast running out, confessed that the only advice he could give was that Napoleon should show 'prompt determination' and move on 'as speedily as possible'. Becker said that his own powers had now lapsed and that it would be foolish 'to wait until agents are sent in pursuit' and Napoleon 'would be exposed to new dangers.'

* * *

Gourgaud had meanwhile been sent on a fool's errand to ascertain the readiness of the frigates. Napoleon did not even wait him to return and tell him there was no suitable offshore wind, that there was no useful wind further out in the Basque Roads, and that the British ships were spread watchfully across the exit channels. He decided to hustle the whole party out to the Ile d'Aix, a small, fortified island about a mile beyond the anchorage of the frigates. There would be temporary safety there; the stretch of water would inhibit any attempt to seize or even assassinate him. He would, moreover be in a position where he could most easily and directly make contact with the British. The sense that he would be in control there, on his own island as he had been at Elba, may also have been some reassurance. It was manageably secure as a temporary refuge. A crescent of sand and trees, over a mile from tip to tip and a few hundred yards across, it had been heavily fortified by Vauban, with an encircling wall and a fort at either end protecting the little township. The works had even been improved by Napoleon himself, after a state visit in 1808, which was well and kindly remembered by the garrison and fisher-folk.

There was, too, a lingering bitterness against the English. They had stormed and occupied the island in 1757, when they were fighting Louis XIV, and it had been the scene of the dramatic fireship attack in 1809. It still had a substantial garrison of marines and artillerymen: its forts, and others around the bay, were more than adequate to keep *Bellerophon* and her consorts at bay (or even to protect Napoleon if he decided on a final act of defiance and launched a comeback on the French coast as he had done from Elba). Given his record and his character this was not an improbable fantasy for his enemies, but given the situation it was unlikely in the extreme. The Bourbon flag was already flying from steeples and mairies across the marshes of the Charente, and it would soon be hoisted over the nearby port of La Rochelle.

* * *

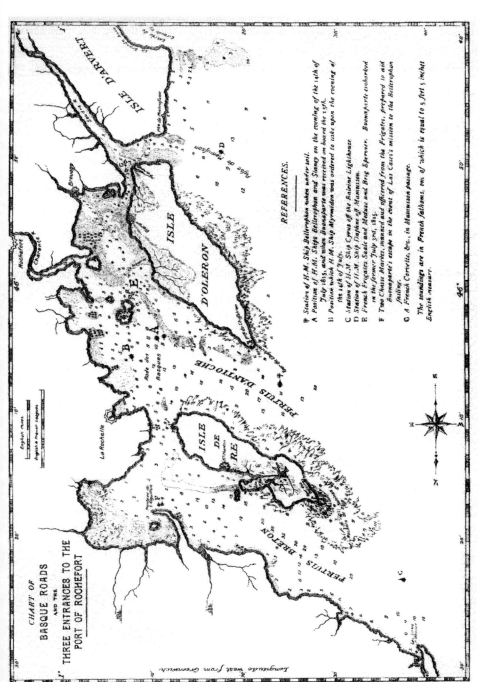

Maitland's chart of the Basque Roads

The frigates, anchored a mile or so off Fouras, had been given notice that, after so many delays, Napoleon and his whole retinue were on their way. The log-book of *La Saale* records that, with this expectation, the ships' boats of *Saale* and *Méduse* were sent across to Fouras to lift the oncoming fugitives off the beach. This was almost literally the case. The oyster-beds of Fouras stretch out in mud at low tide, and when the party began to reach La Coue beach at 5 pm the boats of the frigates and a miscellaneous collection of fishing-craft were waiting out in the shallows. The way in which the emperor, his aides, the ladies and the children were carried out pick-a-back by the sailors and the fishermen was long recalled as a tragi-comic scene. Of all the possible ways in which Napoleon might have left the shores of France this was probably the most unlikely and bizarre.

Once all were aboard the bobbing flotilla it proved hard for the oarsmen to make headway against the wind that Captain Philibert was always citing as a reason for prevarication; and it gusted enough to drench the passengers with spray as the boatmen rowed into it. They had been told to make directly for Ile d'Aix, but after nearly two hours they were still only abreast of the Enet fort, half way across from Fouras, and only a few hundred yards from the frigates. Napoleon now had no choice. He had to lead his entourage on to *La Saale* in what was an unavoidable but undignified scramble; though Philibert's crew welcomed him with cheers and a guard presented arms his dragoman Ali thought the reception was 'muted' and that Philibert himself appeared to be 'apathetic and indifferent'. Napoleon, as was his habit, inspected the ship, asked if it would be possible to sail that night if the wind was favourable, made sure that the vessel was provisioned for a long voyage, and saw that his party was settled in as far as possible in a makeshift and hurried arrangement of the cabins. The breathless impression of a hurried departure was heightened by the way boats came out all through the night carrying servants and the baggage which was to be loaded on the *Méduse*. It probably seemed that the column that had set out from Malmaison had after all reached its journey's end – all sixty of them. Becker, for one, was distinctly satisfied. He felt, he reported to Paris, that he was fulfilling his delicate mission 'under the double commitment of my duty to the emperor and the government… to the satisfaction of both.'

Napoleon, however, was still restless. The next day being fine and calm there was no effort to break out the sails, and – early on deck as was his wont – he took the opportunity to examine the roadstead. Using a glass loaned by the midshipman of the watch, for the first time he clearly saw his nemesis, the vessels that he had been warned about for the past two weeks. Out there, beyond the massive Fort Boyard which dominated the channel, were a large man-of-war and a frigate, closing the exit to the Atlantic as Captain Philibert had said they did. He decided to continue on as he had set out the night before. Rousing Las Cases, Bertrand and Gourgaud, Napoleon decided to make an immediate reconnaissance of the island.

Ashore, on the green parade-ground between the fort and the three small streets of the township, he found the garrison troops at their Sunday morning exercise, and he was welcomed with loud shouts and drums beating the general salute. He walked about the little streets of one-floor cottages, acknowledged greetings in the easy way that was one secret of his popularity, and paused to consider the fine house he had ordered to be built for the commandant when he made his previous visit. Here he was overtaken by a breathless and seasick Becker, alarmed on waking to find that Napoleon had left the ship without saying where he had gone and what he was doing.

* * *

At dusk the little party went back to *La Saale* to be greeted by Bonnefoux with a fierce letter from Decrès. 'It is of the utmost importance that the emperor leaves the soil of France,' he wrote in what was to be the final ultimatum sent before Fouché and his colleagues were superseded by the incoming Bourbons. This minatory tone fitted poorly with the dithering list of possibilities which followed. If Napoleon couldn't leave on a frigate, could he slip away in a small boat; if that suggestion did not appeal, perhaps he 'prefers to go on board one of the British ships or go directly to England,' although if that was his choice he must apply formally in writing (to whom?) so that it would appear to be his idea and not a decision which Fouché and his colleagues would appear to have forced on him. In a mood of anxiety, Decrès then repeated the same points in the next paragraph, saying that these proposals were for an 'urgent departure … founded in interests for his own personal safety.' An accompanying order emphasised the need for haste '… within twenty-four hours at the latest' (Fouché's writ would no longer run after that). The only significant clause revealed the anxiety of the government in case Napoleon, now virtually beyond its reach, might yet put himself at the head of a rising among the armies along the Loire and the Gironde. 'Napoleon must not, on pain of treason, disembark at any point on French soil.' Becker, whose appointment had now run to its close, was told that he must not leave Napoleon's side, 'until he has either been taken aboard an English ship or disembarked in England.'

Napoleon either had to comply with the last of the sequence of confused and anxious orders that had followed him from Malmaison or defy them. The discussion continued after Bonnefoux went back to Rochefort to await any further muddled and out-dated instructions.

* * *

The discussion about the future went on, grew stale as fragments of fact were stitched together with guesses. Since Napoleon could not bring himself to a decision, and neither faction had much new to say, the balance of argument tipped towards negotiations with the British. All other possibilities seemed attractive but ... but... but how? Late into the night of 10 July Napoleon woke Savary and Las Cases and sent them off to the *Bellerophon* under a flag of truce. They were to make a formal but futile enquiry about the passports: Napoleon continued to attach great importance to this issue, as if the documents would somehow legitimise his departure, even if he must have known they were never coming. In fact, the British government had formally turned down the request on 30 June. The visit was also intended to give Las Cases a chance, since he knew English well enough from his years in exile, to form some impression of how Napoleon might be received. With his long record of war against Britain, and the hostile feelings that he knew were expressed in cartoons and articles in the newspapers, anything might be possible. For some reason Napoleon had a conviction that the British would receive him well, that they would restrain their allies and the Bourbons from ill-treating him. In this he was probably right, but such hopes could not be defined or quantified. At the end of the day it was one guess to set against another.

13

Rendition?

Nothing in Maitland's career had prepared him for the discussion which began as Las Cases and Savary came aboard *Bellerophon*. At that moment he 'could not be sure that Napoleon was somewhere close by,' he might be there somewhere ashore with a substantial force, or without any protection at all, he might have these two frigates at his command and might well be proposing to use them to break out of the estuary. Maitland had been able to watch the ships taking on stores and would know a long voyage was intended. Had these two envoys then come to deliver a challenge, or a request? He felt unsure what to say, or what to do. He knew that six weeks ago Lord Keith had given him powers 'to seize and detain' Napoleon but that was easier said than done now the emperor was almost within his grasp. Was he entering on to a stage of diplomacy or preparing himself for the sudden eruption of gunfire if, as he guessed might be the case, in the last resort Napoleon would try to shoot his way out? Above all, he was anxious lest he might make a culpable blunder with the best of intentions despite a strict adherence to what he believed was his duty. Years later, recalling these events, he was still rehearsing this edgy state of mind.

In fact the meeting went easily. The initial exchanges were courteous, the envoys were welcomed to breakfast, and in a few minute Las Cases had explained their purposes and handed over a letter of protocol from Bertrand. It said that Napoleon had abdicated, that he proposed to seek 'a refuge' in the United States on the frigates which were anchored nearby, and that he was enquiring about the passports that he had been 'informed' would be supplied (the word 'informed' was the first of the semantic points that Napoleon would later use to claim that he had been misled). Bertrand also asked, if there were no passports, 'whether it might be the intention of the British government to impede our passage to the United States.'

Maitland, who was an agreeable and sensible man, led the envoys into a relaxed conversation – since both were in mufti there was no question of naval ceremonial – remarking that he had met Savary in Egypt in 1799, when they were both serving for three weeks on the commission which negotiated the surrender of the French expeditionary force that Napoleon had left there. It would have been a typical 'old soldiers' approach to break the ice before Maitland settled down to read Bertrand's letter.

Maitland knew he was taking several kinds of risk when he had no idea of Napoleon's status – prisoner of war, a fugitive from the French government, an enemy of state: some were later to suggest that he should have been treated as a pirate! A simple slip could easily put the British government into grave diplomatic difficulties, to say nothing of the damage a false move would make to his own career. What he must do was temporise, to strengthen this unforeseen contact with Napoleon, do nothing to scare him away: he could no more send a party of marines ashore to search out the emperor than he could take these men as hostages. The flag of truce had to be respected. Meanwhile he had some formal questions to answer. He could not permit 'any ship of war to pass out to sea' nor any merchant vessel carrying 'a person of such consequence.' And then he was rescued by some naval routine. The envoys had scarcely settled to talk when the sails of the *Falmouth* were seen, joining from Quiberon Bay and undoubtedly bringing new orders from Sir Henry Hotham, the squadron commander.

Maitland had to be careful he did not reveal the substance of Hotham's signal, fudging his distracted reading of it into the conversation. He had to be careful, moreover, that he did not inadvertently disclose the orders that Hotham had sent him, which were filling part of the gap in his knowledge of what to do next. The central and reassuring point was the repeat of the over-arching orders Keith had issued back in May. Any captain fortunate enough to intercept Bonaparte 'should keep him careful custody... return to the nearest port in England with all possible expedition.' It was the ensuing sentence that could have sent Napoleon off into any hasty alternative line of escape he could find, for they were not the words of an admiral whose country was proposing to offer asylum to a defeated enemy. The captain 'should not permit any communication with the shore, and he will be held responsible to keep the whole transaction a profound secret until their Lordships' further orders shall be received.' With such stark words immediately to hand Maitland still had to present a cordial face to the envoys, trying to avoid giving them any reason to feel antagonised and at the same time doing his best to jolly them along with chitchat about life in England – a topic in which, given Napoleon's assumptions, they were right to be interested.

Maitland had quickly come to the conclusion that the envoys were under greater pressure to conceal the weakness of their position than they chose to reveal: Savary kept talking about Napoleon's newfound interest in peace and tranquillity, his desire to avoid further bloodshed; Las Cases tried to convince Maitland that Napoleon could well go back to leading an irredentist army in France on the Loire if he felt rebuffed. Maitland was shrewd enough to discount such talk. 'It appears to me from their anxiety,' he reported to Hotham, 'that they are very hard-pushed either by the government in Paris or from the approach of the armies.' Maitland felt that this point had come out clearly when he put the only difficult and most pertinent question: 'Suppose the British allowed him to get off to America, what pledge could he give that he would not return, and put England, as well as all Europe, to the same expense of blood and treasure that has just been incurred?' Maitland certainly spoke for his government, and anticipated much of the press comment on Napoleon's surrender. Savary made a long dissembling reply. Napoleon was no longer a man of influence. 'He would prefer to retire into obscurity… ending his days in peace and tranquillity.' This bland imposture seems to have been too much for Maitland. 'If that is the case,' he is alleged to have said in passing, perhaps tense in his irritation with Savary's pretensions, 'why doesn't he seek asylum in England, a peaceful place with a moderate climate.' Savary seems to have had no sense of humour and replied with an extraordinary and ill-conceived tirade. 'There are many reasons… the climate is too damp and cold; it is too near France; he would be… the centre of every change and revolution that might take place there, and would be subject to suspicion; he has been accustomed to consider the English as his most inveterate enemies, and they have been induced to look upon him as a monster, without one of the virtues of a human being.' In short, no cordial reception could be anticipated.

Since Maitland's casual, slyly teasing comment has been repeatedly cited as an attempt to entice Napoleon into surrender (even if there is no confirmation of the actual words said to have been used). It should be set against Savary's abrupt and ill-mannered outburst in the same conversational exchange. It is not evidence of considered bait, even though Maitland was certainly making an effort to be agreeable, to soften an inevitably stressful situation. He did not want to see Napoleon slip off the hook on which his plenipotentiaries had just impaled him. Las Cases was clearly searching for an assurance of good intent. He had been telling Napoleon day in and day out that he could expect goodwill from the English, feeding Napoleon's own assumption on the point, and he snapped up any crumb of proof that he was right. He wanted an assurance that Napoleon 'would be well-received'. When Maitland conceded that point, Las Cases turned it into a positive assertion. In any case too much can be read into Maitland's reactions to the questions the envoys were firing at him. While the discussion was continuing he was trying to write a report of his significant encounter to his senior, Sir Henry Hotham, excusing himself for any confusion 'as the two Frenchmen constantly address me with new proposals.'

* * *

Savary and Las Cases took back Maitland's reply to Bertrand. He told them explicitly that he could not answer for the intent of his government. He gave no reply to the question about safe-conduct. He insisted that he could not 'permit any ship to put to sea from the port of Rochefort... without the sanction of my commanding officer.' He sensed the two men had been sounding him about his reaction if one or both frigates attempted to force a way out, and he was giving fair warning. He did not consider it proper to mention the new instruction which meant he must carry the emperor off to Torbay – under the prevailing rules of war there was no obligation on him to play this card.

* * *

Back on *La Saale* the question of a fighting escape was being discussed for the last time. Most of the suite were still pressing for negotiations, Montholon and Lallemand made a final plea that the emperor should make a run for the army on the Loire. Captain Ponée seems to have pressed the scheme for one frigate covering the other in an attempt to bypass *Bellerophon*, and this project was apparently still in play that night. While Lallemand was sent off yet again to Le Verdon, to make a last check on the state of Baudin's scheme to escape from the Gironde, the frigates seem to have been suddenly brought to readiness about 9.30 pm. The logbook of *La Saale* notes that the decks were cleared for action and topsails set. At 10.30 a boat was sent over to Chapus to pick up a pilot who could take ships through the difficult narrows (away from a direct confrontation with *Bellerophon*). The captain of *l'Epervier*, moreover, was warned to be prepared for action, and Philibert wrote an odd note to Bonnefoux saying that Becker 'had been unable to carry out the task assigned to him' – which may have been his standing orders never to leave Napoleon's side until he quit the country. It seems as though everything was suddenly committed to an attempt to leave by the narrowest and most risky of the exits of the Charente. Maitland, indeed, was alerted, for his lookouts had seen suspicious activity on the frigates and next morning he felt his concerns were justified, for four fishermen came on board to tell him that the best pilot for the Maumasson passage had been taken out to *La Saale*. He sent *Myrmidon* to stop the Maumasson exit, and brought *Slaney* and *Bellerophon* to weigh in the Basque Roads. From a distance of about three miles, he wrote, 'it looked as though the frigates were perfectly ready to put to sea, should an opportunity offer; having their sterns covered with vegetables, their top-gallant yards across, studding sail gear rove… all indications, well-known to professional men, of preparing to sail.' His ships, therefore, were 'kept with slip-buoys on their cables and everything kept ready to make sail at a moment's notice… guard boats were kept rowing all night, as near the frigates as they could venture.'

It is not known exactly what happened, but whatever had been proposed before midnight must have been abandoned by three in the morning. The most probable explanation is that having come close to accepting the Ponée plan, on being confronted by an attempt to implement it, Philibert had made a dramatic decision. Savary recalled that Philibert had suddenly cited secret orders to the effect that he was not 'to go out if the ships ran any danger.' Philibert also explained later that in the circumstances (that Napoleon had in any case left by other means) that he would overlook 'the act of mutiny' on the part of Ponée and his crew. One result of this double-shuffling, however, was that Napoleon abruptly decided that it was too risky for him to remain on *La Saale* – Philibert might yet find he had another secret order to arrest him. He took the decision to move the whole party over to the Ile d'Aix. At four o'clock in the morning, apparently, Napoleon had boarded the schooner *Sophie* without telling Philibert where he was going. It was this process of transferring the entourage before dawn that was observed by Maitland as 'numerous boats' shuttling between the ships and the shore.

* * *

The commandant's house on Aix was suitable and agreeable for the final nights of the journey, as can be seen to this day. The largest building apart from the forts had room for Napoleon, the Bertrands, the Montholons, Savary, Gourgaud and Becker: the headcount was coming down to the core of the little court. Other members of the party were lodged in the

The commandant's house on l'Ile d'Aix

cottages across the street. From the balcony Napoleon could look out over the roadstead, and see *Bellerophon* and *Myrmidon*, reminding him of their solidarity with the Bourbons by firing salutes and hoisting the white flag to mark the return of Louis XVIII to Paris. Napoleon was taking a morning salute of his own, under the tricolour, from a party of marines. At the same time, in the course of the upheaval of arriving on the island, he was having domestic difficulties – petty jealousies, rows about rank and, in the group which was clearly about to go into exile, anxieties about the future of the women and children, who might have to be left behind.

Some urgency was given to such issues by the fact that an irregular escape was still a possibility. Though Lallemand had not yet come back from the Gironde, Joseph had turned up again with a now-or-never proposal to take Napoleon and two or three of the generals to Philadelphia. Napoleon would not consider such a scheme, any more than the aborted plot to sail out at night in a lugger.

Both rejections were fortunate. If Napoleon had gone over to the Gironde he would have found that Maitland had sent *Patroclus* and *Erebus* to blockade Le Verdon. Had the *Bayardère* scheme been betrayed? The six officers with the luggers were certainly betrayed, and imprisoned. There was, in Gourgaud's phrase, 'a lot of mysterious palaver' going on as the various plans were taken up, examined and put down again. It was Becker's view that a tide of sentiment had now set strongly in favour of the negotiations with Maitland. There was really no alternative, Becker recalled. 'The attraction of England for his companions in misfortune, the hope of an honourable reception which they flattered themselves they would receive, and finally their fears of being taken prisoner during the long sea voyage had always made them prefer English hospitality to a passage to America.'

It was Napoleon's choice. He decided to send Las Cases and Lallemand across to the *Bellerophon* at dawn.

14

An Incomparable Event

In the morning of 14 July, when Captain Maitland saw the *Mouche* coming out before the dawn light that lit its flag of truce, he at once summoned Captain Sartorious of the *Slaney* to come over as a witness to whatever the envoys might now propose. This was a wise precaution since he had no idea what direction the talks might take: he had waited for weeks in the hope that such a moment might come, and he rightly feared that some slip might ruin it. The best he could hope, a remarkable even historic hope, was that Las Cases had come back to start making arrangements for Napoleon's surrender. He would not be coming if negotiations were to be broken off – unless another meeting might be a tactic for delay and deception, even to cover the fact that Napoleon had somehow stolen away in the night. 'My duty became peculiarly harrowing and anxious,' he later reported to Lord Keith, 'owing to the numerous reports of his intention to escape in vessels of various descriptions.'

When Lallemand came aboard with Las Cases there was another 'old soldiers' meeting, for Lallemand had also been a prisoner under Maitland after the Egypt campaign, and there was then some desultory discussion which seems to have gone over much the same ground as the previous exchanges with Las Cases. Ostensibly there to ask again about the passports, the envoys went on to ask again how Napoleon might be received in England. While Maitland again assured them that he had instructions to convey Napoleon to Britain if that was what he wanted, he refused to be drawn about his treatment on arrival – which was the real question the two men had come back to ask. Maitland, supported by officers from *Slaney* and other ships of the flotilla, seems to have said something like 'there was not the least doubt of Napoleon meeting with all possible respect and good treatment… the English people possessed a generosity of sentiment and a liberality of opinion.' Lallemand took this as an assurance that the emperor need have no hesitation in proceeding to England 'so as to be able to continue his voyage to the United States.' Maitland did not report any mention of America, but recalled that the meeting concluded with Lallemand saying he had 'little doubt that you will see the emperor on board the *Bellerophon.*'

The Frenchmen returned to another council of war, where Lallemand made a last attempt to persuade Napoleon to take Baudin's offer of the *Bayardère*; Gourgaud, more from his hostility to the 'pro-English' faction than from any clear idea of what else might be done, was Lallemand's only supporter. Savary's recollection showed the hold quietism had gained on the whole group of advisers, who had succumbed to 'seductive illusions.' He quoted Napoleon as smugly saying, 'I only seek for repose,' and going on to claim 'I am offered a quiet retreat in England' and making the astonishing claim that while he was not acquainted with the Prince Regent, 'from all I have heard of him, I cannot avoid placing reliance on his noble character.' That evening on the Ile d'Aix was clearly a dream world.

* * *

Napoleon, and Bertrand, had in fact settled the matter already, for the documentation was ready for Las Cases to take to *Bellerophon* that afternoon. Accompanied by Gourgaud, a footman and a page (his son) to provide a little pomp Las Cases arrived to present the decisive letter and announce the end of the skimped negotiations. 'His Majesty will proceed on your ship with the ebb tide tomorrow morning.'

There was a last flurry of fuss about the passports. If they had arrived, Las Cases said to keep up the pretence, then Napoleon 'would be happy to repair to America.' If they were still withheld, 'he will willingly proceed to England as a private individual there to enjoy the protection of the laws of your country.' As Maitland was to insist in his official reports there was no hint of seeking or being offered terms. If there was any misunderstanding at this moment it was in the assumption that Las Cases had made, and already grooved into Napoleon's appreciation of his reception –that an asylum-seeker in England would automatically enjoy 'the protection of the laws,' as many famous exiles had done in the past. What Napoleon failed to appreciate was that these figures either held opinions which were of no relevance to English interests or were actually favourable to them, like the reception of the famous Corsican patriot Paoli, whom Napoleon took as an exemplar of his case. This mistaken belief – one that would really matter a few days later – was the idea that a right of asylum began to apply as soon as a man set foot on a British ship anywhere in the world.

It is hard to guess how Maitland would have responded if Las Cases had raised the point of asylum at either of their two meetings. Should he, in fact, have anticipated such an error and gone out of his way to disabuse Las Cases about it? That is the view of French authors who argue that Napoleon was deliberately deceived, lured on board under false pretences. Yet Maitland was under no kind of obligation: Napoleon had approached him unconditionally. As an officer serving under King's Regulations and the Articles of War he would have a keen respect for his duty. He would not, however, have received any instruction about the common law or right of citizenship. His duty, which he performed to the letter, was to state 'explicitly and clearly that I have no authority whatever for the granting of terms of any sort, but all I can do is to carry him and his suite to England, to be received in such manner as his Royal Highness may deem expedient.' That said, of course, a lot of other things were to be said on the nine-day voyage to England. Many of them – in the informal conditions in which the French passengers were sailing aboard *Bellerophon* – were pleasantries and the kind of gossip common to travellers heading for a strange country. There were also failures of communication, due partly to stilted translations. It seems fair to say that nothing was done to make Napoleon and his party uneasy about their prospects. Courtesy does not imply enticement. Maitland was like many other Whigs in the Royal Navy – patriotic but favouring conciliation with France.

* * *

Before the meeting moved on from its dramatic start Maitland had to deal with the business that had brought Gourgaud on board. He was on a special mission, carrying a letter that Napoleon had written late the night before, when he decided to give himself up next day. It was a personal letter to the Prince Regent, and Gourgaud was expecting to take it to London and deliver it, explaining as he did so that the emperor would like to go to America, and 'failing America' he would prefer to live in England. In the presumptuous style of the ruler-to-ruler network to which he was accustomed, Napoleon set out what he wanted from the Prince. 'I wish to live in a country house, about ten or twelve leagues from London... in the strictest possible incognito. I shall need a big enough house to accommodate all my suite.' Gourgaud was not told specifically to mention Hartwell House, which had just been vacated by the late exile Louis XVIII, but it was to be implied that something on that scale would be acceptable, somewhat grander than Thornbury, where Lucien had lived in Shropshire for more than five years.

There was nothing secret about the letter. Maitland had it copied before Gourgaud was hurriedly despatched to England with Captain Sartorious in the *Slaney*, which would also be taking Maitland's first official report of Napoleon's surrender. As the package was sent off Maitland once again reminded Las Cases that he was not 'authorised to stipulate as to the reception of Bonaparte in England, but that he must consider himself at the disposal of his Royal Highness.' Given his hopeful state of mind Las Cases must have taken the reference to the Regent as a quite proper referral up the chain of authority, for he said he was 'perfectly aware' of that prospect and that he concurred.

The presumption was implicit in a very condescending line of the letter.

> 'Your Royal Highness,' it began. 'A victim to the factions which distract my country, and to the enmity of the greatest powers in Europe, I have terminated my political career, and I come, like Themistocles, to throw myself upon the hospitality of the British people. I put myself under the protection of their laws, which I claim from your Royal Highness, as the most powerful, most constant and most generous of my enemies.'

The comparison with Themistocles was a characteristic flourish of Napoleon's classical knowledge, of which he was proud. He was accustomed to exercise it when it took his fancy to compare himself with Caesar, Frederick the Great, and other generals who had left their mark on the face of history, Themistocles was the apt comparison for the moment. He was the Athenian victor at the battle of Salamis, who was later cast out by his own people to find a comfortable exile at the court of Xerxes, whom he had defeated in the historic battle. It was a revealing letter, and he was never to know how it failed its purpose. When, with its flattering mock-modesty, it finally reached the debauched and vulgar prince, he dismissed it with a wave of the hand and a coarse laugh. For the moment, however, it served Napoleon's purpose as an indication of intent. It was the first move in his plan to present himself as a figure of great dignity who, through no fault of his own, had fallen on hard times, who now wanted no more than a modest and harmless retirement, a benefactor who had deserved better of the world and now sought to be done better by history. It was a complicated role, given his record, that even to his own frustration and discomfort he was to maintain all the way from Rochefort to the final fall of the curtain on St Helena.

* * *

With Gourgaud gone Maitland and Las Cases settled to the main business, formally presented in a letter from Bertrand. There were no ifs and buts in it. 'His Majesty will repair on board your ship at four or five in the morning.' Once again it was announced that he would be arriving as 'a simple individual, to enjoy the protection of your country's laws.' The most worrying aspect of it for Maitland was the appended list of fifty persons who would also be seeking this protection at the same time. There was the entourage itemised, all down to the last pastry-cook and lamplighter; all come from the Elysée and Malmaison. Maitland had expected a fallen emperor: he was getting his whole pretentious little court.

It was taken for granted that somehow the whole party could be accommodated and carried off to England: Las Cases had arrived ready to stay on board and share the housekeeping problems with Maitland, like a head-waiter overseeing preparations for a wedding. As *Bellerophon* had been cleared for action, in this uncertain period when she might have to engage the frigates, cabins had to be set up again, and furnished as far as possible – starting with the makeover of Maitland's fine stern-cabin for Napoleon. The protocol as well as the practical problems were great. The cabins were graded by rank; how should they be graded for the five generals? Where were the footmen and the cooks to be put? And what was to be done, on a ship already crowded with nearly a thousand men, about a dozen maids? and then there was all the baggage that had been traipsed down from Malmaison. A carriage and two horses? Napoleon's coronation robes? There had been some extraordinary sights on the *Billy Ruffian* over the years, but the hustle and bustle to get all these arrangements made must have been quite remarkable, a splendid test of the Royal Navy's capacity to fit-as-fit-may at short notice. Maitland would have been pleased with the way his officers and men accomplished such a transformation, as if they were engaged to produce some sort of nautical pantomime. There were to be no complaints from dissatisfied passengers, even those unaccustomed to a voyage northward into the chops of the Channel. Presumably any reasonable accommodation was now acceptable to these remnants of imperial glory, who had been on the move for two weeks, huddled emotionally as well as physically into a jolting carriage-ride across France, beset by rumours about what was going to happen to them all. From Napoleon downwards it must have been a great relief.

* * *

The rush of administrative duties occasioned by this incomparable event was left to the competence of Andrew Mott (who came to feel an affinity with the way Bertrand ran the formalities of the little court, just like a ship!). Maitland's gracious consideration of the feelings of the exiles – also eased the business of boarding and what might have been a very awkward passage. For Maitland, personally, it must have been the most exciting time of a lively career. He had to receive Napoleon in two capacities: as a host and as commander of *Bellerophon,* which raised personal as well as professional problems. A young Scotsman who had spent much of his life at sea was now confronting the most famous man in the world, a 'Corsican Ogre' in the eyes of the British, a hero who had brought unparalleled glory to France, a revolutionary who had tamed a revolution into an empire, above all a military genius whose victories had cost Europe a fortune and three million lives. They would meet on a few square feet of an oak deck on one of the ships whose untiring efforts for fifteen years had helped to bring down an empire that had once stretched from Madrid to Moscow – an empire that without the Royal Navy might even have been pushed beyond Egypt to India. 'If it had not been for the effort of your navy,' Napoleon admitted to Maitland in the course of the voyage, 'I should have been the ruler of the Orient!'

On what terms would they be meeting, when he had been at pains to tell Las Cases there were no terms? How was Napoleon to be greeted? A slip of protocol – too reserved, too unbending, too considerate – could have serious consequences. Should Napoleon, perhaps, be treated as a visiting dignitary, a person to whom the French word *redittion* might mean voluntary surrender? Or as a prisoner-of-war? Did he, in fact, have a proper title? Maitland of course knew it was British policy to regard Napoleon simply as 'Buonaparte' not as an emperor, but did he still carry the rank of a general, or some other courtesy title that indicated the style and rank to which he was entitled? Once aboard, how much freedom was he to have to roam the ship, to talk to the officers, even to members of the crew, as was said to be his habit? Who should decide who should be invited to dine with him, and in what order should they sit? What would happen to the captain's personal prerogatives, jealously recognised by all the 'Billy Ruffians' but presumably unknown to presumptuous landlubbers coming in from a foreign court? The questions must have rolled at Maitland faster than he could improvise answers to them. How, again, should Bonaparte and party be entertained? Could he, or anyone in his court be permitted to ask about matters of substance, however casual? There were pitfalls in almost any topic that could come up in conversations about English landscape and climate, work and customs, the rules of hospitality, table manners, the popularity of the government. Napoleon was certainly going to talk about the reports of country life brought back by his brother Lucien from his long internment in England from 1808 to 1813. Such was the style he was expecting for himself.

In the event Napoleon himself proved more tactful than some of his own staff, and he found it easy to talk away about the design and working of *Bellerophon*, and other ships, the way that officers were trained, the discipline of the crew, the sailing points in good and bad weather. He also spent a good deal of time in his cabin, as aloof and no more approachable than an admiral ensconced in protocol. It was Bertrand who continued to regulate the affairs of the little court. Once at sea, Maitland's anxieties seem to have blown away. All the letters and diaries that survive give a surprisingly agreeable impression of a voyage which might easily have been intolerable. One officer described the voyage as 'halcyon days'.

15

Just in Time

It must have been the worst day of the whole journey for Bertrand. He had been cool and competent through all the fits and starts of the whole affair, from Waterloo to the Atlantic, coping with Napoleon and his colleagues, managing the logistics as well as the political arrangements, even fending off the near-hysterical outbursts from his wife who wanted nothing but to discharge the whole enterprise into the English Channel. Now, in the chaos of sorting and packing, preparing to deliver the entourage to *Bellerophon* in the orderly form it was presented to Maitland, he was at least relieved of the problems created by Napoleon's indecision. The emperor seemed settled in his mind, reassuring the doubters, saying again that 'corrupt men' had played fast and loose with the 'independence and glory of France,' but claiming that the ship's people were still 'stout-hearted and magnanimous,' repeating that the Prince Regent had 'nobility of character', and saying that once aboard the *Bellerophon* 'I shall be on British soil; the English will be bound by the laws of hospitality.' Having persuaded himself into the last and greatest of his illusions he retired for a few hours from the bustle of preparation. At that moment neither he nor anyone else knew how close things had come to disaster.

* * *

For nearly three weeks the crisis had been proceeding by remote control. Decisions had been made by way of the intermediaries between Fouché and Napoleon, by couriers, despatches and even, latterly, by telegraph. But because the scene shifted day by day there was a curious shunting of events: Napoleon and the column of fugitives never quite out-distanced

Fouché and his colleagues but they never quite caught up with Napoleon. Just as Fouché had to write his orders guessing what the situation would actually be like when they arrived, so Napoleon had to anticipate what they would say. This leap-frog process went on right up to his arrival at the Ile d'Aix, when Decrès had signed off with the last confused message before he cleared his desk and made room for the vengefully royalist Marquis de Jaucourt, who had come in vowing to settle 'the Napoleon business' and set about it. There was to be no more toing and froing with, he believed, the old Jacobins round Fouché scheming to get their former leaders out of the country, and the staggered movements between Rochefort, *La Saale* and Aix almost gave him his chance. The longer Napoleon prevaricated the more his margin of safety evaporated: by 12 July the time-lag had shrunk. In three days time it would be down to a matter of hours.

Before the Bourbons returned there was a series of imprecise understandings between Wellington and Fouché. Almost until the last day of the provisional government Fouché avoided an explicit commitment to seize Napoleon and deliver him to Wellington or Louis: this was no longer the case. What may have been collusion with Wellington had been replaced by formal collaboration between Louis and Castlereagh – to put it personally, between Jaucourt and Sir John Croker, the secretary of the Admiralty who had come to Paris as determined as Jaucourt to settle the matter. On 13 July the pair of them drafted an elaborate plan for apprehending the runaway: put into effect four days sooner it would have done the trick.

The time-lag was still against them. They had to cover a number of problems with guesstimates. First, there was a specific decree that Napoleon was not to board any British ship. Jaucourt plainly feared that if he was once aboard, it would prove very difficult to reclaim him. A new prefect, Baron Richard, was appointed to collaborate with Bonnefoux at Rochefort, and they were to be joined by a Captain de Rigny, who (with other military officials) was posting down from Paris with warrants and pistols in his pockets. To the last a time-lag was creating problems. Jaucourt did not know whether his orders might cover some kind of mutiny that had already occurred or some conspiracy that had not yet been played out. The tenses, indeed the fiery uncertainty of the warrant, show this confusion. It seems to assume that Rigny would find some half-baked event in process and stop it by threatening dire consequences. He was to go out to Aix under a flag of truce to inform the officers that the new regime had 'no hostile intentions' towards them and their men. Napoleon personally was the sole object of the exercise. The local soldiers and sailors were to be told that they were 'allies' unless (what did Jaucourt imagine had happened?) their organisation 'made it necessary' take extreme measures.

At this point the document took off into wild speculations about shots being exchanged with British ships and the killing of British sailors in consequence of 'open rebellion'. On the assumption that matters had now got out of hand, and that Napoleon had fled on one of the frigates, Rigny was told to seek help from Brest... or even from Lord Keith in Plymouth Sound! Set against the actual situation in the Basque Roads it shows why people thought the Bourbons stupid as well as incompetent. Even with the participation of the sober and generally sensible John Croker the search for Napoleon had degenerated into a farrago of nonsense.

All the same this scheme of entrapment played its part in the final hours. Alerted no doubt by telegraph, Bonnefoux anticipated Rigny's arrival and went out to the *Saale* late in the evening of 14 July. The fragmentary records show that he and Philibert were well aware what was happening over on Aix. They were intending, at least, to connive at Napoleon's midnight flit to *Bellerophon*, and reluctant to do Rigny's work for him. Bonnefoux afterwards said that he was unable to go across and detain Napoleon because the tide was setting in and there was no wind once again. Yet they sent Bougnis Desbordes, a cousin of Philibert and one of the lieutenants of the *Saale*, over to tell Becker that the emperor must leave at once, and to rouse Jourdan, the captain of *l'Epervier* (which was to carry him out) to hurry – an injunction he took so seriously that he fouled an anchor and had to cut the cable.

By their ambivalence Bonnefoux and Philibert had neither helped nor seriously hindered Napoleon during this muddled transit of Rochefort, though for one reason or another they had failed to get him away. At the last however they had saved him from the attentions of Rigny, and his two accompanying officers, who arrived too late. Finding themselves cheated they next applied to Hotham on the *Superb*, who told them their mission was now pointless since Napoleon had gone beyond their reach. There were, of course, enquiries about the failure to catch him, which never made up into a coherent account of what had actually happened that night. The frustrated royalists had to be satisfied in the end by handing down minor penalties to most of those involved. The only record of the failure is the handwritten order from Jaucourt in the French naval archives, cancelled in red ink.

* * *

Napoleon had gone before dawn. He was dressed in his favourite uniform of a colonel in the Chasseurs de Garde, his decorations catching the early light, a tricolour cockade in his iconic hat. The little official family walked up the street through sentimentally emotional and applauding crowds and out through the gate in the wall, coming to the slipway on the south point where three boats were waiting to take them out to *l'Epervier*. Most of

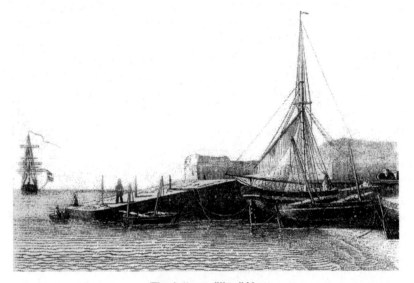

The jetty on l'Ile d'Aix

the party had already left before the generals and their ladies, going out to the *Sophie* in the darkness with their baggage: when the small coach and horses were loaded the last trappings of imperial pomp fell away. There were now tears rather than cheers and Becker, who had done an honourable and steadying job through all the travails on the way from Paris, offered to comply with his orders and accompany Napoleon out from the last rocks of France to the *Bellerophon's* wall of English oak. Napoleon declined. 'It must not be said that France handed me over to England,' he said cryptically and inaccurately.

16

Billy Ruffians

'At the break of day, on 15 July 1815, *l'Epervier* French brig-of-war was discovered standing out towards the ship, with a flag of truce.' When Frederick Maitland wrote those words in his memoirs some years later he must still have felt the thrill at the look-out's cry of an approaching sail. He would also have remembered his uncertainty. After the negotiations with Las Cases and Bertrand's formal letter which said that Napoleon would board next day, there could be little doubt that he would actually present himself. But in what manner? Giving or expecting what kind of impression? On *Bellerophon* all was 'expectation and excitement' a midshipman recalled. Everyone was running to his station, eager to miss nothing of the moment, while Andrew Mott made sure that the ship was dressed exactly as Maitland wished.

It was to be a muted ceremony. There was a marine guard at the gangway but they would not salute. The officers would stand ready for introductions but they were not to remove their hats, as they would normally for a visiting dignitary or high officer. And the crew were not to man the yards as they did in a traditional welcome. Maitland would soften the snub by explaining later that full honours only began after the colours had been hoisted at 8 am. He had tried to calculate the proceedings to a button in case there might be an unwitting recognition of rank for which he might be called to account. He had to work out the details himself, for there had been no comparable occasion in the long tradition of the Royal Navy – and he had to stage-manage these proceedings within those traditional dimensions. To cap all these worries, the sun that was rising behind *l'Epervier* was also lighting a distant set of sails coming in from the ocean. It was a full-rigged ship that could only be the *Superb*, summoned by

Maitland's report that the emperor was about to give himself up. Midshipman Home, who left a full report of that day, was not above a young man's point-scoring in his autobiography, and he made a snickering comment that Maitland stifled an oath when *Superb* was sighted as if he feared that his superior officer was hastening up to claim the prize.

* * *

It was in fact Mott who took hold of it. *L'Epervier* was making an easy but slow crossing from Aix, crabbing out with a falling wind as the ebb turned. There was certainly much the same anxious anticipation on the

Lt Mott collects Napoleon in the pinnace

brig. Napoleon was at his most controlled, concealing a budget of apprehensions, patronising Captain Jourdan and the crew with solicitous questions, as was always his habit with his *grognards*, asking Jourdan about his years as a prisoner-of-war in England, comparing the vessel to *Inconstant*, a similar brig which had carried him back to France from Elba. He seemed resigned when Jourdan asked him why he had made no effort to escape – saying he would happily have volunteered to lead such an attempt. 'Too late,' Napoleon said, looking out to *Bellerophon*. 'They are waiting for me.'

Bellerophon's moment in history

He had taken care to present himself with his accustomed dignity, with a white waistcoat and breeches, a green jacket with a scarlet collar and facings, an olive greatcoat and the cocked hat with a tricolour cockade. He wore the Grand Cross of the Legion d'Honneur and some lesser self-awarded decorations. However anomalous this costume may have looked in the shabby crowd and the darkness of the quai at Aix, he held himself at this dramatic moment as if he was at a parade on the Champ de Mars: Napoleon was a great man for ceremonies.

* * *

The encounter could not come quickly enough for either Maitland or Napoleon but time was dragging out as *l'Epervier* slowed with the tide, and Maitland decided to launch his own pinnace with Mott in charge to row over to close the bargain. Pulling hard, with Napoleon's distinctive figure standing erect, the oarsmen brought the crowded boat alongside the gangway. Answering Maitland's anxious call 'Have you got him?' Mott sent up Bertrand and Napoleon, and as the farewell cheers from *l'Epervier's* sailors came faintly across the water, the silence on board *Bellerophon* was broken only by the shrill pipe of the bosun's whistle.

Bertrand was the first to go up. 'The emperor is on board', he said formally, moving aside to allow Napoleon to come face to face with Maitland. 'He pulled off his hat,' Maitland recalled, 'and addressing me in a firm voice said, "I am come to throw myself on the protection of your prince and laws".' He had begun as he meant to go on, announced by title and repeating the most vital phrase from the previous day's letter to the Prince Regent.

The moment of formality passed, as the two men moved across the quarterdeck to the cabin with the casual comments appropriate to the reception of a house guest. Napoleon made a suitable appreciation of the great cabin's style and comfort and offered a graceful pleasantry about a painting of Maitland's wife. After the remainder of the suite had come on board, and introductions had eased the inevitable embarrassment of the moment – there was no mention of transit to the United States or repetition of rigmarole about his peaceful intentions. Maitland was glad to take up Napoleon's request to be shown over the ship, a custom often observed on such occasions; and there was the usual run of small talk – comments about the smart discipline of the crew, the appearance of the ship, a comparison to a French vessel, which seemed to go well beyond the stiffness that could be expected from a recently defeated enemy. If Maitland was all anxious good manners Napoleon had certainly set out to be ingratiating as a means to make his position more congenial, an attitude that was to last until sharper questions began to be asked as *Bellerophon* came up to the coast of Devon. This agreeable social tone was picked up by the officers, each astonished by the presence of the emperor relaxing in the courtesy of their deck. They could not have guessed that after fifteen stressful years of war against the Corsican Ogre he would turn out to be a man skilled in the effect of charm – and this was the first occasion when he used it to his captors, the first demonstration of how he proposed to rework the English image of him. He was, of course, a familiar figure from years of caricature. At forty-six, Midshipman Graebke wrote to his mother, he was 'a fine-looking man, inclined to corpulency... hair turning gray and a little bald on the crown of his head, no whiskers, complexion French yellow, eyes grey, Roman nose, good mouth and chin, neck short, big belly, arms stout, white hands and shows a good leg...' Others noted him as dignified, that though short he had 'a commanding presence' and that his expression was 'solemn and almost melancholy.' The reaction on *Bellerophon* was generally favourable. 'From the time of his first coming on board my ship,' Maitland reflected, 'to the period of his quitting her, his conduct was invariably that of a gentleman... in no one instance do I recollect him to have made use of a rude expression, or to have been guilty of any kind of ill-breeding.' Such a testimonial, which came a long time after the event, shows how Maitland was affected to reciprocate. It also explains the unexpectedly comfortable way a ship's company and its extraordinary passengers were to pass their days together.

* * *

There were more formalities before the voyage began. One observer recalled that Napoleon seemed very anxious for the ship to be off, glancing at the shore as if he could only be safe once the *Bellerophon* had sailed; but that was probably someone being wise after the event. The hue and cry that Rigny was raising ashore had only just begun, and starting so late it had no chance of success. There was, however, a distraction that caught his attention, and he watched closely as Maitland went across to *Superb* to greet his admiral, Sir Henry Hotham. Here was another awkward meeting which might indicate how he was to be treated, and another set of relevant decisions on that point which Hotham and Maitland had to make in a few minutes' discussion.

'I hope I have done right,' were Maitland's first words to Hotham, 'and that the government will approve of my conduct, as I considered it of much importance to prevent Bonaparte's escape to America, and get possession of his person.' Hotham was reassuring. 'Getting hold of him on any terms would have been of the greatest consequence, but as you have entered into no conditions whatever, there cannot be a doubt that you will obtain the approbation of His Majesty's Government.' Maitland was glad

Surrender: the incomparable event

of Hotham's endorsement. It meant that the pair of them would be sharing the praise or blame if there were critical questions about what they had done in these tricky circumstances. Hotham then relieved Maitland of another anxiety, generously (for he was the senior) asking if he would like to pass Napoleon over into his care. 'Certainly not,' Maitland said at once. 'I have had all the anxiety and responsibility of conducting the matter to this issue.'

When Maitland returned and told Napoleon that Hotham was anxious to meet him, Napoleon sent Bertrand across to make the protocol arrangements; and when Hotham came over that afternoon with his flag-captain and his secretary it was again Bertrand who formally arranged the audience. He would have known that Hotham was only one rung down in the naval hierarchy from Lord Keith, the commander-in-chief, and might be expected to speak with more authority about his prospects. It was already clear to Maitland that things would go more smoothly if Napoleon was allowed to set the pace, and both he and Hotham were too anxiously polite to stop the initiative passing to Napoleon. The first day, Maitland wrote, 'Bonaparte, viewing himself as a royal personage, which he continued to do while on board the *Bellerophon*,' presented himself as host, arranged the seating and treated his guests to a meal prepared by his French chef presented on the plate and porcelain he had brought aboard. Maitland noticed that Hotham remained uncovered in the presence of the ex-emperor, and that Napoleon kept his hat on all the time save when he was actually eating.

'Under the circumstances,' Maitland remarked, 'I considered that it would have been ungracious and uncalled for in me to have disputed this assumption of royal dignity.' He was not aware until too late that these acts of courtesy were being taken as more than a precedent for shipboard behaviour. By the time he realised that he was being outwitted, it was then too late to revoke the implicit permission for Napoleon to bring the imperial court and its manners on board. It had been an unwise genuflexion that sustained the false hopes which had encouraged Napoleon to give himself up. The Admiralty was in no doubt about this when Maitland's role was later scrutinised. Melville had reason to think that there was a deferential style about the procedures. Savary said that Hotham 'rendered the emperor the honour due to a crowned head'; and that 'such great care taken by the British to please us led us to hope that the reception in England would be no worse.'

Maitland was still uncertain about the question of deference when next morning Hotham invited Napoleon and his suite over to *Superb* for breakfast. He noticed that the gunports of *Superb* were open and the tompions removed from the guns, as if ready to fire a salute, that ropes had been prepared for the crew to man the yards, and the ship's band was ready on deck. Concerned about this, since he had 'received Bonaparte without even the guard presenting arms,' he sent an officer to ask Hotham whether he intended to salute Napoleon as he went aboard *Superb*, and whether the same should be done as he left *Bellerophon*. Naval protocol was being judged to a nicety. Both men were undoubtedly as worried about what the Admiralty might consider proper as they were about upsetting Napoleon. Hotham replied that he would only man the yards, as a token of respect, and that Maitland might do the same when Napoleon returned to *Bellerophon*.

At 10 am the captain's barge was ready for the crossing, but on his way to the gangway Napoleon tarried at the marine guard, quizzed the marines in his customary way and, to their astonishment, put them through a part of their customary drill. Small gestures such as this had the same

Napoleon exercises the marines

effect on the crew that his presentable manner was having on the officers, accustomed to the navy's strict bounds of discipline.

The sight of the manned yards on *Superb* evoked another round of naval questions from Napoleon, interrogating the officers, inspecting the ship. The advantage of such an easy attitude was to put aside the stiffness of what could be an embarrassing encounter and postponed more formal and potentially difficult questions. The only business that was discussed was formal matters like the arrangements (unfulfilled!) to transport to England the horses and carriages left at Rochefort.

* * *

On *Bellerophon* the symbolic moment had arrived. Maitland was ready to weigh anchor and sail, to take the ship out to sea through a warm summer evening towards the sunset. Everything was done with precision and in silence, as always when a ship brings up the anchor to the cathead and begins to ease through the water. The quiet efficiency seems to have been a surprise to Napoleon and his officers watching from the poop. 'What I most admire,' he remarked, 'is the extreme silence and orderly conduct of your men – on a French ship everyone calls and gives orders and they gabble like so many geese.'

The two long days, which had been pregnant with so many difficulties, were passing off as well or better than could have been expected, and Maitland noted that Napoleon did not seem depressed as they passed out beyond the Chassiron lighthouse. At 6 pm they all went in to dinner and Napoleon was 'in very good spirits,' going over old battles and telling anecdotes about himself. He even unbent to the point of playing cards, *vingt-et-un*, which Maitland refused to join in on the jokey grounds that he had left all his money with his wife. Whereupon, Napoleon offered to lend him some.

The more easily things went, however, the more Maitland worried that he had been so accommodating that it would later prove embarrassing, and three days out he drafted another letter of self-justification to Lord Keith, describing in great detail how he had managed the blockade at Rochefort and (as his instructions had demanded) 'seized' Bonaparte and was taking him back to England. Once again there was the fretting insistence about 'stating in the most clear and positive terms that I had no authority to make any sort of stipulation as to the reception he was to meet with.' Maitland believed, rightly, that much hung on this form of words. He was repeatedly to refer to it when doubts arose about the implicit conditions on which Napoleon had 'given himself up… surrendered… been seized… been enticed… or simply accepted on board.' The distinction between these definitions of Napoleon's status might have no practical effect once he was aboard: it was a case of 'finders-keepers' as the *Bellerophon* carried him away; but they had very different political and diplomatic implications.

As Maitland realised, any one of them might be accepted or rejected by Lord Keith, or the Admiralty, or even in a court of law. Given such concerns Maitland unavoidably created ambiguities but seems to have behaved with considerate dignity towards a great man in adversity. On other ships, under triumphalist captains there could well have been more vengeful resentment for the years of war.

* * *

The most striking evidence of this civility, in which the cheerful boisterousness of the midshipmen off duty contrasted with the austerity of the working of the ship, was the staging of two eighteenth century farces. The titles – *The Poor Gentleman* and *Raising the Wind* were sardonic and only accidentally relevant. They were probably part of the repertoire of plays kept on board. Amateur dramatics played a bigger and refreshing role aboard ships then is commonly realised. It is a tradition (still maintained) that goes back at least to the seventeenth century: it is recorded that the staged premiere of *Hamlet* was on HMS *Dragon*, a British ship off Sierra Leone, in 1607; and when Sir John Franklin's ships were icebound in the Arctic the crews exchanged performances to pass the time. There were similar diversions on Royal Navy ships which sustained the years-long blockade of Napoleon's France. All the ship's assets would be deployed, carpenters to knock up furniture and scenery, sail makers to run up costumes, and it seems the performances were often open to crew as well as officers (see Appendix I).

On *Bellerophon* a marine lieutenant – 'a fellow of great taste' according to Midshipman Home – was responsible for getting the production up and presenting it on the restricted space of the gun-deck. The performance was much appreciated by Napoleon and his party, Fanny Bertrand standing in to interpret for them. The French were much amused by the boys who took the female parts. Home remembered well, since he was one of them, the 'smooth-faced younger gentlemen' who were 'rather of the Dutch build.' There were other moments of cheerfulness 'regardless of the future', Home said 'the daily turnout on the quarter-deck was quite gay and reviving, not least because the Bertrand children had the run of the deck and the younger midshipmen played games with them.' The social scene was livelier and more casual than might have been expected in the circumstances, and the exiles seemed to see in this a promise that they might indeed be 'well-received'.

* * *

Yet there was also pathos. Early in the morning of 23 July, seven days out from Rochefort, the ship was just abeam of Ushant when young Home came on watch to see Napoleon emerge to stand on the poop. 'He took out a pocket-glass… looking eagerly at the land. In this position he remained from five in the morning to nearly midday, without paying any attention to what was passing around him, or speaking to his suite, who had been standing behind him for several hours.' Home had a conventional reaction to this 'last view of France! What must have been his feelings in those

The cartoonist does the crew of Bellerophon an injustice

few hours. How painful the retrospect, and how awful the look forward!' He thought of the fallen emperor as 'deserted and betrayed', and said that 'his emotion was visible… he hung upon the land until it was only a speck in the distance… he uttered not a word as he tottered down the poop-ladder; his head hung heavily forward, so as to render his countenance scarcely visible, and in this way he was conducted to his cabin.' Home continued to ruminate on 'the loss of his throne, his empire, his soldiers, on all of which his ambition has fed until it knew no bounds.' It is curious that there is no hint of *schadenfreude*, of bitterness or triumph against the man who has been 'keeping Europe in ferment these last twenty years.'

By and large, the 'Billy Ruffians' were well aware, almost proud of their role in bringing all that to an end, without fuss or malice.

Maitland, properly and sensibly, keeping as aloof as possible in a ship so unusually and awkwardly overcrowded, never allowed himself to get too close to Napoleon. For all his dry coolness he permitted himself one consoling gesture, waking Napoleon in the early hours as the profile of the Dartmoor hills came into view. He fetched Napoleon from his cabin in a dressing gown, showing him the moors and the Devon coastline. Maitland noticed how few naval ships they had sighted on the nine-day voyage; 'had he passed the squadron off Rochefort,' he wrote ten years later, 'he would have made his voyage in safety to America.' Napoleon may very well have had similar recriminations at seeing so much of the Atlantic open to any audacious attempt he must have made... At that point his mind was probably far from the might-have-beens. What *Bellerophon* had done or failed to do was irrelevant. She had done her duty, to the best of Maitland's ability. The question now was not what had happened back in France but what would happen next day when *Bellerophon* dropped her anchor in the sheltered fleet anchorage at Torbay.

17

Seized and Detained

A secret message brought the news of Waterloo to the banker Rothschild in London on the night of 19 June, to his immediate profit and the later knowledge of the government. The news was in the broadsheets and spreading through celebrating crowds in the next two days, and it had been received by Lord Keith, the naval commander-in-chief at Plymouth, by telegraph on 21 June. No one yet knew what had happened to Napoleon but it was generally assumed that with this last spasm of violence the long sequence of French wars, which stretched back through Napoleon and the Revolution to Louis XIV, was at last over. At the same time the signing of a peace treaty with the United States meant that the unnecessary and unpopular war of 1812 – itself an offshoot from the struggle against Napoleon – was also at an end. There had been a false dawn in 1814, when Napoleon had been rounded up and put on Elba, but the stunning victory in Flanders meant a real prospect of peace, even at the price of near bankruptcy, and social unrest. The Napoleonic wars had worn Britain into a kind of shabby unity, that had cost around 1,000 million pounds and more than half a million casualties, the last 60,000 in the Waterloo campaign. A narrow-minded Tory government had finally carried the war through to its end, making the most of its navy and compensating for its military deficiencies by financing and marshalling reactionary dynastic allies in a series of coalitions against France. The Tories had been struggling against the spreading infection of the Revolution, and then against the imperialism of Bonaparte, and their government was a reactionary compromise between the Hanoverian monarchs and the limited democracy of the powerful landed interest. Nevertheless, it tolerated a feeble opposition of Whig grandees and radical publicists. Lord Liverpool, as its prime minister, was contemptuous of the Prince Regent, whom he rightly thought a dissolute sot of Whig sympathies, and consulted him as little as possible. Two of the Regent's brothers, the dukes of Sussex and Essex, were themselves ardent members of the Whig oligarchy, and though Charles James Fox, the great advocate of conciliation with France, was dead, his nephew Lord Holland had taken on that role, and there were other prominent Whigs in the Lords and the Commons, who had the not-quite-adequate makings of an alternative government, and a scattering of popular figures in the Commons who sat for the few seats with a wider electorate.

The allies make a meal of their enemy

Napoleon does not seem to have been too well-informed about British politics, though a good many of the Foxites and radical intellectuals had left their calling-cards on him during the brief Peace of Amiens: at one point in the peace there were over 5,000 English visitors in Paris. It certainly suited him to pretend to a favourable view of the Regent which was not generally shared. If he had been more aware of the political weakness of this debauchee whom he addressed fawningly in his letter from the *Bellerophon*, and to whose expected generosity he often referred in discussions about his future, he would have been less optimistic. That letter, when finally delivered, evoked no positive reaction at all, though Lord Keith's judgement on Napoleon's charm and the Prince's susceptibility was that if they had managed to meet 'they would have been the best of friends in half an hour.' Liverpool's opinion was that it would have been far more dangerous to let Napoleon get into a position where he might be able to stir up disaffection in the opposition generally. This was a government noted for its repressive measures against radical agitators and seditious pamphleteers – and it would get more severe in the unruly peace that followed the war. The English may have been a poorly-educated people but many thousand copies of Tom Paine's *Rights of Man* had been sold, and even wartime suspensions of *habeas corpus* could not disrupt the rule of law which dated back to the Glorious Revolution of 1688.

This was the context in which an inflexible government had to decide what to do about the sudden appearance of Napoleon on its agenda. Where was he? What should be done if and when he was seized and detained? In these explicit and unchallengeable words the Royal Navy had been told what to do, for the task would almost certainly fall to the service which had struggled longest and most effectively against him. Liverpool, and the small clique of close colleagues in the Cabinet who had brought the country through the last stages of the war, would have to deal with the new challenge quickly, and secretively. Even before Waterloo it is clear that Liverpool was thinking about an ultimate victory, and wondering how the allies might finally dispose of Napoleon when it had been won. He had been over this ground before, in March 1814, and for good reason had been dissatisfied with the choice of Elba. Now, with Napoleon likely to fall into British hands, he was insisting that this time a final place of detention must be found, and that meanwhile the Corsican Ogre must be kept out of the country and denied any contact with possible sympathisers ashore for fear he might set off disturbances, or worse.

There was no disagreement in the Cabinet about this policy. Liverpool was in daily touch with Wellington and Castlereagh in France; Bathurst, the Secretary for War and the Colonies, was a severe man; the Lord Chancellor, Eldon, was there to cope with legal problems that might arise (see Appendix) and Melville, with relevant experience at the Admiralty, was watchfully responsible for all the policies and decisions that ran through the Royal Navy's chain of command as it sought to seize Napoleon and detain him until his ultimate fate was determined. Liverpool himself had substantial departmental experience as Home Secretary and Foreign Minister and had been a confirmed antagonist of revolutionary notions, since, as a young man, he had seen the fall of the Bastille. He was determined to keep this final act of war under his strict control, a task made easier by the fact that he had prorogued Parliament in early July, so that there could be no formal debate about his activities either in the Lords or the Commons.

* * *

In general terms, of course, the government's intentions were in the public domain, because it had been a party both to the Congress declaration of 13 March and the Treaty of Vienna of 9 June. Each document had defined the criminal status of Napoleon and how he was to be treated. By violating the Treaty of Fontainebleau he had destroyed 'the only legal title on which his existence depended.' The March document said that Napoleon had 'deprived himself of the protection of the law ... delivered himself up to public vengeance.' In June the allies were insisting that the war would go on 'until Napoleon had been disposed of and the peace of Europe made secure.' The details of these manifestoes were of course left until the occasion for enforcement arose, but there was ample justification here for any punitive action if Napoleon escaped death in action or became a prisoner. There was certainly sufficient excuse for the Prussians, for instance, if their patrols caught and shot him; the Russians and the Austrians could have no legal problems, and though a restored Bourbon king might be foolish, he still could launch a trial for treason. The allies, in fact, had framed a catch-all indictment, and it was a matter for Liverpool to decide whether he and his colleagues should act jointly with their allies, act independently within the framework of the Vienna indictments, or make their own arrangements without bringing Napoleon within the ambit of British law. That is why he was to be kept in secrecy and isolation, and why the government was to act with such haste.

Before the news of Napoleon's surrender reached London there were anxious letters between Liverpool and Castlereagh in Paris. On 7 July, running over the possibilities, Liverpool argued against entrusting Napoleon to France or other allies: 'we should think it better that he should be assigned to us... that the discretion should be invested entirely in ourselves, and that we should be at liberty to fix the place of his confinement.' It is not surprising he insisted on the means to make that confinement effectual, even though he could not prevent the newspapers from speculating how that could be done. Both in the War Office and especially in the Admiralty officials were searching out maps, reports and other information for Liverpool to decide what to do when Castlereagh's hurried despatch of 17 July confirmed that Napoleon had surrendered to Maitland on the *Bellerophon*. That was good news, but embarrassing. The *Courier*, the well-informed minsterialist paper, took up at once the point that was the focus of all the negotiations about and with Napoleon in the next few weeks.

If Napoleon had voluntarily given himself up as a prisoner of war, the paper argued, the Law of Nations prescribed that 'as soon as your enemy has laid down his arms and surrendered his person, you have no longer any right over his life.' Even if he had violated the Laws of Nations himself, that 'would afford us no justification in violating them ourselves;' and that his reception by Maitland meant that 'we shall afford him an asylum – that his life will be spared – but that we shall have him in such safe custody, that he shall not be able to disturb again the repose and security of the world.' It was not to prove as straightforward as the *Courier* assumed but the newspaper had at least come to the crux of the matter: even before *Bellerophon* dropped anchor in Torbay the government had decided what to do, how to set about doing it, what problems to expect in the doing of it, and how it could be justified.

* * *

The task was set out by Liverpool in a further letter to Castlereagh on 21 July. He accepted the allies wish 'that we should have custody of him... allowed to judge the means of it,' but there could be no question of detaining Napoleon anywhere in the British Isles. There were 'very nice legal reasons... which would be particularly embarrassing'; and, aside from that, Castlereagh 'knew enough of the feelings of people in this country not to doubt that Napoleon would become an object of curiosity immediately, and possibly compassion.' Keeping Napoleon in Britain or anywhere else in Europe, 'would contribute to a certain degree of ferment in France.'

In any case, both Melville and John Barrow (second secretary of the Admiralty) 'decidedly recommended St Helena as the place in the world best calculated for the confinement of such a person.' It was not merely isolated, a few square miles of volcanic rock some seven hundred miles out in the South Atlantic, it was also fortified, and it had only one settlement where a landing was possible. 'At such a distance and in such a place all intrigue would be impossible.' Thus, essentially, Napoleon's destiny was settled before he even set eyes on the coast of Devon.

A more detailed memorandum from the Foreign Office noted the island's compact form, its towering cliffs, its powerful shore batteries, its difficult paths… Finally, there was the great asset of its system of telegraphs, linked to observation posts 2,000 feet above the sea, where any ships within a radius of thirty miles could be seen, checked and reported to the governor. There was no real possibility of escape. In fact ten years before, Napoleon had approved two French naval expeditions which approached the island and sheered off without any attempt to take it. One can see why the Whitehall officials considered it an ideal place for a State Prisoner – as they were now calling Bonaparte.

All the necessary preparations were being put in hand, first locating a ship which could transport Napoleon and party, *Bellerophon* being too old and crank for such a long errand. Troops for the garrison had to be selected, ships had to be watered and victualled. And formal changes had also to be made because the island did not belong to the Crown but to the East India Company, which used the patterns of wind and current to break the long journey to and from its territories in India. Such routine stops would be a great convenience if Napoleon and his court were to be marooned there for years. Casual callers were to be excluded; only EIC and naval vessels were to use its facilities. The island, however, could not be left in private hands, and it would have to be governed and garrisoned by the British army. Bathurst had already chosen the governor, Sir Hudson Lowe, a bureaucratic martinet, who became notorious for his ill-tempered feud with his eminent prisoner, and by 25 July the government had acquired formal rights to the island. The Directors of the EIC handed it over to the Crown in a curiously indeterminate fashion, enabling it and its residents to be treated as if the place were the site of a British overseas garrison such as Gibraltar or Malta. One of the consequent oddities was that its inhabitants were not British citizens and they had no rights to proceed in British courts under British law. This point was a matter of serious interest to a government which was just embarking on a course of action where questions of residence and access to the courts could become a serious issue.

It was to recur as a source of legal challenge in modern times. The removal of a state prisoner beyond the rules of war (the Geneva Convention) and the rule of law in the detaining state was nothing new: it was quite the custom in the archaic regimes that Bonapartism had challenged across Europe. It became clearly unacceptable under the developing concept of personal rights in Britain and the United States, and in Britain the forceful (Napoleon explicitly required the use of the word 'forceful' to make this point) style of deportation evoked an immediate objections as a disruptive and damaging precedent. The questions then raised, however hurriedly and inadequately, were to arise again in modern wars against ideologies and regimes that were themselves outside the laws concerned.

* * *

The government's timing could not have been more prompt. Three nights earlier the *Slaney* had carried Captain Sartorious into Plymouth Sound, bringing the despatches from Maitland and Hotham which described Napoleon's surrender. Lord Keith was naturally excited, the more so when Sartorious told him that Napoleon might be expected to arrive on *Bellerophon* in Torbay any day soon – it had been a slow passage. For Keith this would be the highlight of more than sixty years at sea. As commander-in-chief of the Channel Fleet he found himself in control of all aspects of this historic operation, and he managed it with dignity and efficiency. Immediately, keeping Gourgaud with Napoleon's letter to hand, he despatched Sartorious off to Melville's private house near London, where the First Lord was to be tumbled out of bed at 3 am. Taking Sartorious for a quick visit to the Prince Regent (and no doubt showing him the 'unofficial' copy of the petition from Napoleon), the pair of them went on to break the news to Liverpool and the Cabinet.

The reactions were immediate. Melville and Barrow made sure every arrangement would be in the hands of the Royal Navy from first to last – there was to be no doubt where the credit lay for seizing and detaining Napoleon, down to fobbing off both the generals in Plymouth who tried to snaffle him for their own and the army's glory. Keith, moreover, was now preparing his official role in Napoleon's arrival. He had already received Melville's instructions for dealing with the *Bellerophon*. The old first-rate was to be kept anchored off the little fishing-port of Brixham, about a mile out, and no one – in Melville's phrase – 'was to be suffered to come on board' or leave the ship. She was, in short to be 'quarantined' for political rather than medical reasons. The first sign that there was something odd was that the ports on *Bellerophon* and *Myrmidon*, which had come in together, were being closed. This was unusual for an arrival, since the shore boats always swarmed out with bread, tobacco, fruit, even women, and traded with the crew through the ports. Now the shore boats were being warned off and before long, armed patrols were put out to keep them away. In one of the boats was a local boy, John Smart of Brixham, who left one of the few detailed descriptions of what happened. He told how he and another boy had put out in a baker's boat which made several attempts to come close to *Bellerophon*. Then, through one of the ports not wholly closed, they saw a man secretively signalling to them. As they came round for a closer view, with the patrol boat astern, the man threw a small black bottle into the sea and the boy picked it out of the water as it drifted past. In it was a small roll of paper, with the words 'We have got Bonaparte on board.' Five minutes after the boy was back on shore 'there was not a soul in Brixham, except babies, ignorant of the news.'

Certainly, this first known leak shows what might have happened with a laxer rule regulating contact. A more serious lapse occurred when Midshipman Home went ashore with the cutter taking Lieutenant Mott to land with despatches for Keith and the Admiralty. On that day, already, Melville was telling Keith for his 'private information' that 'in all probability the ex-emperor will be sent to some foreign colony… we shall not apprise him immediately of his future destination.' Home gleefully recalled that as soon as Mott had left the boat it was beset by excited young women, who carried the impressionable and irresponsible youth off to a Devon cream tea, and plied him with questions about Napoleon as well as scones. 'What was he really like… were his hands and clothes covered in blood… were we not frightened of his voice like thunder?' Home replied that he was a handsome man, with charming fingers and a musical voice: 'if by chance they could get a look at him by the gangway they would fall in love with him directly.' Such incitement made the young women hustle Home down to the beach and he had the pleasure of seeing the cutter 'crammed with the young charmers of Torbay.' Coming to his senses at the thought of the reception that might greet him back on board Home stiffened his resolve and had the crew lift the would-be sightseers over the side.

No one was permitted to follow the cutter's trip ashore but word that Napoleon was in sight spread rapidly and hundreds of local residents began crowding down to the beach, and fishermen could turn silver by taking them out in boats. This had been anticipated by John Barrow as soon as news of the *Bellerophon's* approach reached London on 24 July. He imposed even more scrupulous restraints on ship to shore contacts. Maitland was told that he was 'to prevent all communication with the shore, but through him, and by him, and through the agency of Lord Keith.'

In the event this constraint was easier to enforce than the clause which followed it: 'proper measures are to be taken to prevent boats and small craft from crowding too near the *Bellerophon*.' Barrow's anxiety on this point was justified. In the event the swarm of spectators was to be the most notable public feature of Napoleon's appearance on the coast of Devon. Melville himself, writing to tell Keith personally what the Cabinet proposed to do about Napoleon, also sent even more forceful instructions for 'close surveillance of Napoleon and his troublesome guests,' though they were to be permitted any goods or services which might contribute to the comfort expected at their rank.

Other orders on the way provided that for reasons of security *Bellerophon* should not linger in Torbay but, accompanied by *Slaney* and *Myrmidon*, should transfer from the open bay to the larger and more regulated anchorage in Plymouth Sound. Immediately under Keith's eye, it enjoyed quicker telegraph and courier access from London. Some of the messages were concerned with the manners and protocol of Maitland's reception of Napoleon in the Basque Roads, about which the Admiralty was to be as fussed as Maitland was anxious. It was essential to establish that Maitland had not unwittingly prejudiced the conditions on which Napoleon was to be received.

* * *

Whatever the niceties of the formal reception the informal welcome was threatening to get out of hand, on these lovely summer days, as the news spread along to Plymouth, to Exeter, eastwards to Somerset and Dorset. Coaches were coming down from London, Birmingham and Bristol, swaying along with a press of passengers. The anchorages at Torbay and the Sound, one person remarked, had 'become the rendezvous of all the curious people in England,' as they lined the beaches, put out in boats, called out and waved, as word of mouth and newspaper reports brought more spectators every day. The mood of the crowds was extraordinary – what Napoleon at first took to be jeers were for the most part cries to attract his attention. 'A large portion of the spectators,' the *Morning Post* regretted to say, 'not only took off their hats but cheered him, apparently with the view of soothing his fallen fortunes and treating him with respect and consideration.' Musicians played in some of the boats, people stood tottering in them because there was no room to sit, others were singing songs. An impromptu gala which might have been taken for crowds celebrating Waterloo or welcoming the peace astonished Napoleon. As many as eight thousand were estimated at Torbay, more at Plymouth; at the peak there were said to be almost a thousand boats. Napoleon was allowed to play to this waterborne gallery, appearing regularly at the gangway, bowing and raising his cocked hat as though he was orchestrating this astonishing performance. There seems to have been little control aboard *Bellerophon*, the sailors being permitted to hold up informal bulletins on chalked boards: 'Resting', 'On Deck' and the like.

There are many descriptions of this concourse, paintings too, which persisted in the face of sometimes brutal interference by heavy dockyard boats, even shots in the air, as attempts were made to sustain a cordon about three hundred yards away from the ship. There were upsettings, even drownings. Lieutenant Mott dived over to rescue two young women from a sinking boat: others were not so lucky. The commonest reason given for such a daily demonstration was curiosity. Napoleon was probably the best known and most recognisable person in Europe, an image presented in hundreds of caricatures and cartoons; and more than an image, he was a great general, Britain's most persistent and now defeated enemy, who embodied the French Revolution and made himself master from Madrid to Moscow. Wellington later put it neatly: 'Napoleon was not so much a personality as a principle.' It is no wonder that crowds packed the harbours and jetties for this once-in-a-lifetime event, wrote to their families and friends about it, and were shedding the diabolic fears held through years of war in favour of a more compassionate, even a more favourable opinion – just as the Prime Minister feared they would. Lady Charlotte Fitzgerald, who saw Napoleon at Plymouth said 'seeing Napoleon for themselves had shown John Bull that Bonaparte had neither horns nor hoof,' but she feared – like Liverpool – that allowed ashore 'he might have been a rallying point of conspiracy and treason, leading the fractious population into a violent jacquerie.'

It was curiosity that continued to stir the public. In the next year an exhibition of Napoleon's clothes and souvenirs, taken around on a national tour in his carriage, brought in over 100,000 visitors; smaller but similar shows and museums, as well as Napoleonic plays and concerts, were regular money-spinners that became widely popular as the exile on St Helena dragged out. This decline in hostility was accompanied by a similar if less dramatic rise in pro-Bonapartist sentiment, which came to see

Napoleon as the heir to the radical republicanism of the revolutionary years, the opponent of feudal and theocratic regimes across Europe, a champion of liberty against despotism, the maker of a new legal pattern and sponsor of new scientific and educational ideas. His gestures towards liberal constitutionalism during the Hundred Days had also enhanced this progressive reputation. Once seen as the iconic enemy of liberty within a generation he was being converted into a paragon of reform.

The British middle and the lower classes, who could scarcely be called an electorate, did not enjoy much influence in the British parliamentary system. For almost half a century, they suffered from the corruption and reaction of one government after another, and were liable to swingeing laws and penalties against sedition; yet even then they sustained a surprising level of political interest and the first groundswell of social change, lifted mainly by newspapers that had national sales and often tens of readers (or listeners) per copy. Together with the aristocratic and merchant Whigs, supporters of the American revolution and sympathisers with Napoleon, this loose alliance of liberals, democrats and radicals was a force to be reckoned with: hence the anxiety of Liverpool and Castlereagh about the response if Napoleon once set foot ashore. As it was, these restless liberals were following events on the Devon coast with sharp interest, many apparently wishing to see Napoleon come ashore, to 'have his rights', and to prevent what was seen by many as his illegal deportation without trial. 'If they can illegally snatch Napoleon abroad from Devon what is to prevent them snatching Cobbett from Surrey?' asked the great radical journalist, whose *Weekly Register* sold as many as 40,000 copies a week.

Napoleon must have been to some extent aware of this surge of sentiment, might indeed have looked to such sympathisers to help him; and for all the restrictions imposed on correspondence with the Hollands, the eminent lawyer Sir Samuel Romilly, Sir Francis Burdett and other Whig publicists, he was able to make contact with them with appeals for help somehow smuggled away from the *Bellerophon*. It was Las Cases who was the greatest help. During the ten years he spent in Britain and America between the Terror and the Empire, he had made a network of friends, partly through his work as a freelance teacher, partly through social connections. The most helpful at this time was Lady Clavering, born French but married to an English baronet, who had been one of his pupils and now became an effective intermediary. It must have been all the more depressing for Napoleon to feel that help was there, within sight, almost within reach.

18

Strict Regime

Napoleon had certainly allowed himself to be misled and by the generous courtesy shown the party on the *Bellerophon*; he was keen to see how he would be treated on arrival, and was shaken by the harsher tone that was adopted the instant *Bellerophon's* anchor dropped. This would normally have been the moment at which an official reception party might have put out to the ship, or at least when Maitland might have looked out for it. He became reserved, even downcast, and the courtiers relapsed into a similar mood. They had all been upset when Gourgaud reappeared, returned to the ship with his letter formally undelivered; he had not even been sent to London, let alone allowed to reach the Prince. With him, moreover, he brought a bundle of newspapers, few of them friendly and some with hostile speculations about exile to St Helena or elsewhere. Napoleon kept his dignity, but he now began to protest against his treatment as a prisoner and object to the prospect of deportation. The members of the party who had argued so strongly at Aix for travel to England now looked, and were, crestfallen – especially Las Cases who had spoken so eagerly for it. Lallemand and Savary – 'the two villains' Castlereagh had called them – were cynical and disilliusioned. They had predicted some such fracture of hopes as this, and from now on they focused on saving themselves. If they were not chosen to accompany Napoleon further into exile they feared they would be returned to France, where they were on the list of Bourbon death warrants. Fanny Bertrand, who had been in high spirits as the ship sailed towards England was now edgy, anxious, taking every chance of pressing her own case for going and staying ashore.

Worse was to come after two days. At 4 am on 26 July a messenger brought Melville's order that *Bellerophon*, *Slaney* and *Myrmidon* were to up anchor and sail round the coast to Plymouth. The movement as they put out to sea aroused some of the party, who thought it a sign that they were moving to a larger port with more facilities – such as a senior officer who was in contact with Whitehall by telegraph and courier – while others took it as an ill-omen that they were moving further away from London. Fanny Bertrand was distressed by the idea that they were already setting sail for St Helena without notice and made another scene. 'Everyone seemed to be studying us with gloomy interest,' Las Cases recalled, 'the most sinister rumours had reached the ship.'

Anchored now between two frigates, the *Liffey* and the *Eurotas*, and within a tighter cordon of guardboats, *Bellerophon* was still in view of the sightseeing crowds, now increased by a long line standing just about water level on the unfinished jetty that poked out into the Sound. There were still no visitors to the ship itself, except on official and ship's business. An exception was made for Mrs Maitland to go alongside, and Napoleon addressed a pleasantry to her, but even Lady Keith was annoyed to find she got no nearer than the deck of the *Eurotas*.

* * *

Napoleon had now asked three times for an interview with Keith himself as the senior officer and he seemed agreeable enough: he had sent a polite message via Maitland to thank Napoleon for ensuring that medical help had been given to his nephew at Waterloo. Napoleon thought it might be possible to set protocol aside temporarily. 'I shall be satisfied to be a private person, until the British government has determined in what light I am to be treated,' he said to Maitland. Keith could not accede without instructions, and these were delayed while the government remained undecided what status Napoleon should enjoy.

* * *

The doubt arose from the manner in which Maitland and Hotham had received Napoleon when he surrendered, and the Admiralty was still not certain whether or not they had prejudiced the occasion. The issue had arisen when Lieutenant Fletcher, the officer Hotham had sent off with despatches on the *Slaney*, had delivered the reports and been questioned about them. When Melville talked to Fletcher he was disturbed at what seemed like the generous, almost the obeisant way they had greeted Napoleon, when all the orders sent out to the patrols had insisted that any ship which seized him must restrain and isolate him. On 25 July, when Napoleon had already come within Keith's command, Melville wrote him a severe letter. Bonaparte should not have visited *Superb*; the yards should

Waiting for the verdict: a midshipman's sketch

not have been manned; Napoleon should not have been welcomed with royal respect or permitted to host Maitland to dinner in his own cabin on the imperial plate. These were errors that may have seemed trivial, and slipped past in the intensity of the moment, but Melville regarded them as serious breaches of protocol in these circumstances, when precedents were being established and the parameters of detention were being set.

One important reason for Melville's severity was the mistake made in Elba by Colonel Campbell, the commissioner appointed to watch over Napoleon who, lulled by his charm and familiarity, let him escape. That was the army's fault: Melville was determined that the navy should not repeat what he called the 'follies' committed last year by 'some officers in the Mediterranean'. In an accompany-ing note Melville had been even more explicit, saying that 'Bonaparte had been allowed to assume a great deal more state, and even authority, and had been treated with more submissiveness than belongs to his station as a prisoner of war, or to his rank as a general officer, which is all that can be allowed to him in this country.'

Of course, he conceded that no British officer could treat a captive with inhumanity, that 'the station which Bonaparte had so long held in Europe would naturally, almost involuntarily, lead an officer to abstain from any line of conduct which could be construed into an insult... but such indulgent feelings must be restrained within proper bounds.'

Since the same despatch told Keith that Sir George Cockburn had been appointed to command at the Cape, and that he would be accompanying Napoleon to St Helena to remain there until Sir Hudson Lowe arrived, it is clear that by the time *Bellerophon* came into Torbay the whole matrix for coping with Napoleon had already been put in place. These reprimands were designed to lock its provisions into the minds of the men who for a few more days would be handling the day-to-day relations with a prisoner who, effectively yet without being told, had been judged and sentenced without a hearing or a right of appeal. In fact, once Melville had made this clear, he became less severe, relieving Maitland of his professional anxiety by saying that his conduct in the Basque Roads had been given Admiralty 'approval'. Maitland still felt that his name should be cleared once and for all, and he wrote further justifications of his actions in reports to Keith and in the account of Napoleon's capture that he gave in his memoir. It is curious that Melville never raised the point that Las Cases and Napoleon stressed so often – that Maitland had deceived, misled or enticed them to board *Bellerophon* for England. Yet this concerned Maitland so much that he was at repeated pains to rebut it. He was certainly sensitive about his sympathies with the Holland House liberals (in fact many navy officers were Whigs, and even sat as Whig MPs), and his cousin Lord Lauderdale had been an outright supporter of the Revolution as a young man. Even now Lauderdale was an outspoken sympathiser with Napoleon in his decline.

There could have been a source of unspoken embarrassment here if Maitland had felt a touch of unwitting deference might discredit him professionally.

With that problem behind them Maitland and Keith now had the task of implementing the strict regime enjoined by Melville, and while Maitland's courtesy was sustained, he was at pains to distance himself from Napoleon and the entourage. With Keith he now had the responsibility of preparing Napoleon and a selection of his aides for departure to the other end of the world, and it cannot have been easy for him. The doubling up of guards, the continuous circling of boats and the newspapers that came aboard made the whole party aware and depressed at its prospects.

* * *

Even so, there was delay. Keith decided that now he had an official prescription of Napoleon's status he could meet his prisoner without awkwardness. He knew what to expect, because Napoleon had already rehearsed his case to Maitland – Napoleon claimed again that he could have joined the army on the Loire; he could have escaped; he only wanted permission to go to the United States; all the same, he had 'thrown himself on the humanity of England.' If he was now to be sent to St Helena, 'he would prefer death.' He would be content to be sent to the Tower, but he would above all like 'to live in private in any part of the kingdom.' In fact, when Keith went aboard *Bellerophon* on the morning of 28 July, Napoleon went well beyond this mantra to talk 'about many subjects, Toulon, Egypt, East Indies etc.' It was Napoleon's first opportunity to impress a senior officer with direct access to Whitehall; and yet it ended with the same plaintive pleas. 'I am no more and can disturb nobody. Cannot I live in England?' He then went on to ask Keith to inform the Prince Regent that he wished to become a British subject. 'That would be irregular,' Keith said officiously, but he offered to transmit any letter to the government. He then had to refuse an even more hopeless though superficially reasonable request. Napoleon said he would like to go for a walk ashore – the last idea Keith wished to entertain. Even if Napoleon was unaware of the legal implications of setting foot on English soil (he almost certainly was), Keith knew what might be involved. A third request was then refused. Could Keith tell him how long it would be before he and his companions were told what was going to happen to them? Keith temporised, saying there were still some time-consuming details to be settled with the allies. This was true. Castlereagh was in the process of drafting – and signing on 2 August – a compact which made Napoleon their common prisoner, only to be released by mutual consent.

The crowds ashore had as yet no notion of the decisions that were keeping Napoleon and his party detained on *Bellerophon*, without any means of effective protest against their fate. If the questions that Napoleon had been asking had been put to the demonstrators they might well have evoked the same kind of sympathetic response that was being made by the radical journalists who were trying to delay or prevent a final decision. What the papers were printing was based on guesswork or smuggled messages, but the news and the editorials were drastic enough to make Keith send Maitland instructions 'to double your vigilance.' To Keith's especial annoyance a copy of the letter to the Prince Regent had got out and been published: the leak, he insisted, was not from his office, but it may well have come from Las Cases who had made the original copies. There were also leaks at the London end, probably from clerks in the Admiralty and War Office, and there were open controversies in the press. The *St James's Chronicle*, for instance, urged that the record should show 'no stain… blot of malignity or vindictiveness', and that 'the British should forgive him who never forgave, and generously treat him who was generous to none.' A fierce letter in *The Times* declared that 'the age will be forever disgraced, and the cause of justice will endure a fatal shock, if Napoleon Bonaparte is not brought to a *solemn trial* and to *public execution*.' This writer's excitement carried him over into a second tirade. 'Now that we have paid for his guilt by a more lamentable waste of gallant lives than were ever before lost by us, in any single battle, now we are to become his protectors!… He trusts himself to those he has most injured.' Against such a background of mixed sympathy and abuse Napoleon continued to look composed when he appeared at the gangway. On a sunny Saturday there were more boats than ever. But there was now an air of restlessness about an event that was turning into a historic performance.

* * *

Maitland and Keith both noticed this change, on shore and aboard, where the members of the retinue were daily becoming more uneasy about their futures. A small-minded yet self-important group, Keith thought them, as anxious for generous treatment for themselves as they were concerned for the prospects of their leader. Some knew they would be taken away, others expected more pruning from the party of fifty-five to produce the final set for St Helena. So the tensions and jealousies which had been intensifying in the retinue all the way from Malmaison were now breaking out into open rivalry, into jockeying for the most favoured roles. Bertrand, as always, was steady and loyal; Montholon and Gourgaud were at open odds with each other; both were critical of Las Cases, who seemed to have ingratiated himself as secretary and scribe, adopted by Napoleon to tell his version of the last phase of his career. They were all irritated by Fanny Bertrand's hysteria. She had become so distraught that on 30 July Maitland had been obliged to report her demand that Bertrand should be omitted from the party bound for exile, since he had told her he intended to follow Napoleon to the last. Maitland said he 'was actuated only by the distress in which he beheld an unfortunate woman who declares that she would poison herself in preference to quitting Europe, and that she had taken this step without the knowledge of her husband.' Fanny persisted. Her next protest was to scream at Maitland that 'the Emperor is a monster of egotism, and would see women and children perish without feeling a thing.' Two days later she made a rush to throw herself through a window into the water and had to be held back by Montholon.

Napoleon himself remained outwardly calm, though those who saw him every day judged that he was increasingly depressed – very different from the sociable, self-confident person on the crossing from France. He had been noticeably upset when he was told that the letter to the Prince Regent was still being held in Plymouth. In the circumstances it had been a vain hope. Though he did not have the apparent familiarity with the Prince's character and attitudes that he had boastfully assumed in the discussions back on Aix, he may have had an idea that the Prince was at odds with the Liverpool government and on better terms with the Whig peace party. He was undoubtedly frustrated by the way he had no access to officials and ministers: as Melville had intended everything had to be done through the mediation of Maitland and Keith. His resentment increased day by day with no official note being taken of his remonstrances. He might well have felt that he was already caught in a curiously insubstantial trial, in which the case for the prosecution was inferred, the case for the defence was avoided, and the means by which a verdict might be handed down, or the time when a result might be expected, were simply ignored.

By now, indeed, he seemed to be thinking less of the result, which could never have been in much doubt, than of starting to prepare his case in a different jurisdiction – in the court of public opinion, because he thought that way, even 'at the bar of history'.

It is significant that in all the complicated exchanges in this critical phase of his detention neither Napoleon nor his custodians ever mentioned the word 'trial'. Both parties were probably aware that, whatever the situation in Berlin or Paris might be, there was no basis in English law (without new legislation) that would permit resort to such proceedings if the government was prepared to act arbitrarily. That remained to be demonstrated, of course, but meanwhile it all assumed the air of an impromptu court martial. Even today, in the UK, let alone then, there remain serious difficulties about the arraignment, trial, conviction and sentence of state prisoners for offences committed outside the jurisdiction of the detaining powers. As we look back on 1815, the pace at which arrangements were being made for hastening Napoleon out of British waters shows the government's fear that delay might lead to more than embarrassment, perhaps to the disruption of the whole process.

That was the complaint of the Tory newspapers, which would have no truck with uncertainties. The *Courier*, always in the lead against Bonaparte, insisted that no Britain 'can view Bonaparte with a least feeling of pity or respect... is he not fallen by his own inordinate and remorseless ambition, which was not to be sated at less price than the conquest of all Europe and the ruinous subjugation of this country?' The *Times* of 31 July fumed with similar ferocity: 'instead of bringing him to justice, we are to impose upon ourselves the disgraceful task of conveying his body to a distant island, and there watching it... Turn him loose again upon the continent and let him work his worst... may the next man who catches him be actuated by a more proper sense of his atrocious and criminal life!' At the other extreme of opinion, on 31 July the *Independent Whig* denounced 'the banishment of Napoleon to the island of St Helena, merely at the will of the Crown... The character and dignity of the country is not only outraged in such an assumption of power, but the Bill of Rights is actually made a dead letter.'

It might be thought that Napoleon deserved no justice, that retribution was all. That was not the whole motive of the verdict that a messenger would deliver from London next day. Revenge was only part of a sentence of lifelong exile.

19

Verdict

At 10 am on 31 July the verdict arrived. It was not in the form of any legal proceedings. It was simply a letter from Melville to Keith, dated 28 July, which had been brought down by Sir Henry Bunbury, a dignified and considerate general who was Under-Secretary for War; and it was simply left to Bunbury and Keith to decide how its contents –curtly described as 'being convenient to General Buonaparte that he should be apprised without further delay of the intentions' of the government – should be so communicated. No document in either English or French was offered. In the event, Keith made a stuttering start at an impromptu translation and Napoleon asked the more linguistically skilful Bunbury to continue. At the end Napoleon confessed himself sufficiently informed to dispense with a written translation. Napoleon, Melville had said, 'must be restrained in his personal liberty... denied the means or opportunity of again disturbing the peace of Europe and renewing all the calamities of war.' He would be allowed to take three officers and twelve domestics to St Helena: 'the climate is healthy and the local situation will admit of his being treated with more indulgence than would be compatible with adequate security elsewhere.' Detailed instructions would follow when Sir George Cockburn arrived on the *Northumberland*.

Napoleon then began to deliver a long 'solemn protest' in its usual formulas. He had arrived voluntarily to 'obtain the rights of hospitality', 'come to this country as a passenger on board one of your ships of war, after a previous negotiation with its commander' who 'lured him into a trap.' It would kill him to be sent to St Helena... he demanded to be received as an English citizen; let the Prince Regent put him in a country house under surveillance. He might even offer his parole, he said in a grudging

184

way. In St Helena the climate was too hot; he could not take his usual twenty-miles ride; what would be the good of his death since he was no longer a sovereign, only a private individual? All that said, he repeated its salient points, adding appropriate remarks about the 'hospitality and generosity of the British people,' saying thus killing him would destroy the 'honour and justice' of England. He need not have given himself up. He still had an army at his disposal, or could anyway have evaded capture, but he preferred to settle as a private person in England. He then repeated the main points again, especially his deception by Captain Maitland, and complained that he had been deprived of his rights as a sovereign. Even though at the last he had only been an emperor in Elba, a small imperial state, he had quitted under the clear impression that the admiral was to land him in England. 'You found me free, send me back again… or let me go to the United States!' It is understandable that Keith considered that he was 'hot, agitated, violent and repetitious in the extreme.' Keith was in fact relieved when for some minutes Napoleon came down to such practical questions as the date when the *Northumberland* would sail, and whether there would be sufficient time for his protest to reach Whitehall. 'After some pause,' however, Keith and Bunbury found that he was breaking out again, denouncing Maitland for misleading him and the illegality of sentencing him to death or imprisonment, extolling the peaceful intentions with which he would now live in the English countryside – adding a promise that he would have no political dealings with France.

A concise and fair-minded summary of this farrago was taken back to Melville. Once again Keith found it necessary to remind Melville that Napoleon was erroneously insisting that Maitland was 'ordered' to receive him as a 'snare', whereas no one could have foreseen that it would be a particular ship which would encounter him. It was proving almost impossible to distinguish 'capture' from 'voluntary surrender'. Keith went on to describe how he had assured Napoleon that the British government wished to render his situation 'as comfortable as is consistent with prudence.' Whereupon Napoleon 'immediately took up the papers from the table and said, with animation, "How so St Helena?"'

* * *

Napoleon was not yet done. When his visitors had left he called in Bertrand and dictated his brief as a reply yet again, insisting that he had only come as 'the guest of England' because Maitland had asserted 'that he had orders to receive me on board and convey me to England with my suite, if I presented myself for this purpose… From the moment that I was freely received on board the *Bellerophon* I was under the protection of the laws of your country. I would rather die than go to St Helena or be shut up in

First a close shave, then a scalping

some fortress… It is in the honour of the Prince Regent, and the protection of your country's laws, that I put my trust, and I still continue to do so.' Giving this letter to Maitland, Napoleon expostulated over it, in what Maitland called his 'jerky, passionate tones… his apparently disconnected sentences… seemed to follow his train of thought with difficulty!' He raged about 'the perfect horror' of St Helena, '… worse than Tamerlane's iron cage… they have no right to call me general, they may as well call me archbishop, for I was head of the church as well as the army… Banish me to an island in the Tropics! They might as well have signed my death-warrant at once!'

Maitland expected him to be prostrated but he later took his usual evening walk, seemed calm over his dinner, and then retired to his cabin, where he had his assistant Marchand read Plutarch's account of Cato's death. It was not the only time his associates feared he might use the vial of poison he had brought with him from Paris – he was fairly free with saying he would die rather than depart, and there had always been an unverified report that he had incompetently poisoned himself at Fontainebleau before he was forced to leave for Elba. On this occasion there were more threats by Gourgaud, Montholon and Lallemand that if he did not die they would make sure that he did not let them all be driven across the seas.

Maitland did his best to calm the group, but then had to deal with the different problem of Savary and Lallemand, who had now been told they were not to sail without being given any assurance against their repatriation to France. They had openly expressed their anxiety after they learned they were on the death-list in Paris and were given no idea what omission from Napoleon's sailing list implied for them. Savary, by some means, managed to get a long plea out to the eminent Whig lawyer Sir Samuel Romilly – who appears to have had a private word with the Lord Chancellor on their behalf – and Maitland felt his honour obliged him to write a letter supporting them.

'I acted in the full confidence that their lives would be sacred, or they should never have set foot in the ship I command.'

In the event the two generals and some lesser officers were taken off to Malta and detained for seven months, kept out of the way declared Savary (who had run secret police himself) so they could not give evidence that the British had trapped Napoleon until he was too far away and it was too late to do anything about it! Being informed of their agitation, and of Fanny Bertrand's weeping fits, Keith told Maitland that the sooner all the arrangements could be made the better, even such a small matter like finding Napoleon another surgeon because Dr Maingault, the man he had brought from Paris, was homesick and seasick. With some despatch, since Napoleon had struck up a comfortable relationship with the surgeon of the *Bellerophon* – O'Meara was an Italian and French speaking Irishman in the navy – he should be permitted to take up the appointment since, unlike other people, he actually wished to go to St Helena (He was to become one of the most comprehensive and dubious chroniclers of the years of exile).

* * *

While the party on *Bellerophon* became more restless the preparations for dealing with them became more advanced. Sir George Cockburn in London, only recently back from his expeditionary activities in the United

A circus animal to perform on St Helena

States (where he had burned the White House!) was now preparing to get himself and Napoleon off to St Helena, and to deal with all the logistical problems involved. The *Northumberland* was the chief of these. Back in the Medway, after long foreign service, she needed a refit and a repaint, then working round to Spithead and on to Plymouth. This took time, but more than that: it took firmness and patience dealing with a disgruntled crew who thought they had come home from long service and were due to be paid off. The notion that they were now to be called on to sail to the South Atlantic, without any foreseeable end to patrolling duties, was enough to provoke a mutiny. Twenty-four men deserted ashore, as many more were guilty of mutiny aboard, more again had to be discharged or transferred to other ships. Even those kept as crew were in such an unreconciled state that there were to be outbreaks of trouble all the way out to St Helena where, having landed the official party, *Northumberland* was kept on as a circumnavigating guardship.

At the end of July an anxious Keith had written to Melville complaining about the continuing crowds in the anchorage. 'I must be particularly vigilant, for the "General" and his suite are convinced that once they set foot on shore, no power on earth can bring them back again. They are determined to disembark. It is all they will talk about and they are becoming very aggressive.' By return Melville sent a strict and anxious signal. 'On no account to permit Buonaparte to come on shore. In some newspapers a notion is held out that he may be brought out of the ship by a writ of *habeas corpus*. The serious public inconvenience and danger which would arise from such an occurrence, even though he may not escape and be remanded by the judge as a prisoner of war, render it indispensably our duty to prevent it.'

The laws of England were more complicated than Napoleon and Las Cases had any idea – in any case despots are accustomed to bend or ignore laws to suit their purposes – while Lord Liverpool, reactionary though he was, realised that he was in an extraordinary situation: politically and practically he knew what he intended to do about Napoleon, but he was unsure whether it was lawful. He had started to ask this question of his legal colleagues before Napoleon reached Torbay. They were a formidable team of lawyers, and they were obliged to scratch through precedents to find which might apply. Eldon, the Lord Chancellor, was a member of the Cabinet, and had the task of collating the opinions of his brother Sir William Scott, head of the Admiralty court; Ellenborough, the Chief Justice; the Master of the Rolls, and the Attorney- and Solicitor-Generals.

The process of advice went on long after Napoleon had sailed away, being debated right up until April, because it was also related to the Treaty of Paris (which had to be sealed as well as signed) and to the question in Parliament, whether the government had behaved legally, or infringed the law in ways that had to be retrospectively indemnified (see Appendix III).

It was the government's intention from the outset to treat Napoleon as a prisoner of war – a designation that had the advantage that he could not claim protection of *habeas corpus* (which in any case was suspended in time of war). Could he be thus characterised? The lawyers had their doubts. One question, which never came to be pressed, was whether Britain was legally at war, since the parliamentary decision in May 1815 had been only for the purposes of defence, not foreign expedition. If the country was at war, however, with whom was it at war? France? When the King of France was in exile, and being helped to recover his throne (though this was not specified in the Vienna Treaty and was not the stated policy of the other allies). Was it against Napoleon, who had no sovereign power because he had forfeited his rights by breaking the treaty that had installed him on Elba? What then was he?

The lawyers inclined to the view that he was a pirate, or a vagabond, but pointed out that there was no provision in the law of nations for war against such a person. That line of thought was superficially attractive because they had found a relevant characterisation. Emmerich de Vattel in 1797 described those 'scourges of the earth, fired by a lawless thirst of power... sport with the quiet of mankind.' One such could be 'repressed or chastised by a general confederacy... depriving him of a power which he so enormously abuses.' In short, by creating exactly the sort of alliance that the four powers had signed in Vienna. The problem was that this had no bearing on the fate of the troublemaker once detained; and in particular when it was a question of detaining him long after the state of war. For instance, if such a confederacy defeated him, could it reduce him from sovereign to bandit, since there was no provision in the law of nations to make war on bandits?

The more Eldon sought to bring a legally acceptable conclusion out of such issues, the more he felt he had uneasily to agree with what Liverpool was proposing to do, the more he found himself sidestepping from the law into *raisons d'état,* having to accept Liverpool's belief that, so far as Napoleon's fate was concerned, he would have to fall back on legislation to validate what had been done with doubtful legitimacy. Eldon was not satisfied. 'Our bills of indemnity may save our necks,' he said, 'but when a question arises, which the law of nations must determine, bills of indemnity must be considered as good things but not settling all points.'

When it came to the crunch in the case of Napoleon there was no opposition, political or legal, which was strong enough to prevent the government getting its own way, even if it had lingering feelings of doubt about it.

* * *

All this argument was long spun out. In the particular circumstances in Plymouth in early August, however, the government was afraid that there might be a fissure through which Napoleon might insert himself into this repertory of law and precedence and claim the rights if not the duties of an Englishman.

For two or three days, indeed, this anxiety seems to have verged on panic: if Napoleon was not a prisoner of war, all kinds of writs might be raised beside the main law of *habeas corpus*. There was *ad testificandum*, which compels a person to attend court to give evidence; *ad respondendum*, which brings a person from a lower to a higher court to answer more serious charges; *ad deliberandum*, a writ to move a person between different courts; and the most common usage, *ad subjiciendum*, bringing before an open court any person claiming to be wrongly arrested or detained. These devices would certainly be known to radical barristers who sympathised with Napoleon, and would be seeking to find a way to delay if not abort his departure.

So far as the government was concerned, at this precise moment, the question was not whether or not it could win any case brought by Napoleon or on his behalf; it simply could not risk the consequences of the case being brought in the first instance. Once a crucial piece of paper was served – in this situation it would have to be served on Lord Keith as Napoleon's legal keeper – there was no way of predicting how far or how long it would run, or where it might lead politically as well as legally.

The legal advice was obviously to move Napoleon out of Plymouth, so there could be no question of him being within the jurisdiction of British law (the question whether his presence on *Bellerophon* gave him that protection, as he certainly believed, was not put to the test. Nor was the argument that being held aboard ship he was subject, in the British system, to the different jurisdiction of Admiralty Law).

The argument in the press, as Melville noted when he wrote to warn Keith of mounting unrest, was increasing day by day. The *St James's Chronicle*, for instance, was already claiming that a new act of parliament would be required to authorise the continued custody of Napoleon, and that it could not be put through when parliament was not sitting (it was not passed until 11 April 1816) and in the meantime, as the newspaper pointed out, the government would be acting on its own responsibility, not lawfully. The most powerful campaign began on 30 July, in the *Morning Chronicle*, a radical newspaper, where a prominent barrister named Capel Lofft – a collaborator of Fox, Wilberforce and other anti-slavery reformers – insisted that Napoleon could not be regarded as a prisoner of war. Even if he was, Britain did not treat her prisoners thus. Could he be tried, sent to lonely imprisonment on a deserted far distant island? Lofft went on to insist at length that Bonaparte was within British 'local allegiance' with 'the concurrence of the Admiralty… within the protection of English law.' He insisted that 'deportation, or transportation… cannot legally exist in this country, except where the law expressly provides it on trial and sentence.' Going over Napoleon's voluntary presence on *Bellerophon*, Lofft said there were no grounds to hold him isolated, as if he were subject to the objectionable practices of European despots, condemned without a hearing. The polemical William Cobbett added his conviction that 'once the waters of the ocean bore him into the constitutional jurisdiction of this country… he was now entitled to all the rights of the law.' Hundreds of other correspondents took up the same cries.

The *Courier*, taking the lead against the liberals, wrote columns against 'those who think the tyrant of the human race an object of compassion,' could view Buonaparte 'with the least feeling of pity or respect,' or think that 'the violator of all laws' should be entitled to the protection of 'one of those great laws.' Like the government, the *Courier* took its stand on treating Napoleon as a prisoner of war, who might have had a claim for consideration 'were he not such a prisoner and such a man – had he not broken his parole at Elba and involved Europe again in warfare and slaughter, for his own selfish and ambitious purposes?'

That charge, echoing the words of Castlereagh and Wellington, was the heart of the political case and the last words made the contrast with the liberal sympathy with the fallen eagle. 'When a ferocious and dangerous animal is taken, with what justice can he complain of restrictions that prevent him from continuing his career of cruelty and crime.' *The Times*, in a cooler tone, made the point (the main point the government was choosing to make) that it was better to start by assuming that Napoleon was a prisoner of war before going on to debate his rights. The *St James's Chronicle* shifted the ground to argue that Napoleon was detained under 'a law of a much more extensive and general kind… the law of nature and nations.' Capel Lofft, coming back to the argument on 3 August, accused the hostile papers of trying to drive Bonaparte to suicide and insisted that *habeas corpus*, the Bill of Rights and the Common Law all denounced 'unequal and arbitrary punishment'; and a less shrill protagonist spoke of the spoiled generosity of a British prince and government treating 'so distinguished an actor in the theatre of the world… like a paltry felon.' The diatribes in the London prints were matched by the rumour-mongering and shouting of the Plymouth crowds – who seemed to expect the imminent appearance of the Prince, or the royal dukes known to sympathise with Napoleon, even Napoleon himself.

* * *

It was not the simple and unlikely prospect of an escape that was worrying Melville. The risk of some kind of legal coup had been canvassed in London for some days, and Melville now sent an official warning that Bonaparte might come on shore, 'by virtue of a writ of *habeas corpus* and that serious public inconvenience and danger, would arise from such an occurrence.' The most telling statement in the letter was an admission that for all the government's insistence that it was acting within the law it was still not quite sure. 'We may possibly have to apply to Parliament for their sanction to what we are doing respecting Bonaparte and the safe custody of his person, but we must do our duty in the meantime.'

An urgent order from John Croker told Keith that *Bellerophon* should set to sea in company with his flagship *Tonnant* and some smaller vessels, and cruise off the Devon coast until the *Northumberland* should at last come up and the prisoners could be transferred to her for their long voyage. It was a measure of the urgency felt in London that Keith was also encouraged to remove the persons (Gourgaud, Montholon) using 'violent and threatening language,' and – an instruction which showed the really anxious mood that was developing in Whitehall – if any of the party escape to shore 'your Lordship will take the most active measures for securing them and sending them back on board ship.' Keith must have reported the incidents of strangers (including a Frenchman) who had been found attempting to board *Bellerophon*, and Maitland had been sufficiently alarmed one night to check whether Napoleon was actually in his cabin, and to station a special watch-boat off the stern.

The state of alert was justified by an escapade which came too close to success for comfort.

* * *

It is thought that it was Capel Lofft that devised the scheme, but the actual process-server was Anthony Mackenrot. It is customary to describe him as a crank, and he was eventually detained as a demented person in Bethlem and finally put out of the country, but he had been coached to a clever move of last resource to extract Napoleon from the *Bellerophon*. He was a lawyer who had been a minor judge on Tortula in the West Indies, a man of contumacious disposition who had quarrelled with Admiral Cochrane, accusing him of cowardice years before in failing to attack a weaker French squadron commanded by Admiral Willaumez with Jerome Bonaparte on board.

Cochrane, himself a radical and controversial figure (who had commanded the fireships in the fireship attack at Rochefort) sued for libel. At this point Mackenrot went to the Court of King's Bench and secured from the Chief Justice a writ (a *subpoena* not *habeas corpus*) requiring the attendance as witnesses, on Friday 10 November, of Admiral Willaumez, Jerome Bonaparte and Napoleon Bonaparte! No matter how absurd such a demand might seem, the absurdity could only be put to the test if the witnesses were actually called and did not appear. If they were within the jurisdiction they could be obliged to attend, and anyone detaining such a person would be equally obliged to produce them. Once such a writ was served on Keith he would have to land Napoleon and produce him at the November hearing.

This was not Mackenrot's original intention: the writ was taken out in June when Napoleon was inaccessible in France, apparently as vexatious ploy, but Lofft had seen its new possibilities. On 2 August Mackenrot was hurrying down to Plymouth to serve it on Keith, who was responsible for detaining Napoleon. Warned of this possibility Keith had decided that in addition to getting Napoleon away to sea on *Bellerophon* he should go as well, so that he could not be reached by any writ-server. He had left home already when Mackenrot arrived, referred on from Keith's dockyard office, and neither the admiral's secretary nor his wife could say exactly where he might be found.

The secretary, James Meek, aware of what was happening, got word to Keith on *Tonnant*, which was waiting for a wind to clear the big ships out of the anchorage. Keith watched while Mackenrot rowed out to *Bellerophon*, where he had the 'inexpressible delight' of seeing Napoleon through the cabin window while he was being waved away by a patrol boat. When he hailed the ship the officer of the watch threatened to shoot him but incautiously revealed that Keith was to be found on *Tonnant*. Before Mackenrot could come alongside he had been seen by Keith who clambered down the other side of the hull into a boat that took him swiftly away towards the beach at Cawsand, followed by Mackenrot's slower craft. Hot and harassed Keith got to the point at Rame Head and got on board *Prometheus*. He sent Maitland a chit: 'I have been chased all day by a lawyer with a *habeas corpus*... keep all sorts of boats off, as I will do the like in whatever ship I may be in.'

Meanwhile Napoleon was catechising Maitland about the way he was being spirited out to sea without warning, and Maitland in turn was trying to get him to render the final list of those chosen to accompany him over into *Northumberland* when she eventually arrived.

After another attempt to reach *Bellerophon* while this hide-and-seek was taking place, Mackenrot went back to the King's Arms Tavern in Plymouth and wrote a formal letter to Keith regretting he had missed him, adding that 'an evasion' of the writ would 'amount to high contempt' against the court, and that he proposed to renew the application next day – with an implied threat of legal harassment if Keith again failed to accept it. The Admiralty's fear had been very narrowly avoided, but the issue lapsed as Maitland, Napoleon and Keith were now well out on the sea and beyond Mackenrot's reach. If he had in fact served the writ on Keith there would certainly have been 'serious public inconvenience,' or at least serious personal inconvenience to Keith if he defied the summons of the Chief Justice. At best the whole timetable for transfer to *Northumberland* and departure to the South Atlantic would have been hindered if not completely disrupted – and the level of public protest would have risen to a new pitch.

Napoleon signs his abdication

20

Gone

'Bonaparte is giving us great trouble at Plymouth,' Liverpool wrote to Castlereagh, explaining why the *Bellerophon* had been hurried out to sea to await the arrival of *Northumberland*. 'We have abundant proof that it would have been quite impracticable to have detained him here, without the most serious inconvenience.' The telegraph had been busy with urgent signals all along the coast, not least to hurry *Northumberland* on to the rendezvous. As her commander Captain Ross wrote to a friend in Jamaica, 'from the anxiety of ministers to get him away you would have supposed their lives depended upon it.' Certainly in the loading of his own ship, with troops aboard to make sure the recalcitrant crew would actually raise the anchor to leave Spithead, there had been barely enough time to rush on board the tons of meat, sugar, salt, flour, wine, tobacco and all else needed for several months at sea. Even then, she had not taken on sufficient water and some of the naval ships coming out of Plymouth to the rendezvous had to top up her casks.

On 5 August, as *Bellerophon* and her attendant squadron headed east, the fine weather broke in a grey mist and a sullen sea, in keeping with the mood of the French party who were only too aware that they were heading for a final separation. Napoleon, brooding in his cabin – unwell, with swollen legs, Fanny Bertrand reported, complaining that he was unfit as well as unwilling to be shipped away – talked mainly to Bertrand and Las Cases about the selection of his travelling companions, and prepared new complaints about his treatment. There was still gossip about his intentions, ashore as well as aboard. *The Times* that day was scoffing at the prospect of suicide: 'this great man may be too great a villain to die by any other hand but his own.' A correspondent thought St Helena 'too good for this atrocious monster who should be loaded with chains and shut up for ever in a dungeon from the light of day... to be employed in the difficult work of stirring up repentance in his blood-guilty soul.' The *Morning Post* was almost as violent in its farewell sentiments – 'nothing ever preceded his footsteps but horror and massacre, nothing ever followed them but desolation.' Capel Lofft, meanwhile, was preparing to follow Mackenrot's repulse at Plymouth with more heated complaints against the illegality of the whole affair.

Keith was still wondering whether there were still loose ends left behind his enforced flight from Mackenrot, and was writing to reassure Melville that there had in no way been a legal presentation of the writ, even despite Mackenrot's final attempt the following morning, getting a fast rowing boat to take him ten miles out to sea and rowing all round the squadron. As the *Northumberland* came up on 6 June, and salutes were exchanged, Keith wrote with relief to his wife. 'All our troubles will soon be at an end now, and we may return to quiet again.'

* * *

There were still problems, however. Napoleon had yet to be brought to agree to his deportation, and failing that would not furnish the final list of his travelling companions. He insisted that Maitland should provide the written orders transferring him to *Northumberland*, so that he could claim he had been 'forced' to leave *Bellerophon* – this was one of the first problems that Cockburn had to discuss with Keith when he joined him on *Tonnant*, and Bertrand finally came over to settle the personnel problems. There were other housekeeping difficulties. Bertrand had to accept a search for arms (a precaution against escape attempts), though Napoleon was not to be 'insulted' by a request for his sword. The search also had to extend to the accounting of money and jewels, with Cockburn cursorily serving as a kind of customs officer, and taking the treasure into custody for later use for additional expenses on St Helena. One item that was not included was Napoleon's transfer to Las Cases of the 200,000 franc diamond necklace given as a parting present by Hortense at Malmaison. A more substantial domestic matter was the delivery of the terms and conditions which Bathurst at the War Office had laid down as the occupation rules for St Helena. This was a long document, extending to such details as the return of Napoleon's body to England if he died on the island. On the way through to this gloomy conclusion it provided for various searches and the censorship of mails, laid it down that anyone going to St Helena in the official party must expect to stay there, ruled that complaints and proposals must be submitted to the government in London and, to limit clandestine messages or visitors, no foreign or private ships would be permitted access to the island.

Such transactions were routine for the senior officers involved, and it seems that they conducted them as far as possible in a way to avoid humiliating the prisoners. The best example of Keith's attitude at the time of the transfer was his comment, when Cockburn was impatient that Napoleon was keeping everyone waiting, was: 'No, no; much greater men than either you or I have waited longer for him before now; let him take his time.'

There were also the last-minute arrangements for Dr O'Meara to sail on *Northumberland* with a naval salary and his prospects in the service unimpaired. Since he had been on the official St Helena list the change left a space for Las Cases. A failure to include the officious scribe would have been disastrous. This completed the list of deportees, with Gourgaud protesting jealously for his place. Bertrand and Montholon, their wives and the four children, and in the retinue of valets, a butler, a cook, footmen, a steward, an usher and a lamplighter, there was a total of twenty-one in the group besides Napoleon himself.

Bertrand was upset that the accommodation, even for fewer persons, was so much less commodious than that provided on *Bellerophon*, but Cockburn – who was determined the voyage should proceed under strict conditions – said this was the best a general could expect on such a distant voyage. There were additional guards too: Cockburn was well aware of the need to keep a clear separation of the passengers from the turbulent crew he had been given.

* * *

Las Cases was still weaving his way through the shipboard confusion with messages for the record. Early on the morning of 7 August he brought Maitland another letter from Napoleon. In order for it to be received and passed on to Keith, Maitland had to go across to *Tonnant* and get permission to receive and transmit it. This was a final summation of the points made in the 'solemn protest' drafted just before *Bellerophon* sailed. Once again, it was intended more for history than to extract an answer from either Keith or Melville.

He asked first for Las Cases to be given the 'deed' signed by the authorities who without 'prior investigation', without hearing Maitland or anyone else present at Aix have 'arbitrarily declared that I am a prisoner of war' though 'it is obvious that I came of my own free will and in good faith, as is abundantly proved by my letter to the Prince Regent.' (Which had at last been officially despatched on 27 July) Declaring him a prisoner, he said was 'directly contrary to the laws of the country and those of hospitality' and putting him 'on a rock lost in mid-oceans, in tropical heat' was 'obviously a death sentence.' Once again, he linked the alleged faults of Maitland to the denial of *habeas corpus*, since he was now 'under your flag, in your harbours, with the offer and the promise of the captain' and could 'only be removed, deprived of my freedom, led and exiled in accordance with your laws and in due form.' Besides, he was now being deprived 'of his properties', and he and his suite were made subject to 'hardships likely to shock any refined man.' He was appealing 'formally to sovereigns and peoples in regard to this strange and singular affair.' Saying that Keith had expressed 'pain' carrying out these orders, he called him as an advocate 'in order to get their hastiness, rigours and injustice invalidated.' Neither in this letter, nor in any other of the protests against the sentence imposed on him, did he ever make any mention of the decrees of 'outlawry' proclaimed by the Congress of Vienna, under which the British government might also have claimed the right to imprison him.

When Las Cases arrived on *Tonnant*, and handed over this letter he reverted, yet again, to the alleged misdeeds of Maitland at Aix. 'We were standing,' he said afterwards, and so it was not surprising that 'Lord Keith listened to me with marked impatience… his frequent bows were evidently intended to make me retire!' Napoleon claimed that nothing Maitland had said excited 'a suspicion in our minds that we were to be prisoners of war… we came on board voluntarily and in confidence,' and that the letter to the Prince 'must necessarily have created tacit conditions, since he made no remarks on it.' This was too much for Keith's patience and he irritably protested that Maitland was carrying out his instructions from Keith as commander-in-chief. This drew a tart reply from Las Cases, who said that in this case Keith should be severe with himself about his instructions for 'all the officers whom we saw at the time conducted and expressed themselves in the same way.' Not surprisingly Las Cases then 'relieved the admiral of my presence in order not to prolong a subject which his lordship's conscience rendered painful to him.'

Las Cases had come to the end of the road so far as Keith was concerned, having reduced the whole of this dispute to an attack on the integrity of Royal Navy officers. Yet it could not be left there: a substantial reply to Napoleon had to be delivered before he moved on. From Maitland's letters, Keith wrote, 'nothing like a promise or what could possibly be construed into a promise was made on his part, but on the contrary a simple offer of good treatment, and being carried to England, and I am happy in thinking that both these objects have been fulfilled with all possible kindness and attention... Of the Laws I am not able to judge – my habits are of a different nature, but my study has always been to observe them in all the different countries I have visited... it was always a painful duty to communicate anything of a disagreeable nature to anyone, and I hope you will do me the justice to believe it true.'

Keith was to discover later that Las Cases had prefaced his implication of dishonesty with a direct and shocking challenge to Maitland, as if the whole process of the surrender had hinged upon Maitland's false dealing, whether it was personal or part of a British scheme of entrapment. He came up to Maitland on deck and said flatly that Maitland 'had assured him that Napoleon would be well received in England and allowed to reside there'. Maitland never challenged Las Cases with seeking to cover up his own mistake in giving Napoleon this impression: he was content to ask Las Cases 'how you could so far misunderstand me... as I constantly stated that I could make no promises whatever; that I thought my orders would bear me out in receiving him on board and conveying him to England... I acted very much on my own responsibility. You questioned me frequently as to my own opinion, and as I was quite ignorant on the subject, I could only say I had no reason to believe he would be ill received.' Las Cases retracted saying there had been a misunderstanding. Maitland could do no more with an issue on which so much had been made to turn. 'If there was a misunderstanding (which I cannot allow to be the case),' he wrote in retrospect, Las Cases had only himself to blame, and he turned the charge of deception on its head. He recalled that Las Cases deliberately concealed his knowledge of English, when he first came on board, and that, 'as I had considerable difficulty expressing myself in French, could only be intended for the purpose of throwing me off my guard, that he might take advantage of any expressions that fell from me... Even after he was on board… though he acknowledged he could read English…he affected not to be able to speak it.'

Still after this exchange, Maitland remained hooked on this line of defence. On 8 August, once the protagonists in this dispute had sailed south over the horizon and Keith was coming back to Plymouth, Maitland felt obliged to make another attempt to set the record straight, in the form of his official report closing the story of the Rochefort episode. It was almost wholly devoted to recounting the events of 14 July, with one significant variation. Asked if he would permit Napoleon to go to the United States in an English ship of war, he replied, 'I have no authority to permit any of these measures, but if he chooses to come on board the ship I command, I think, under the orders I am acting with, I may venture to receive him and carry him to England; but if I do so I can in no way be responsible for the reception he may meet with (this I repeated several times).' Maitland denied that he, in any way, entered into conditions with regard to Napoleon's reception, nor 'at that time was it finally arranged that he was to come on board the *Bellerophon.*' Pressed by Las Cases to say whether he would be well received, Maitland simply turned the words back and said, 'I had no reason to suppose he would not be well received.' He reminded Keith that he told Las Cases bluntly that 'I have no authority for making conditions of any sort' and that no one had challenged that, until Las Cases had suggested otherwise in their conversation on 6 August. He reminded Keith that even Napoleon had conceded this in their last conversation. 'Certainly I made no conditions; how could a private individual make conditions with a nation I wanted nothing from them but hospitality… I threw myself on the hospitality of the British nation… my only wish was to purchase a small estate.'

After that issue had been trailed for hundreds of miles by Las Cases covering his own mistake Maitland was glad when, just before Napoleon left the ship, Montholon came to express Napoleon's thanks and his regrets that he had not seen the Prince Regent, for he had hoped to ask him to promote Maitland to rear-admiral. It was, in the circumstances, even more gratifying, when he told Montholon that he had been hurt by the accusations of Las Cases, he got an unexpected reply. 'Las Cases is disappointed in his expectations; and as he negotiated the affair, he attributes the emperor's situation to himself but I can assure you that Bonaparte feels convinced that you acted as a man of honour throughout.' Even so, Maitland had to make the final comment of an injured party: 'it is extremely unpleasant for me to be under the necessity of entering into a detail of this sort…' Keith had given him the opportunity to clear his name in the official record, but the allegations still festered when Las Cases later wrote his *Memorials* on St Helena.

* * *

In the morning of 7 August the maritime carousel on *Bellerophon* was winding up to its climax with a final inventory of the belongings to be ferried across to the *Northumberland* and a round of tearful farewells, letters, even formal audiences to officers who had served Napoleon to the end. Feelings were running high among all those who had made this extraordinary journey from Paris by way of Basque Roads. Bertrand, trying to snatch a breakfast in the course of a dozen tasks, found himself once again berated by his wife, making a last plea to remain in England. As Bertrand shrugged off this demand for the last time she turned on Maitland, for whom it was too much. 'Madame Bertrand,' he said stiffly, 'I have from the beginning endeavoured to avoid meddling in the very unpleasant discussions that have been going on for some days. But as you demand my opinion… I must acquaint you that I think, if your husband quits his master at such a time as the present, he will forfeit the very high character he now bears in this country.' Turning out on the deck he found her following him with another of her demands. 'Why is the emperor not to have the whole after-cabin on the *Northumberland*?' Maitland replied that Admiral Cockburn had been so ordered by the Admiralty. 'They had better treat him like a dog,' Fanny Bertrand shouted, 'and put him down in the hold at once.' This was too much for Maitland, who had absorbed such gibes for three weeks. 'You talk like a very foolish woman; and if you cannot speak more to the purpose or with more respect for the government I have the honour to serve, I request you will not address yourself to me.'

* * *

It was a relief to have Napoleon thanking him and the ship's company for 'kindness and attention,' although 'my reception in England has been very different from what I expected.' There was no irony here, though Maitland must have been glad to reach closure on that issue. While Napoleon was having his final exchanges with his followers Maitland had to make sure that this time the ceremonials had been rightly judged. There was a captain's guard of marines with a drummer boy, the officers ranked on the quarterdeck, and much of the ship's company drawn up in the waist and forecastle. Keith, just arrived in his barge, joined Cockburn and Maitland in full dress. Bertrand summoned Keith to escort Bonaparte from the cabin. At the last he was still objecting to his treatment and asking about opportunities to appeal his fate, still formally insisting he would not leave the ship. 'You must take me by force.' Keith protested that this was

Bellerophone returns to Plymouth

unthinkably disagreeable. 'Oh, no! But you shall order me,' Napoleon said. Keith paused. 'I order you to go.' Napoleon nodded. 'Let us go.' That said, he delayed again, for a private word with Bertrand, and to deal with some letters.

In a while he came out to the waiting audience. The most telling account of his appearance was left by Midshipman Home, who found him 'sadly changed from the time we had last seen him on deck... he was scrupulously cleanly in his person and his dress; but that had been forgot – his clothes were ill put on, his beard unshaved, and his countenance pale and haggard. There was a want of firmness in his gait, his brow was overcast, and his whole visage bespoke the deepest melancholy; and it needed but a glance to convince the most careless observer that Napoleon considered himself a doomed man. In this trying hour, however, he had not lost his courtesy or his presence of mind.' Home, who had developed a warm sympathy with him in the course of the voyage from France, felt that he caught the feeling of the crew. 'What a horrid gloom hung over the ship. Had his execution been about to take place there could not have prevailed a more dead silence... a proof how the attention of every man on board must have been riveted.' Even in this hour of misery, Home recalled, he made his farewells with his 'indescribable charm.' Looking back from the Admiral's barge he 'saw heads crowding out of every port, and he lifted his hat and inclined his head to the ship's company.'

Maitland watched the barge moving towards the *Northumberland*, mulling over his feelings in the past three weeks. How could a British officer, prejudiced about 'one who had caused so many calamities to his country,' sit with him at table for nearly a month and not feel 'a sensation of pity, allied perhaps to regret, that a man possessed of so many fascinating qualities, and who had held such a high station in life, should be reduced to the situation in which I saw him.' The impact on the crew was more extra-ordinary, given that the men had been cooped up in port, in an overcrowded ship, and with only a sight and a gossip about him. Maitland noticed the hush, and asked his servant 'what do the people say of him?' Ship's hearsay can be telling. 'I heard men talking this morning,' the servant replied, 'and one of them said: "They may abuse that man as much as they please, but if the people of England knew him as well as we do, they would not hurt a hair of his head".' The phrases may seem forced, but they would have echoed through the crowds that had watched day after day in Plymouth. It was a dull wet evening as *Bellerophon*, *Eurotas* and *Myrmidon* turned away leaving *Northumberland*, *Bucephalus* and the *Ceylon* about to head south on their long journey from autumn into spring. Such a sizeable and extensive fleet had never before been assembled for one man, and there were still more people come out to wonder at it, their small boats weaving among the big ships and guard boats. One had several of Keith's nieces come as close as they could get. Suddenly, another rowboat that had come out with a party of eight from Torquay rounded the bow of the *Northumberland* and was smashed by the schooner *Nimble*, serving as a despatch boat. Two of the young women were drowned. The ship's first lieutenant leaped into the sea and saved a woman and a child, and the *Nimble's* crew saved the rest. It was a sombre end to a sombre occasion.

Napoleon at St Helena

Epilogue

For the third time Napoleon was going through the ceremonials of joining a British man-of-war, and this time the impact he made scarcely matched the occasion. Captain Ross of the *Northumberland* confessed himself disappointed with him... 'pot-bellied... rather clumsy... very sallow, greasy-looking brown hair, and altogether a very nasty, priest-like looking fellow.' It is clear that the atmosphere on board would from the start be more reserved than the curiously relaxed impetus that Napoleon had brought on board *Bellerophon* with his false expectations. There were no illusions now, and the situation was not helped by the grim mood of the crew and the floggings that Napoleon was later to find repulsive.

The first awkward hours were taken up with a curious *tête-à-tête* between Napoleon and two members of parliament, Lord Lowther and William Lyttelton, friends of Cockburn who brought them aboard as guests for the event, and in a casual kind of way he had cooped them up in a cabin to have an unexpected colloquy with Napoleon – one that they found as difficult to get started as he did. The talk staggered on through lunch, the young men firing questions at random and Napoleon producing his routinised answers. At the end of two hours – which were no doubt of interest to the purchasers of Lyttelton's published report – Napoleon had run through his repertoire of conversation and only allowed one flash of sarcasm. Saying, rightly, that *Northumberland* seemed to have been fitted out in haste, and getting the answer that she was a good fast sailor, he grunted: 'They might have sent a ship in better condition.'

At least Lyttelton spoke fluent French. For most of the voyage the assorted passengers would be trying to improve their language skills. The ship's surgeon, William Warden, spent the journey with long sessions teaching Bertrand to read *Roderick Random* in English. The dinner table topics seem to have been limited – battlefield memories, an interrogation of the chaplain about the Reformation, Waterloo of course – and regular games of cards at which Napoleon won or lost with equal good humour and equal mistakes in totting up good and bad scores. What seems notable about the whole stretch of seventy days was the air of resignation, broken only by the lively enjoyment of 'crossing the line', though Napoleon left the homage to Neptune to his generals and the children. For most of the time the future was settling into the rules of the game laid down by the War Office and, now to be implemented, with a relentless boorishness and lack of consideration which were to make Sir Hudson Lowe infamous as governor of St Helena.

* * *

Lowe was not yet ready to leave from London where competing factions sought to brief him for a task for which he proved professionally and psychologically unsuited. For one thing he had commanded a battalion of Royal Corsican Rangers against Napoleon and resented his defeat, and despite that he seemed smugly content to condescend from his mainly garrison experience to Napoleon as a battlefield commander. No amount of briefing was to suit him for his task. This seems not to have mattered to Bathurst, the Secretary of State for War, who gave Lowe instructions of a severity that began the declension from detention into punishment. It did matter greatly to the opposition party, led by Lord and Lady Holland who, having failed to find any means to keep Napoleon in England, had turned their Bonapartist sympathies to ameliorating his lot and helping his acolytes escape Bourbon retribution.

It was the energetic Lady Holland, the model of a society hostess, whose salon at Holland House was the focus of liberal political and intellectual life, who took the lead. She and her husband had previously given Napoleon support in Elba, and in the process had made use of the unfortunately relaxed British commissioner Colonel Campbell as an intermediary. Now she attempted the much more difficult task of lobbying the stiff-necked Lowe into giving her access to Napoleon once he was installed on St Helena. In the course of the autumn she gave a series of dinner parties at which Lowe was courted in distinguished company – from Cabinet ministers, opposition leaders and public figures carefully graded towards such intellectuals as Byron. Her aim was to create a situation in which Lowe might be persuaded to allow an easier regime and permit the Hollands to supply the prisoner with books, newspapers and comforts – even visitors, perhaps, as was the case on Elba.

The campaign was a signal failure. The most interesting feature of its last stages were the deployment of Captain Maitland as a dinner guest, an obvious enough choice to coach Lowe in the ways of his future prisoner, but one that Lowe rejected on the grounds that Maitland was 'prejudiced', presumably in Napoleon's favour. By now he must have known – a fact generally concealed (like Maitland's audience with Napoleon at a levee in Paris 13 years before) – that Maitland through his cousin Lord Lauderdale had longstanding sympathies with the Holland House set. This casts no doubt on his attention to duty, but it may account for his patent civility towards Napoleon and his anxiety that he might be thus liable to reprimand.

* * *

The debate about the treatment of Napoleon had certainly not finished as he sailed beyond the immediate reach of law and politics and even after he reached St Helena on 17 October. Capel Lofft and his supporters were still filling columns with protests about his illegal treatment; the *Courier*, *The Times* and the *Morning Post* still led the campaign which mixed a final round of abuse with justification of what the government had done. There – to all practical purposes – the debate ran on and ran out, except, significantly, within the government. Liverpool had never felt completely comfortable during the shambles at Plymouth, and now Lord Eldon, who had given him the legal support he needed at the time, found that he too was uneasy. Mulling the matter over, while he was on sick-leave shooting partridges on his estate, Eldon wrote on 6 September to his brother, the Master of the Rolls, saying he was not satisfied, and that as Lord Chancellor he could not put the great seal on the convention (treaty) which the allies had signed in Paris, and that there was some dissatisfaction with the provision made in it for the treatment of Napoleon. He returned to the earlier suggestion, that the government might require an act of indemnity. Two weeks later Liverpool replied to his comments, by saying that he had always thought that for all the confusion there was only the choice: between treating Bonaparte as a French subject (and returning him to France) or as a 'captain of freebooters or banditti, and consequently out of the pale of the protection of nations.' His limited sovereign rights, Liverpool was convinced, had been forfeited when he broke the treaty conditions which placed him on Elba. Either he had to be treated as a French rebel (and returned to France) or as an outlaw *hostis humani generis*. Liverpool agreed that an act of indemnity was necessary to settle outstanding doubts but it was a sign that doubts persisted, 'I trust we have one good ground to found it on, if not two.' Eldon was equally concerned about justification, telling his brother Sir William Scott 'to do the thing that is right is really the matter of most concern to me.'

The last challenge came in February 1816 when an Act of Indemnity declared it was lawful for the government to commit Napoleon 'to such persons, and in such a place, and under such restraint' as the Crown saw fit. Having covered all possibilities, without troubling to justify the case, it added complicated clauses defining attempts by Napoleon to escape as capital treason and (an unusual prospective indemnity) more legislation designed to deter others from such escape attempts. When the bills came to the House of Lords (passed on 11 April 1816) it was clear that they were fudging over the uncertainties which Eldon had been trying to resolve, Castlereagh contenting himself by saying that Bonaparte's detention (whether as a sovereign prince or a prisoner of war) was 'justifiable in a technical sense, according to the law of nations... imperiously called for by a due consideration for public safety and general peace.'

Castlereagh had no problems with this specious obfuscation in the Commons, but there was opposition in the Lords, where both Holland and Lauderdale claimed that the legal conundrums had not been resolved – whether his status as emperor of Elba had or had not been resolved, whether and when he became a prisoner of war. It was clear that for all Eldon's desire to do the 'right thing' he had given up attempts to resolve the ambiguities, cynically describing the bill as 'necessary... sufficiently plain and distinct,' merely inserting a preamble saying that 'for the preservation of the tranquillity of Europe, and for the general safety... Napoleon Bonaparte should be detained' and that his custody was 'lawful'.

Whether or not Napoleon had been held under the law of nations or as a British prisoner of war, the British parliament had decided he was lawfully held. What the British parliament says is lawful, was and remains lawful, whatever anyone else may think, and whatever challenge might be made in defence of the prisoner in St Helena.

Footnote

Two questions about Napoleon's capture remain. If Captain Maitland had previously met Napoleon, why was nothing said about it, despite the much-

A prisoner-of-war in fact?

expressed Admiralty anxiety about his treatment of Bonaparte as an ex-emperor rather than a prisoner-of-war. It is reported that on 7 October 1802 the *Moniteur*, the official gazette in France, included Captain Frederick Maitland in the list of persons 'received in audience' by Napoleon. Given that Maitland's cousin, the Earl of Lauderdale, was a noted Bonapartist and, like several thousand other English tourists, visited France during the Peace of Amiens, Maitland's presence is plausible. He was a liberal-minded Whig, like many other naval officers, and he was an accepted dinner guest of Lord and Lady Holland, the leaders of the Whig Bonapartists. Against this, the *Carrère* – the captured French frigate which Maitland was commanding before the Peace of Amiens – was only paid off on 4 October 1802. Unless he had actually left the ship some days earlier Maitland could not have been in Paris on 7 October.

The second unsolved question concerns the two frigates, *La Saale* and *Méduse*. The query is whether it was by lucky chance that they happened to be at Rochefort in June 1815, or whether they were brought up for possible use if things went wrong in the Hundred Days. It is usually reported that Napoleon sent Bertrand to 'ask' Decrès for the use of the frigates, an errand which assumes that he already knew of their whereabouts. If not, did Napoleon only ask in a general way for 'ships' – and there is some reason to think Bertrand specifically asked about American ships or ships sailing for America? Or did Fouché know about them and at once see the opportunity to impose a plan that could lead to Napoleon being trapped in seeking to flee on one of them. If they were specifically stationed there by Fouché that would be very strong evidence of a plan of entrapment; even so, not conclusive evidence. There is no way of reading Fouché's intentions. It is possible that at the outset Fouché did favour Napoleon's escape to the United States, and that the known changes in the orders to the frigates did reflect changes evoked by his dealings with the allies.

Bibliographic Note

Bibliography
Over a period of two centuries thousands of books have been written about Napoleon and his times. Currently, the most extensive listing can be found in *Napoleon: The Myth of the Saviour*, Jean Tulard, London 1981. Other titles with listings relevant to *Fallen Eagle* are: Rory Muir, *Britain and the Defeat of Napoleon*, London 1956; Gregor Dallas, *1815: The Road to Waterloo*; Inès Murat, *Napoleon and the American Dream*, London 1981. Some of the titles printed below have different publication dates for English and French editions.

Memoirs
The most important memoir of the events at Rochefort is the volume written later from notes, a journal and ships' logs by Captain Frederick Lewis Maitland. The first edition of *The Surrender of Napoleon*, London 1826, is rare; a later edition of 1904 is somewhat easier to find. Apart from an autobiographical introduction the text contains all the essential details of the negotiations with Napoleon, communications from Lord Keith and the Admiralty, and extensive summaries of Maitland's relations with Napoleon. Few historical events of this importance so escape the confines of state secrecy. There is a similar ventilation of detail by other participants in the events of 1815, who wrote, dictated or endorsed ghost-written recollections, and these are primary but often unreliable sources for anecdotes, conversations etc. The *Memorials of St Helena* were nominally the result of Napoleon's dictation to his amanuensis, Emmanuel Las Cases, but while their overall effect has been accepted it is also clear that the text was contrived to present the account favoured or even invented by Napoleon. General Bertrand was closer than anyone to Napoleon, serving as his court chamberlain from the start of his exile in Elba, and his *Les Cahiers de Sainte Helene*, Paris 1949, is an undistinguished record of Napoleon's rambling remarks. Armand de Caulaincourt was a sober man, and the high

point of a generally reliable account in his *Memoirs*, London 1950, was the comprehensive account of the Fontainebleau abdication in 1814. Baron Fain wrote three important accounts of events leading up to Waterloo, *Manuscrit de 1812*, Paris 1827, *Manuscrit de 1813*, Paris 1825 and *Manuscrit de 1814*, Paris 1823. Fleury de Chaboulon wrote his *Memoirs*, London 1819, while Napoleon was still alive and able to comment sarcastically on his self-important claims. It was not to be expected that the head of the secret police would write a revealing or comprehensive autobiography, and Fouché's *Mémoires*, London 1892, are no more to be trusted than their author, who was accomplished at concealing the truth. General Gourgaud was as jealous and place-seeking in his *Journal*, Paris 1899, as he was in attaching himself to the emperor. J. Hanoteau edited the *Mémoires de la Reine Hortense*, Paris 1927; John Cam Hobhouse wrote an English eye-witness account of Paris in 1815 in *Recollections of a Long Life*, London 1909; Midshipman George Home recalled the passage of the *Bellerophon* in his *Memories of an Aristocrat*, London 1838; Lavalette, who saw everything from the vantage post of Minister of Communications, had a hair-raising escape, and *An Adventurous Life*, London 1931, is a gripping read; the Marquis de Montholon, a man of erratic loyalties who has been much suspected of being a Bourbon agent and the murderer of the emperor, wrote a questionable memoir of *The Captivity of Napoleon at St Helena*, London 1947. The *Mémoires* of Louis Marchand, Paris 1952, *In Napoleon's Shadow*, San Francisco 1998, are reasonably authentic, and contain much useful domestic material up to and on St Helena; General Savary was involved all through the flight from Waterloo to Plymouth; inclined to be dull and self-regarding, he made the most of what he knew in his *History of the Emperor Napoleon*, London 1828, and his *Mémoire sur l'Empire*, Paris 1821, and also like others writing accounts of this sensitive period during the Bourbon restoration he made sure his text was acceptable by omissions and the expression of suitable opinions. Prince Talleyrand was Fouché's equal as a mendacious intriguer but at least his *Mémoires*, New York 1891, were edited by the duc de Broglie and were based upon an authentic text.

Biographical
Napoleon so dominates the scene that biographies and books on the war and politics of the period are unavoidably enmeshed. Among these are many books with a significant biographical emphasis on Napoleon and

British contemporaries, C. J. Bartlett, *Castlereagh*, London 1996. René de la Croix Castries, *Lafayette*, Paris 1918. Ray Cubberley. *The Role of Fouché*, Madison, 1969. David Cordingly's *Billy Ruffian*, London 2003, is a well-documented 'biography' of a ship, which includes the Rochefort surrender. R. F. Delderfield, *Imperial Sunset*, London 1968. Roger Fulford, *Samuel Whitbread*, London 1967. Pieter Geyl, *Napoleon: For and Against*, London 1949. Tangye Lean wrote an unusual account of radical English opinion in *The Napoleonists*, London 1976. This can be supplemented by Robin Eagles, *Francophiles in English Society 1778 – 1815*, Manchester 2000, In *Flight with the Eagle* by R. Horricks, Tunbridge Wells 1988, is a guide to Napoleon's entourage. *The Iron Duke*, by James Lawrence, London 1992, is one of many modern revisions of Wellington's role in the emperor's downfall. *The Escape from Elba*, by Norman MacKenzie, Oxford 1982, is one of the few books which specifically describes this dramatic episode, with an extensive bibliography. *The Road to St Helena*, by J. David Markham, London 2008, has many appendices but the main story oddly stops short at Napoleon's arrival in England. *Napoleon and Talleyrand* by Barbara Morrison, London 1977, couples the conspirators to good effect. Charles Petrie, *Lord Liverpool*, London 1954, shows how implacable Napoleon's enemies in Whitehall had become after years of war. In *Napoleon: The Last Phase*, London 1900, a British Prime Minister (Lord Roseberry) reviewed the chroniclers of life on St Helena. J. H. Rose, in *Napoleon's Last Voyages*, London 1966, describes the passages into exile on Elba and St Helena. There is similar coverage in the earlier *Napoleon and His Fellow Travellers*, London 1908, in which Clement Shorter created a miscellany which includes George Home's account of the *Bellerophon* and the letters of William Warden, ship's doctor on *Northumberland*. Michael J. Thornton's *After Waterloo: England and the St Helena Decision*, Stanford 1968, is the most serious and well presented account of the political melée at Plymouth. It should be set alongside the similar books by Jean Duhamel, *The Fifty Days: Napoleon in England*, London 1969; and Gilbert Martineau, *Napoleon Surrenders*, London 1971. Norwood Young, *Napoleon in Exile*, London 1915, includes many of the cartoons etc from the Broadley collection.

Context

There is such a range of choice that a few titles will represent the field. For instance, the scene is closely viewed from a Bonapartist standpoint in

The Fall of Napoleon by David Harcourt-Williams, London 1994. There is also the standard Anthony Brett-James account of *The Hundred Days*, London 1964. The classical contextual history is to be found in the volumes of Henri Houssaye, especially *1815*, Paris 1914, *The Second Abdication*, London 1918, and *The Return of Napoleon*, London 1934. Two modern titles are by Henry Lachoque, *The Last Days of Napoleon's Empire*, London 1966, and *Waterloo*, Paris 1976. Claude Manceron's 'faction' style is well displayed in *The Last Choice of Napoleon*, London 1966. Harold Nicolson's *The Congress of Vienna*, 1946, remains a popular account. Mark Philp, *The Revolution and English Popular Politics*, Cambridge 1954, gives a very good background to English opinions of Bonaparte, and Stuart Semmel's *Napoleon and the British*, London 2004, will remain a scholarly classic on the radical opposition to the Tory war. Edith Saunders, *The Hundred Days*, London 1959, has long been a standard text. *The Bourbon Restoration*, by G. de B. Sauvigny, Philadelphia 1966, is a useful source on an aspect of Napoleon's overthrow that receives little attention outside France. Adam Shom's *One Hundred Days*, New York 1993, matches the quality of his *Napoleon Bonaparte*, New York 1997.

Archives
There are many sets of relevant papers. The main sources for Castlereagh's letters and despatches are the Public Record Office in Belfast and the Foreign Office series in the National Archive at Kew. The Keith Papers, edited by C. Lloyd, were published by the Naval Records Society. There are the extensive Admiralty materials at Kew. Wellington's *Dispatches and Supplementary Correspondence* was published in 1865. Such relevant newspapers as the *Morning Chronicle*, the *Courier* and *The Times* are held by the British Library. The official organ in Paris, *Le Moniteur* is in the *Bibliothèque Nationale*.

Appendix I

"Boney and the Billy Ruffians"
The Plays in Historical Context
By Professor Juliana Saxton, University of Victoria

Consider the lot of sailors in the Napoleonic era. Long months or even years at sea with little to do but stand watch, patrol the line of blockade, prepare for battle that might or might not take place and, with all that time, the hours upon hours in which to think of home. It is not surprising that the plays the Royal Naval midshipmen of HMS *Bellerophon* chose to perform were those that reflected not the sea and warfare, as we might expect, but ones that reminded them of a very different kind of life.

We read in the Ship's Logs compiled by Midshipman Francis Wall Justice, who served aboard the *Bellerophon*, that the plays chosen to be performed before Napoleon and his entourage on July 18, 1815, were two light-hearted farces of the era, first performed at the Theatre Royal, Covent Garden. These plays were as much enjoyed by the casts and crews of the ships of the line as they were by London audiences, enlarging as they do upon the fallibility and foibles of human nature and with the added comedic possibilities of the "ladies" roles. Unlike better-known restoration comedies, *The Poor Gentleman* by George Colman (1801) and *Raising the Wind* by James Kenney (1803) were contemporary "meditations" on the charms of life, money and romance at fast-paced play in the English countryside.

The Poor Gentleman by George Colman
A farming family in need of cash takes in lodgers: a half-pay army lieutenant, his sister and his daughter, Emily, upon whom the wealthy squire, Sir Charles, has designs. A case of mistaken identity, a maiden aunt, a handsome but penniless young man, his wealthy uncle, a devious apothecary, and a wood-land duel all have their roles in this "Pythonesque" farce in bringing the young people together and opening a future of comparative happiness for all.

Raising the Wind by James Kenney

In a joyous and brief comedy of fainting ladies, a letter misdirected and received, elopements planned and forestalled and, of course, close and not entirely trustworthy dealings with money, we are introduced to impecunious Jeremy Diddler and his attempts to "raise" some "wind". It is from his last name (and behaviour) that both the verb and the noun are derived. A moral little tale on the dangers and difficulties of "diddling" that a deathbed reversal in the form of an inheritance of ten thousand pounds helps greatly to alleviate.

There has been little research onto this fascinating sidelight into life at sea but we do have glimpses. Before the Battle of the Nile, "every means possible was taken… to keep the men not only in the highest efficiency and in good fighting trim, but also happy and contented. Every evening there were theatricals on board the different ships, or "sing-songs," concerts, fencing and single-stick displays and competitions, wrestling matches and general "sky-larking" aloft… And we know about the watchful eye of a Royal Marine Lieutenant (possibly Lt. John Wilson) known as "The Bard of the *Bellerophon*". *Boney and the Billy Ruffians* offers a unique re-creation of a little known moment in theatre and naval history.

There is a long tradition of performances on board naval ships but very little is recorded about how these performances were staged or produced. We do know from the research that professional actors, dancers and entertainers would come aboard to entertain when ships were in port. And the great traditional rituals of "crossing the equator" made heavy demands upon costumiers and property makers for the large casts required. Innovation and initiative were keys to success. These notes provide some ideas that suggest how things might have been done.

Scenery: There were huge amounts of canvas available and so it is possible that canvas backdrops were "tied" off to beams. Many of the men (and officers in particular) were accomplished draftsmen and artists so that the quality of the backdrops would be of a good standard. These backdrops would be of a size that would allow them to be rolled up for storage and easy touring. There would be, in all likelihood, a rustic interior (wooden walls, smallish uncurtained window, perhaps some copper pans hanging, etc), an upper class interior (walls, window(s), curtains, portraits, perhaps even a pretty table with flowers), and a country scene of woodlands and views. These would be hung one upon the other – rolled and revealed as the scenes change.

Costumes: The men were often accomplished stitchers (mending sails was an on-going activity); they often spent their spare time carving buttons and tie and pigtail holders (tie-pairs), as well as decorating their uniforms with ribbons sewn into the seams of their trousers or shirts. With these skills, costumes would be created with imagination and skill; the materials however, would be what was available and the fits crude. This last because the costumes would have to be "generally" sized so that roles could be exchanged: "He [Napoleon] appeared much amused, and laughed very heartily at our ladies, who were personated by great strapping fellows dressed in women's clothes, and not in the most tidy fashion" (Maitland). Wigs would most likely have been made of hemp and dyed to fit the character. The cast could have borrowed the wigs of the officers, if appropriate, for the older gentlemen. Midshipmen would have had "shore" clothing available but might have borrowed from the officers for the older parts.

Props and Furniture: They would have had to make do with what was available – some of the better furniture and props being borrowed from the officers' quarters. There was a production of *Hamlet* where the ship's bilges were raided to provide gravel for the gravedigger's scene!

Music: Music was a large part of a sailor's life – it was both recreation and an accompaniment to work. Sailors often entertained themselves by making their own instruments and became accomplished players. Fiddles, flutes, fifes and tambours were the main instruments, along with the human voice. There is a fine compendium of music of the time which would serve nicely for both *entr'acte* entertainment and to cover scene changes.

Lighting: Performances took place during daylight hours. Gun ports would be opened as well as the top gratings. Footlights (ship's lanterns) may have provided both a stage demarcation and further enhancement.

The Billy Ruffian

This shanty has been written by Lindsay Macpherson
to accompany the revival of the *Bellerophon* plays

In 'eighty three the keel was laid
(According to the plans of Slade)
Four thousand trees of English Oak
An acre of sail and a mile of rope

A sturdy ship, for soon she'd be
A ship of the line in the Royal Navy
So make the sails, cast the guns
And fight her with bold Cornishmen
Aboard the Billy Ruff i an

The night she launched a tempest blew
No crew was there to save her now
while in her cradle she did rock
and damn near foundered in the dock

God help her now, up went the shout
That now or never she must float
So kick the props, pull the chocks
Ad just five men rushed to her side
And slipped her down into the tide

Oh she slipped in seventeen eighty six
(How I wish I was aboard her now)
A third rate ship with a first rate crew
God knows how many French we slew

Go – darn them all, for we set out
To put the French to bloody rout
So beat the drum, man the gun
We're a fighting ship and will not run
Aboard the Billy Ruff i an

We scoured the seas from coast to coast
(How I wish I was aboard her now)
From Newfoundland to the Firth of Clyde
The Frenchmen could not from us hide

Chorus

And on the glorious first of June
(How I wish I was aboard her now)
Our seventy four guns spoke loud and true
And through the French great holes we blew

Chorus

And when we bore down at the Nile
(How I wish I was aboard her now)
We smashed them with a withering fire
but took a hammering on both sides

Chorus

The year of eighteen hundred and five
(How I wish I was aboard her now)
We took on the French and the Don in turn
A raked 'em through from stern to stern

Chorus

This was Trafalgar's glorious day
How I wish I was aboard her now)
And though the L'Aigle was twice our size
We took her as our greatest prize

Chorus

The Frenchman put up a devil of a fight
(How I wish I was aboard her now)
Our main mast shattered and the Captain lost
And the surgeon working like a man possessed

Chorus

This was to be was our greatest fight
(I wish I was in Truro now)
with blood in the scuppers and a hell of a din
when a bloody great flash took half my skin

Chorus

For thirty years she was at sea
I wish I was aboard her now
Her glorious moment came to pass
as Boney came aboard at last

We had him now, for we'd set out
To put the French to bloody rout
Now he was done, on the run,
And now was had him in our grasp
Old Boney brought to heel at last

And now you've seen the Plays we did
I wish we'd do them all again
To make Napoleon feel at home
'ere o'er the Seven Seas he'd roam

To banishment, it was his plan
To conquer dear old Eng e land
so ends our tale, raise the sails
For we're homeward bound on our final run
Aboard the Billy Ruff i an

Appendix II

Napoleon and America

If Napoleon had accepted his brother Joseph's plan of escape, and abandoned his retinue at Rochefort he would almost certainly have landed with him at Brooklyn on 25 August 1815. It would have been a memorable date for him and for the United States, and both histories would have been different. It is possible he would have been caught on the way, since the American brig *Commerce*, on which Joseph sailed under a false name, was stopped and searched by a British naval vessel, but the search was cursory. Joseph was not even noticed in his cabin, and two British frigates mounting a perfunctory stop-and-search off the mouth of the Hudson were simply brushed aside by the *Commerce* when she arrived. Concern for the fate of his entourage was undoubtedly as strong a reason for Napoleon to cry off the escape plan as the fear that it might miscarry, and two years later Napoleon admitted he had in fact made the wrong decision. 'My greatest mistake was to turn to the English and to wind up in St Helena,' he said. 'If I was in America everything would go well, whereas here it goes badly. It was all an error.'

It is intriguing to speculate just what would have 'gone well' for him in the United States. In the first instance, of course, his arrival would have been an embarrassment to President Madison, who was just signing off from a war with Napoleon's victorious enemy. Even if the President did not worry whether Napoleon might be a possible threat to America's tranquillity, or possibly use the country as a base for intrigues in Mexico or Canada, he would have sought to keep Napoleon at the same official distance that was imposed on other eminent exiles. A relaxed life as what Napoleon called 'a prosperous colonist' would have been open to him, as it was to his brother, but it is doubtful whether Napoleon would have found it as easy to live as a wealthy gentleman-landowner as his less restless and ambitious brother. In the event, Joseph spent trouble-free and cultured years on his estate in New Jersey, greatly preferring it to his term as King of Spain, where he had been reluctantly installed by his brother; and it is almost impossible to conjure up a vision of Napoleon scaling his life down from being emperor of France and commander-in-chief to spending years as an amateur savant, astronomer, botanist and classical scholar. He had brought away scientific instruments, treatises and travel books from Malmaison, and had been reading Humboldt's celebrated *Voyage* to the New World. He had the interests and the aptitudes, no doubt, but not the temperament; his civilising impulses came in fits and starts. It is a gloss on such an attempt at adjustment that hundreds of members of his Guard, who fled France after Waterloo to settle in America, could only briefly maintain the soldier-farmer communities that they set up in Alabama and Texas; and many relapsed into military adventuring, especially with the South American revolutionaries. The call of the trumpet was stronger for them than the demand of the plough.

It was a utopian idea of America as a different kind of place, impatient of the Old World, rejecting restrictive systems of aristocrats and prelates, which appealed particularly to the French. Napoleon had grown up in parallel with the emergence of the United States as a new kind of society: even the *ancien regime* in France had been involved in the War of Independence, and returning soldiers had brought stories about this fresh start in human affairs. Benjamin Franklin, Thomas Jefferson, John Adams and Tom Paine had all lived in Paris and been household words in France.

The American dream of liberty and opportunity, even of happiness as an achievable goal, was actually a better match to English radicalism than to the revolutionary spirit of France, and the Bonapartist addiction to the military ethic and a centrally controlled society. It was revealing that Napoleon spoke of himself as 'Washington with a crown' without any sense of irony – the kind of dissonance that, when Lafayette sent Washington the key to the Bastille, what he got in return was a pair of silver shoe-buckles as an example of American crafts. Lafayette had come back a liberal from his campaigns with Washington, and it was that attitude that Napoleon was rejecting in the abdication debates. When Napoleon relapsed into his despotic mood he was scornful about a country that had no military presence and was held together by a volunteer militia and constitutional federation. 'If the United States were in the middle of Europe it would not stand up for two years to monarchist pressure,' Napoleon declared. 'In the last war against England [1812],' he said sarcastically in St Helena, 'the blows of a few British frigates humbled this confederation of ten million inhabitants to the point of signing a peace treaty amid the smoking ruins of Washington. This was because there was no focus of power in the country: because the first requisite of popular elections without a strong national defence, meant unstable and ineffective government.' It was the same appetite for centralising force that led him to predict the break-up of federal government, prophesying 'dissonance between the northern and southern states' and insisting that if there was no spirit of military glory to bond the system, 'federal unity will be broken by local interests and commercial rivalries.' He would not have been a comfortable citizen of the United States, for all his protestations of peaceful intent and urbanity.

* * *

Joseph Bonaparte, by contrast, displayed just such characteristics. Like his brother Jerome, who had found himself an exile in Baltimore a dozen years before but had been hauled back by Napoleon to make a dynastic marriage, Joseph was attracted by American domestic virtues. He had smuggled in large sums of gold and jewellery, and fetched more later, which sufficed for him to build himself a fine house at Point Breeze, a 200 acre estate on the Delaware River in New Jersey near Bordertown, seventy miles from New York and thirty from Philadelphia. There he lived and entertained in great style. When Madison was asked about receiving such an exile as Joseph his answer was certainly much the same as he would have said about Napoleon himself. 'Prosperity and hospitality do not depend on such a formality, and whatever sympathy may be due to fallen fortunes there is no claim to merit in that family on the American nation, nor any reason why its government should be embarrassed on their account. In fulfilling what we owe to our own rights we shall do all that any of them ought to expect.' Washington society seems to have accepted that considered advice. Among the notabilities in Joseph's social circle were Henry Clay, Daniel Webster and John Adams. Sundays were open house for cultivated Philadelphians, who came up on one of the steamboats that Robert Fulton had vainly proposed to build for Napoleon years before he returned to make them in the United States. The visitors were delighted by the elegance of the house, furnished with pictures by Rubens, Canaletto, da Vinci and Rembrandt, besides a fine collection of furniture and books: and those with a taste for outdoor sports could go hunting and fishing with Joseph. He had a fine life though his wife was not well enough to come out and join him, and after some years he returned to retirement in Europe.

In the meantime, however, he remained the focus of the Bonapartist emigration. He did what he could to communicate with Napoleon, and certainly financed some of the permitted amenities on St Helena. He kept a public distance from futile schemes to lift Napoleon off St Helena, but was undoubtedly informed about them. He gave money to support former officers and officials who were not able for years to return to France, and he was in touch with a few recalcitrant émigrés – notably General Lallemand, who still had a bent for what Castlereagh called 'Bonapartist mischief'. At one point much suspicion was aroused by Joseph's purchase of 25,000 acres on the Quebec border (still commemorated by Lake Bonaparte on the property) which some believed was intended as a base for Napoleon, if he managed to leave St Helena, to plan a disruptive attack on Canada. Joseph was also regarded as a surrogate for his brother, being twice invited to become King of Mexico, which was painfully struggling free of imperial Spain.

Joseph plainly liked his life in James Monroe's America. 'He shows great respect for local customs and manners,' the French consul reported to Paris, 'saying quite often that he prefers his residence here to the flattering and distinguished places offered him in Europe.' Even when his mansion at Point Breeze was burned – supposedly arson by a foreign agent trying to destroy any incriminating letters sent by European rules to Napoleon in his days of supremacy in Europe – he coolly built another imposing property: both were said to be a match for George Washington's Mount Vernon.

* * *

There was, after all, a Bonaparte dynasty in the United States. The nephew of Napoleon and Joseph, the son of Jerome and Elizabeth Patterson of Baltimore, was Charles Joseph Bonaparte. He was a successful lawyer who was a friend of President Theodore Roosevelt, who appointed him Secretary of the Navy in 1905 and in 1909 he became Attorney-General .By then his cousin had come and gone in Paris as Napoleon III.

Appendix III

Lord Eldon's Opinion

This letter from the Lord Chancellor to the Prime Minister, written from his country home where he was convalescing, shows (not clearly but to an extraordinary degree) his difficulty in coping with the problems set by the questionably lawful detention of Napoleon. It describes his uncertainty about affixing the Great Seal, which would ratify the treaty (signed by the allies on 2 August 1815) authorising the perpetual imprisonment of Napoleon, and reveals the legal entanglements which would have enmeshed the government if any challenge by Napoleon, or on his behalf, should reach the law courts. The case was not only without precedent: so was the way in which the Lord Chancellor had to juggle with the confusion of the law. Uneasy, but obliged to come to a decision as time pressed, what he in effect concluded was that there was a *raison d'etat* for the government's action in a confused situation where the loss of the prisoner's liberty should be set against a lifelong threat to the repose and tranquillity of Europe.

1815
Private
Lord Chancellor Eldon
To the Earl of Liverpool – Premier

My dear Lord,
Lord Bathurst will probably have informed you that after hesitation, I have determined to let the late Treaty for the Imprisonment of Buonaparte have the Great Seal appended to it. Provided we make out that Maitland received him upon Terms, entitling us to consider him as a Prisoner of War, I don't think that any Objection can be successfully urged against that Act. And I

have acted upon the Notion that such is the case. I don't mean to say that I should not have so acted, if that could not be made out, because, whatever difficulty there might be in finding a Principle, short of that, which rests upon Necessity, for imprisoning him not only until Peace, but after Peace, I am afraid we must look at as a case, in which Necessity will justify his Imprisonment even after Peace.

Notwithstanding every thing which as occurred to others and been communicated to me, and all, that has occurred to myself, in Meditation here, I cannot bring myself, as yet, to think that, if this Person is to be considered as a French subject and France at War with us, or a French rebel and France at peace with us, he could, upon the general principles of the Law of Nations as applied to cases hitherto occurring in fact be, in the former Case, excluded from the benefits of a peace with France by perpetual subseq^t Imprisonment, or be subsequently so imprisoned, if France, being at Peace with us, had ceased to call upon us as her Ally, to aid against her Subject in Rebellion – Peace with a Sovereign, it may be stated I believe as a *general* Truth, is Peace with all his Subjects – and the assisting a Sovereign at Peace against his subjects in Rebellion is what an Ally may do, at the Instance of that Sovereign, I believe it will be found to be generally true, that Allies can't treat the *rebel* to a foreign power, at Peace with the Allies, as *their Enemy*. And I incline to an Opinion entertained with more confidence than the doubting Lord Eldon usually holds Opinions, that, if Buonaparte is to be considered as a *French Subject*, his Imprisonment after Peace is rather to be justified upon his Case forming an Exception to general rules of the Law of Nations than by any stated Rule of that Law– But then, may it not be *so* justified. Take him to be a *French* Rebel, we have, as to *him*, got beyond (have we not?) the Law "that to his Sovereign he standeth or falleth" –"that his Sovereign & not his Sovereigns Allies are to muzzle & to punish him" – to *this his* Sovereign is incompetent – but then it is said, if so, that must be, because the French Nation would rather have B. their Sovereign than L.^{s} 18. and, by the Law of Nations, you have no right to prevent that People from choosing their own Government. This I say I admit *generally speaking*, but as we have got beyond these *general* Truths: we i.e. Parliament, as I conceive, has determined that *this is a* Case of Exception, because the safety of every other Country requires that the French Nation should not be permitted to act upon the general Rule –and, if *that* be so, can it be contrary to the Law of Nations, whatever are its general Rules, to allow you to *interfere against the French Nation's* having B–e as their Sovereign, that you should adopt (altho you are, or, if you are not, you will be at Peace with France,) *that Measure which, & which alone,* you are bona fide convinced can *make your Interposition effectual*–viz. the placing B–e in durance. –If the French Nation, by *its* disposal of Buonaparte, if he is a Subject of that Nation, could secure us & our Allies agᵗ that Gentlemans machinations to destroy our Peace, I think it would be excessively difficult to justify, according to the Law of Nations, such a Treatment of him *after Peace*: but, may it not be said that all, that has been done, has been done upon the self-same principle, which is to be acted upon, if he is so treated viz. a bona fide, rational, sober Conviction, founded upon strong Argument tending to evince that this *Imprisonment* is of *absolute necessity* to the future *internal* peace & welfare of *ourselves* & of our *Allies*–.

So far, taking him to be a French Subject, or a French Rebel: but is he so to be considered? What say you to that?

He was Emperor of France *de facto*– he abdicated that Character by Treaty –was he *thereby*, thereafter, to be considered as a French Subject to Louis 18th? Was that the effect of a Transaction, in which he became Emperor of Elba, with a stipulated Revenue– If, before the Emperor of Elba entered France, to regain the Throne he was not a French Subject does his Attempt to regain that Throne again make him a *French* subject, or a *French* Subject in rebellion– If, upon Grounds resulting out of the various situations & characters, in which B– has been placed, & with which he has been cloathed, you can consider him as, in no way, in the relation of Subject, or subject in rebellion agᵗ France, then may not the War be considered as a War against *him,* agᵗ *him* as our *Enemy*, without reference to any Character, that he may be alledged to have, bound up in the national Character of France– against *him & his adherents* making, as an Enemy against *us*, an *hostile Attempt* to break down the System of Government, which existed in France, *thereby introducing a System of Govt. in direct subversion of a Treaty with our Allies, founded upon their & our insecurity under any such Government as he would introduce into France?* If we can make this out, (& does there not seem to be ground for saying that we can?) then might we not steer clear of the difficulty, that belongs to excluding from Peace with France or *French Subject* or a *French Rebel*? He would then be a distinct, substantive *Enemy*, independent of any relation to the Sovereign of France, with whom we might be at Peace, or in Alliance? a conquered Enemy indeed, with whom, according to the Law of Nations, we should deal as mercifully as our Security would admit after he was conquered. But then we should only have to determine, as between our selves & him, whether we did so treat, and the rules of the Law of Nations would be to be applied in the decision of *that Question* of *fact*, without reference to any Rule of that Law to him as a Subject of any Sovereign?

I do not know, my dear Lord, whether this long Scrawl is intelligible or nonsense– Just say in one word Yes or No, & how the Matter strikes you, if you have leisure to do so–

I assume in all my thoughts that Maitland has not made a Law of Nations for Buonapartes case by any improvident Measures, or rather thrown difficulties in our Way.

By Quiet, Air, & Exercise I have greatly amended. And, if I can be allowed to stay here next Month, I think I shall be more restored than I could have believed it possible that I ever should be. –

I am, my dear Lord,

Y.ʳˢ faithfully, Eldon

Encombe– Wednesday morning

Buonᵗ was a Subject of France before he usurped the Throne. But he was Emperor of France de facto –If he simply abdicated that Imperial State, it might be said he continued his Character of Subject, not continuing his Rebellion– But, when you consider the effect of the whole Transaction of his Abdication, & all the Circumstances of that Transaction, can you say that the fair effect of it was to restore him to the Character of Subject to Louis XVIII? Would it not have been extremely difficult, regard being had to all the Circumstances, in which he quitted France, to make out that his last Return to it was *Treason* agᵗ Louis XVIII?

I shall write again soon.

Index

Index

Index